Let Me Speak
Notes From A willing Outsider
Dr. Jo Jorgensen

Liberty Street Press

For information about special discounts available for bulk purchases, sales promotions, fundraising, and educational needs, contact Liberty Street Press at sale@libertystpress.com.

Cover Design: Mountaintop Creative Group
Edited by: Evan McMahon

ISBN 979-8-88871-001-2 (Paperback)

Library of Congress Control Number: 2025935264

Published by Liberty Street Press
P.O. Box 44751
Indianapolis, IN 46204
www.LibertyStPress.com

First Edition

Contents

To Emily, my 1st Baby, and Eva, my responsible Rory who raised her impulsive mother as much as I raised her.

Acknowledgements

I'm so grateful to all the wonderful people in my life who helped get me to where I am. Thank you to my brother and sister, Jim and Joy, for putting up with me for so many years, and brother-in-law Ken who's now a part of us. And while they're no longer here to read my book, I of course need to thank my parents.

It would take an entire book to list everyone who was invaluable to the 2020 campaign and everything that led to it over the years, but I would like to single a few people out, starting with Marc Montoni and Michael Cloud, who were invaluable for my U.S. House and VP runs, respectively.

I'd like to thank those who had faith in me in the very beginning of my campaign, including Joe Hauptmann, Stewart Flood, Jeff Dimit, and, of course, my campaign manager Steve Dasbach, who put together a great team including Jesse Mears, who was always by my side keeping things together, and Seth Levy, who got us to where we were going. Elizabeth Brierly was always available on the phone during my midnight (and sometimes 2 a.m.) runs, and Carla Howell helped keep things on message.

Thanks also to Kenna Porter, Jordan Bunch, Brittany Bunch, Katie Prather, and Matt Hudson, graphics design extraordinaire. And to Libby Dasbach, who opened their home as our campaign headquarters. Everyone at LPHQ went above and beyond to help our campaign, including Tara DeSisto, Dan Fishman, and Bekah Congdon.

Special thanks to Marlon for keeping the house running smoothly while I was out running.

DR. JO JORGENSEN

Thank you to everyone at PFL who is helping me continue to spread the campaign message, including Sam Robb, Jim Babka, Tim Hagan, and especially Andrea Holt, who works so closely with me.

Professionally I wouldn't be where I am without my dissertation chair, Fred Switzer, who offered me the teaching position, a job I never thought I would love.

And you wouldn't be reading this book if it weren't for Evan McMahon, who guided me through this process from start to finish and continues to be an invaluable mentor.

Foreword

"A book by Jo Jorgensen? Must be about politics."

Actually, no. Well, of course I couldn't write a book without including something about politics, being the only woman (at the time of writing) in the history of the United States to be on the ballot in all 50 states twice.

This book focuses more on my first love, psychology. The scientific study of the brain and behavior. Perhaps because I have been such an outsider my entire life, I was immediately fascinated by the topic since the first psychology class I took in college, changing my major from biology to psychology during that first class. I finally had the keys to understanding people around me!

Somehow, I found myself teaching psychology 30 years after that first class, and in this book, I share many of the fun and interesting ideas from my classes Pursuing Happiness, Introduction to Psychology, Social Psychology, and others.

It's difficult to separate politics from psychology. Many of my libertarian explanations were based on my psychological training. By understanding people's responses and how they form their beliefs, we can become more successful. I also describe how government policies hurt us all, because they're not based on how humans think and act.

It's also difficult to separate politics from psychology in my own life. I do feel a bit guilty that Wikipedia lists me under "Notable Faculty" of Clemson University, alongside professors who've conducted ground-breaking research, when I've never published. Politics shined a spotlight on my career in psychology. I am honored to be in the company of Thomas Hazlett, also listed.

"*Let Me Speak*" is a take on the "*Let Her Speak*" operation that sprung up during the 2020 Presidential campaign when I was kept off the Trump/Biden debate stage. Ironically, "Let Her Speak" is one of the most recognizable campaign events of 2020, but it was not the work of our campaign – it was coordinated by the new group People For Liberty.

Let Me Speak is a resounding cry for my own life, as well. I was a very quiet toddler (my aunt suggested to my mom that she take me in for testing for what we now call on the spectrum), fairly quiet in grade school who stuttered and stammered when I had to speak in front of the class, to being a wallflower in high school. To say I am a late bloomer is an understatement.

Yes, I was active in structured groups and was even president of multiple groups in high school, but that didn't require any small talk. The tasks were laid out for me – I simply had to fulfill the duties. I've always been a do-er.

Yet even while leading those groups I still felt like an outsider. I'm not going to lie – it was painful being an outsider earlier in life. I even hated my last name – too long and a bit unusual outside of my grandparents' homeland of Denmark. And always misspelled. I've had a lifetime of explaining to people that its "-sen," not "-son."

I learned to embrace the outsider role, though, as I entered adulthood. When I did get married, I actually went through quite a bit of trouble to figure out how to keep my last name, even though my husband had a last name I would've done anything for during my schoolyears. A name that doesn't get misspelled and everyone knows how to pronounce.

Thank you, journalist and author Will Hodgkinson - chief rock and pop critic for *The Times*, who used the term "*willing outsider*" when describing fans of Nine Inch Nails. As soon as I heard him use that phrase, I thought, "*Yes, that's exactly what I am!*" I only wish I had come up with that phrase on my own about 40 years ago. It would've made being an outsider a bit less painful.

I continue to be an outsider, and it's now consciously willing. I'm even an outsider in my job title. On the campaign trail, I was introduced as a "professor," the informal use of professor as being any college instructor, but my job title is technically "Principal

Lecturer." I love my job as lecturer, though, because it means my entire job is focused on teaching, so I get to do what I love – sharing passionate ideas with others.

Introduction

When I was diagnosed with ADHD in my mid-30s, the diagnostician told me I was the worst case she had even seen. I'm not ashamed to tell you that when she told me, I felt my eyes welling with tears. Tears of relief that someone finally understood me, and that I wasn't as "stupid" as some people had thought I was. All my life I'd been aware that something was different about me, that the world seemed to have been designed for other people. Once that feeling had a name, it became easier to talk about what I'd always considered my "outcast past."

As a kid, I was often in trouble for being distracted. My second-grade teacher punished me for looking out the window (I was actually looking at a cute boy) and another grade school teacher told me that she was going to put a stick of dynamite under my chair to get me to start working. I was a diligent, if distractible, student, and busied myself with a little bit of everything: 4-H, gymnastics, sailing, knitting, crocheting, sewing, band, running, an after-school job. At such a small school, I found a place on the basketball, track and field, gymnastics, golf, and field hockey teams.

Even as an adult, I'm chronically short of attention. I once forgot to bring my shoes with me to the Clemson campus to teach and had to stop and buy some sandals. I lost my car keys for three days and had to ask my then-business partner to pick up my kids from school – I finally found them in a plastic grocery bag in the fridge.

When I was getting my Ph.D., my first thesis chair passed me on to someone else because he couldn't get me to focus, but he didn't tell me the reason until 20years later, when I asked him about it for this book (we remain close friends). I've been told by my daughter that after words leave someone's mouth, they travel around the room for a few minutes, then finally get to me.

My difficulty in focusing, problematic though it might sometimes be, has given me a wealth of experiences. I've run for Congress, Vice President, and President of the United States, becoming the first woman in the 247-year history of our country to appear on ballots in all 50 states — twice. I've run a business with revenues of over $2 million a year and closed it down. I've traveled and raised a family. Been married and divorced. I've earned three graduate degrees in three different (though related) subjects and did the work for a fourth. I've learned quite a lot about people, and politics, and why we make the choices we make. And I've fallen in love with teaching — a field I never deliberately pursued — which became a life-changing passion.

It's that desire to teach, and to share experiences, that led me to write a book (well, that, and the publisher constantly asking, "how is the book going?"). Most people who run for national office publish an autobiography, but I never found my life all that interesting. In fact, I turned down an offer from a publisher during the campaign. Others publish a work of political philosophy, laying out a grand vision for society, but it's hard to shape a new, compelling narrative around, "just leave people alone," which is the core of my platform. I also feel compelled to share some insights from psychological research, letting non-specialist readers peek into the most interesting corners of the field I love to teach.

In an effort to be true to my some what-scattered self, and provide the most value to readers, I'm going to do a little bit of each.

I teach a class at Clemson University called, "Pursuing Happiness," which heavily informed the writing of this book, along with social psychology and my graduate work in Industrial/Organizational Psychology, which focuses on coordinating people to meet goals. Students' evaluations of my teaching (we get them every term) are fairly good, overall, though "scatterbrained" does tend to show up pretty often. I think less linearly than most people, and sometimes bounce from example to example in my excitement to convey a concept. You might find the same to be true of the pages that follow.

As you read, you'll hear about the time I bought all the supplies for a kitchen renovation in a single frenetic morning, just five hours after coming up with the idea to do it. The times I went running after midnight on the campaign trail. A near-miss where I almost crashed a small plane into a mountain. And how I delayed a Pink Floyd concert of 50,000 people — completely by accident.

You'll hear about the optimism and idealism (and a touch of naïveté) it takes to run for President on a third-party ticket. In a radically contentious election year. In a pandemic lockdown.

Perhaps you'll find I'm a nutty genius, and that my advice is cogent and important — if that's the case, definitely leave reviews and tell your friends.

This book is NOT a "recipe for success" based on everything I've learned, or a sermon about how to live a good life from somebody who's got it all figured out. I don't. I'm still learning all the time. I make mistakes *all the time,* and I'll tell you about them. I hope I never stop. Every day I try to sort out what makes sense, what feels like it's really true about my own mind, and the world, and whatever claim I just heard somewhere (maybe inside my own head).

But I do want to share some of what I've learned. I've compiled an incomplete, but significant, summary of the best research I could find about what makes people happy. Instead of telling you to "do as I do," I'll tell you what I'm *trying* to do, in my own life. Through my lens as a psychology professor (and a Ph.D. in Organizational Psychology, 2002), and vice-presidential candidate (1996) and candidate for President of the United States (2020), I'll tell you about the interesting, insightful studies psychologists have done to see what makes people better off, both individually and politically.

I'll try to offer some insight into politics, which is psychology with real-world stakes, and economics, which is psychology with numbers. Many parts of human behavior have been studied, named, and categorized.

Psychologists, behavioral economists, and social scientists have an almost uncanny creativity for identifying variables. Experimental design can be marvelously complex, especially if your goal is not to let the subject know he's being studied. (Many times, within this book, and throughout social science literature, subjects are called "participants," because undergraduates don't like being talked about like lab rats.)

But very often, in pursuit of knowledge about our natures, people are treated like rats. In one research study (one of many weird-but-cool studies I'll detail in this book) dozens of participants all stayed in the same hotel, ate the same food, and got the same exercise. Researchers also sprayed the inside of their noses with a cold virus.

Scientists measured their personalities and quirks on a variety of scales, and— this is ingenious! — weighed the tissues they had blown their noses into, to measure the amount of mucus! The finding? People who were happier were better able to resist getting sick, and if they did, had milder symptoms. The power of our brains is truly remarkable, and I love to share all the ways we've come up with to try to quantify that power.

As I write this, the Libertarian Party is undergoing a schism, a crisis of identity. I felt good about being the standard-bearer of that party in 2020. The platform had been mostly unchanged: the platform from the early 1970s was the platform I supported in 2020. I felt confidence in our message and our intentions, and our principles.

But in 2022, the party suffered a hostile takeover by people who immediately changed the platform in ways that can mildly be described as troubling and removed a statement that *"bigotry is irrational and repugnant."* These people are, in short, exactly who you think they are.

Just four short years later, I can't imagine being a voice for what the Libertarian Party has (hopefully just temporarily) become. I finally found my crowd, gave it everything I had, and now, I'm an outcast there as well.

If my life has been a lesson in one thing, it's that no solution, no classroom, no family structure, no state, no medical treatment, can be universally right for the 332 million people who call the U.S. home. There is simply too much variation in our individual values, needs, and temperament for any single policy to be enforced on all of us, and impact all of us equally. People are individuals, not lab rats. And it's wrong to force them to participate in an experiment, no matter what the goal.

Even though I have strong opinions about how people should conduct themselves, I don't have a need to control people's choices. The knowledge that we can't be forced into all behaving or believing the same way is what makes me inherently skeptical of government "help," especially the federal government's. Everything the government touches gets worse. Regulators want to make decisions about gas stoves based on a study or two, but I don't care if you build a campfire in your kitchen. And I certainly won't ban your right to use a stove while writing myself a loophole to enjoy one, as most hypocritical politicians happily do.

When I ran for office, reporters often asked me, "When did you first become interested in politics?" My answer: I'm *still* not interested in politics! I'm running for office as an act of self-defense, to be the voice piping up in these discussions of what people must do or should do, to ask, "What do the people want? What would they do if we left them alone?" Psychology is the focus of this book because it's like an owner's manual for the human mind. I'm fascinated by the behavior of other people. I don't want to control it. I just want to observe it, and understand it, and let people live out their messy, wonderful, wildly different preferences.

The free market, because it's an expression of all our different, individual, competing values and beliefs, can solve problems better than any government. As I often said in my campaign, government has gotten way too big, too bossy, and too nosy. Individuals create and produce wealth — the government just redistributes this wealth that we made.

Smaller government, and less meddling, holds the promise of a more efficient, smoother, fairer, happier society. Everyone should be treated with respect. Everyone can do more, produce more, create more of whatever makes them happy, if they are free to do so. Everybody wins.

That's why I wrote this book. Not because I know what you should do to be happy, or because I have a formula for happiness, I think everyone else should conform to. I wrote this book because I love empirical evidence and psychology and people, and I want to give you all the tools we know of and warn you of what gets in the way.

You can choose for yourself what will make your one life (your beautiful, chaotic, scattered, exciting, eventful life) the happiest it can be.

Gardening the Movement

As I look toward my overgrown garden in the late summer of 2024, I have a chance to reflect. I was chosen as the Libertarian Party candidate for President in May of 2020, at the height of pandemic restrictions, in the first online-only nominating convention in American political party history.

Running for President and continuing to teach my college courses remotely, I crisscrossed the nation for nearly three years (one before the election, meeting delegates, and two after, fundraising and building community), often on a bus with my face on the side, and through a blur of countless planes, taxis, airports, and hotel rooms.

Well into 2022, I was fighting the good fight and trying to keep every other plate spinning. Reviewing conference agendas at my sister's kitchen table during a visit. Reading psychology texts and preparing lecture notes for a brand-new course I was tackling at Clemson, while on the plane between fundraising dinners and board meetings. Texting and attending remote meetings while on the top of a ladder, painting my mom's house.

I collected no speaker's fees and did much of the driving myself to preserve donor funds for Libertarian state parties and our hard-working organizations.

One day, perhaps soon, I'll grow a decent garden again. The few plants I got in the ground this year are leggy and growing down over the sides of the raised garden boxes, their peculiar growth an organic calendar of the time I've spent on the road and away from this home I love.

Investing in the care and growth of the libertarian message and community is a task of hard work, like the sweat and soil of a garden. And like a late-blooming spring, there are sometimes chilly seasons where it's hard to know if all the time you've invested will ever bear the harvest of rich flavor and beauty you envisioned while planting.

Sometimes you put all the care you can into a plant, and it still withers on the vine. There isn't enough sunlight, or the soil has been depleted by whatever came before. The trellis isn't strong enough and the promising fruit drops into the dirt and begins to rot. Sometimes you can rescue a wayward or anemic plant. Train it, build it, nourish it, help it to thrive. Sometimes you try everything you can and it dies anyway, victim of something beyond your control.

It's long been women who have tended society's gardens, doing the quiet work of planting and watering, only to have the harvest scooped up and touted by men.

I experienced this after my presidential campaign, as well. No matter how hard I worked, and regardless of the fact that I was the presidential candidate chosen by delegates, the top of the ticket, it was made clear to me again and again that my voice didn't matter. My opinion didn't count in a room full of men who were sure their way was the only way of doing anything.

Even people who liked and respected me did not stop these things from happening. They were more willing to throw me under the bus so as not to go against or contradict a man, who was not the elected candidate. I was denied high-profile interviews by people who resented that I'd be the messenger, or who didn't have confidence in my ability to carry that message in certain venues. The job of a campaign should be to prep the candidate for the highest-visibility opportunities to reach voters, to understand the candidate's position and polish that message for marketability. Instead, my positions were rejected or silenced, and replaced by those of "more experienced" men, some of whom were not even employed by the campaign.

I was stunned to receive a post campaign butt-dial from a male campaign staffer, who had been high up in the organization. I knew that he had preferred another candidate during the primary (actually, three other candidates, as they dropped like flies), but I thought my successful performance had won him over. After all, in the general election I had received more votes than any other first-time Libertarian candidate, including Gary Johnson, a former elected politician. Worse, I thought he was my friend since he invited me to lunch and a tourist attraction with him while I was in his city visiting family.

But on this unintentional call, as I overheard him speaking candidly to someone else without knowing it was being recorded in a voicemail, I heard there was "no enthusiasm" for me, "low motivation" among Libertarians towards me, and that my record-breaking 2 million votes was "not because of Jo Jorgensen." He attributed the two million votes to the new libertarian vote floor, ignoring the fact that I was the one who got the two million votes.

I admit - I felt crushed. I even started to question my performance, despite having more votes than anyone else out of the gate, despite having an overwhelming majority of excited volunteers from outside the party instead of the usual party members who volunteer out of habit, and despite record interest online. I received more votes than any first-time presidential candidate in the party's history, but many insiders, and apparently more than I'd realized, regarded me as a failure, a disappointment, a liability. I would later learn that the campaign volunteers were overwhelmingly women: in a party that is still over two-thirds men, a large fraction of men didn't get involved to support me. And I still got two million votes.

After overhearing that conversation, I began to replay some of the moments that had seemed to me to be triumphant, like my performance in the interview with John Stossel. And despite my interview performance with John Stossel. Stossel had tried to put me at ease, letting me know that the interview was being recorded for later streaming, and if I stumbled on a question I could start over or even reply with a completely different answer. He stressed there was no pressure, just stop and start over any time I wanted.

But I didn't need the interview to be "no pressure." I was equal to the pressure, and I was prepared. Not once did I stumble during the entire interview, which meant my interview went really fast. We finished so early that John had to ask his producer to get more questions to ask me, since there was so much time left. He said that had never happened before. Suddenly I wondered if my stellar performance still wasn't good enough.

The worst part about my self-doubt is that I have a Ph.D. in psychology. I understand that other people are going to suck sometimes, and it isn't in my control to make them suck less. I can't control their thoughts and behavior (and neither can you) but I can control how I feel about it and how I respond. If anyone should be immune to these feelings of self-doubt, it should be me, given my performance as a candidate and my training in psychology.

But indoctrination is powerful. Our culture is moving in the right direction of empowering women, but we're not there yet. And some of us (slightly!) older women grew up in a time in which women were, subtly and overtly, trained to question and doubt everything we did, knowing it would never stack up to a man's performance.

I did recover from that episode, but I know if I was susceptible to this, then probably many women are. Mental habits that protect happiness empower our movement and guard us against lost potential, which is the inevitable result of infighting and self-doubt.

Women are also judged more harshly than men as we age. Unfortunately, we can't blame society for this, and it may be impossible to shift. There are no known cultures that consider older-looking women as more attractive than younger women, so the preference for youth is likely a mammalian mating strategy. We can implement protections against agism, but we won't overcome it.

Luckily, no one (at least to my face) criticized me for looking old. Usually it was the opposite - people often told me I looked younger in person. I did, however, receive other criticisms. I wish I could say I received the worst criticisms from men, but I didn't. Women can be remarkably harsh to one another, which is at least partially an effect of the imbalance itself: An indie filmmaker friend shared with me that at film festivals if a small number of screenings are reserved specifically for female filmmakers, a kind of crab-in-the-bucket effect takes hold, with women incentivized to tear each other down and ingratiate themselves to men. We see this repeatedly when women are in competition with other women. The power of building each other up and protecting each other from outdated norms takes much longer to realize than the short-term gain of climbing over each other. I am willing to be supportive of others, and to be patient, though it often means getting shoved back down. I got the harshest criticism about my appearance from a woman (an LP member, active in her state), who approached me at a state convention, after the campaign. She pointed out that there were a lot of criticisms about my appearance online, that I wasn't pretty enough to be the presidential candidate, and I dressed too much like a schoolteacher.

I am a schoolteacher.

It's easy to become angry over such episodes. Anger can be very deceiving. It's alluring and invigorating. Anger makes you feel more powerful than you normally do, and you may even feel physically bigger when anger floods you. Typically, though, anger works against us. When we're angry, we tend to become overly optimistic, leading us to take too many risks (and I'm already too optimistic). We become too impulsive, reckless, and prone to making stupid decisions.

But anger can also be deeply motivating. It spurs us to action, to take back what we feel is rightfully ours. To right the wrongs. To slay the dragons. To tackle the injustices and the institutions that carry them out.

The question lies in how to harness your anger into growth. To bristle up and make yourself bigger so you can protect more people. Many species puff up their feathers, arch their backs, and otherwise make themselves appear larger when threatened. To direct the power of anger to move righteously, instead of recklessly. Take on the challenges in your home, your job, your community, your social circle, your children's lives and futures.

Give the anger meaning.

And speaking of anger, no, women are not more emotional than men. Research doesn't back this up. If anything, little boys do tend to be more emotional than little girls, but not by much. But over time, society trains men to channel their emotions into anger and competitiveness instead of empathy and honesty, so it really doesn't do them any favors, either.

Women – don't fall into the trap of allowing yourself to be labeled as more emotional than men – it's not true!

Of course, there are unique positives to being women, where we do not compete with men, some of which you may not have thought about. For instance, out of all family relationships, research has shown that the mother-daughter relationship holds the most potential for happiness. So, men aren't even in the running for this accomplishment and joy! And you've probably heard that the human brain doesn't stop developing until age 25.

Actually, it's age 25 for women. For men? Age 28! Women have an advantage over men in college, even in math. Women can compete with men, but we shouldn't need to be competitive with men. There is too much work to be done to worry about who gets the credit, and too far to travel to be undercutting each other to get ahead on the path. Unfortunately, those who adopt this selfless, "all for one" attitude usually get run over by those who prefer glitter and glory to slog and substance, and short-term personal gain over the long-term growth of ideas.

Women in Politics

I don't believe that innate characteristics like gender or ethnicity are major drivers of who we are or how we behave. Genetics play a role, and social expectations too, but I'm very wary of identity politics, as anyone who followed my campaign will know. Even when I'm treated badly (as happens to all of us, and particularly to third-party political candidates) I don't jump to the explanation that I was mistreated because I'm a woman. (I was often asked during the campaign what it was like to run as a woman, as compared to a man. To which I could only say, "I don't know. I've never run as a man.") I'm fairly self-critical, so it doesn't seem unreasonable that I screw things up, and not everyone will like me. That's natural. Someone's behavior toward me has to be pretty blatantly gendered, before I identify that pattern and attribute it to gender bias.

One such pattern emerged around the 2022 Libertarian National Convention. Traditionally, the presidential candidate is automatically given a speaking slot to address the full delegation at the next national convention after they run. They are expected to give insights from their experience on the national campaign circuit and offer a thank you and some inspiring words to the delegation. That tradition has gone on for at least 40 years. At least until I was the nominee. Not only was I not offered this customary opportunity, but I was also turned down flat when I requested it. No one would even admit to having made the choice. I would be surprised if this would happen to a man. How ironic that just two short years after the "Let Her Speak" campaign, with the purpose of getting me in the national debates with the Democrat and Republican, I'm denied the opportunity to speak in my own party, at what should be the heart of our movement. I had just as many battles to fight inside our tribe as outside.

At various times in my life I've been told, explicitly or implicitly, that the business at the top of whatever field I was in (business, academia, politics) was rightly reserved for men. The calloused hands pointed me away from my interest in a construction job, and toward crafts and cooking. The corporate retreat held at an all-male hunting lodge, which I only discovered after it had occurred. The undeniable barriers and bias against women in teaching and tenure evaluations (though my community at Clemson has been wonderful, the general treatment of women in academia can be dismal). As an undergrad, only one of the many professors in my department was a woman. As Harry Browne's running mate, my voice didn't matter, which was appropriate in a way. But then when I was at the top of the ticket, I didn't have that same power. Often my opinion didn't even guide the messages sent out by "my" campaign, and some of the public statements by my own running mate directly contradicted my positions and beliefs. I often felt I had as much control as the Presidential candidate as I did when I was the VP candidate, which wasn't much. Had my running mates in both situations been women, or had I been a man, I'm sure things would've been much different. Outside the campaign, as well. I was often asked to defend the positions of the VP candidate, even though I didn't agree with his positions. (Reporters don't understand that, unlike the Democratic and Republican parties, the Libertarian Presidential candidate doesn't get to choose her running mate.)

Covert sexism plays out in lots of ways, and I've seen that unfold in different spheres during my lifetime. The inappropriate remarks and endless discussion of my hair, clothes, and even my nails, to the exclusion of my policy ideas. The ever-present implications that I could not be both a great mom to my kids and a top performer at work. A presidential candidate and an adoring grandmother. A divorced college professor and a reluctant feminist.

I was born in 1957, at a time when women couldn't go to Ivy League universities, have their own credit, or serve on juries in all 50 states. Women in science, such as astronomer Vera Rubin, were making significant discoveries which led to Nobel Prizes . . . . being won by men who didn't give credit to the women who helped them get there. (My dissertation chair believes we'd have colonies on Mars and would all be driving cars that fly if women and minorities had been given unfettered access to science over the past 500 years.) The decades of my youth paralleled remarkable progress for women in society. Overall, I've been very lucky in my encounters with overt sexism. Few women are so lucky.

Libertarianism is the single most empowering set of principles for women: the rights to bodily autonomy, to self-defense, to property, to equal treatment before the law. Our philosophy demands a culture driven by consent, from interpersonal touch right up through the consent of the governed, from which Jefferson said government derives its "just powers."

One of my deeper goals is to encourage young women in the movement to become leaders in their own lives and take responsibility for the change that matters to them. I'm offering the best available evidence about how to make yourself happy, so you can influence others from a position of strength. When you're self-confident and self-sufficient, you're less susceptible to manipulation, whether by unscrupulous actors or slimy politicians (am I repeating myself?). By revealing a few personal quirks and missteps, I hope I can reassure you that you deserve a place in the conversation, and to have your voice heard, regardless of who you are or what you might worry your lack. Of the hundreds of women who've come up to me at conventions and signings and fundraisers, sweetly eager to meet "Mama Jo," please know, I'm nothing special. I've got my insecurities and my inadequacies, and I can only ever do my best, just like you. But the cause of liberty needed what I could offer, needed me to be better, and bolder, to embrace the fight. It needs you, too.

If I haven't reassured you yet, read on. We need a movement of people who embrace each other and build one another up. Give each other second chances, but not third ones. We have enough opponents to fend off without inventing them within our ranks. And when we find genuine ones inside, we must expel them. When the roots begin to rot, you must cut out the rot, or it will kill the whole plant. Even if they're still doing what roots are supposed to do, the disease will spread until the plant cannot survive. For the liberty message to spread to the people for whom it is most attractive and empowering, we need to operate a culture that reflects our values. That means getting serious about self-policing and holding each other to a standard of respectful interaction. Draw attention to mansplaining behavior that insults and alienates our brightest young minds. Eliminate harassment and take seriously complaints about violations of consent. Stop greeting women's accomplishments with head-patting, "Oh, good for you, you did a thing! That's so cute!" The impressions we leave are not harmless, nor are they fleeting. We need women to show up and do the work, and we should be willing to give them credit.

If you're not too familiar with libertarian thinking, you will find only the barest outline of those beliefs here. I encourage you to read the classic "*Animal Farm*" by George Orwell, Milton Friedman's "*Free to Choose,*" or anything by Ayn Rand. And while parts of his book are dated, I recommend "*Losing Ground*" by Charles Murray. He was a liberal who set out to show that his policies and beliefs were correct, and to determine the best way to help those who needed it, only to discover that liberal policies were making things worse. There's nothing like a convert! And the best part is he demonstrates how "greedy" capitalism is the most compassionate route. People making their own decisions, rather than government bureaucrats passing down orders from up high, offers the most civility. I'm not offering a political science course here. But I hope you'll see how my own life led me to discover and then deepen this set of principles, and that you'll weigh them honestly against what you know about people and the world.

If you're reading this book because you're already a libertarian of some description, welcome even more. Read this book and build the strength and skills you need to get involved in your community. Confidence isn't something you aspire to; it's something you decide on, and then practice until it sticks. We need you to be your best self, to come alive, and to get involved in creating change. Laypeople often say something like, "According to psychologists, change is painful." Actually, that's a myth. It's not the change that's the problem; it's the uncertainty. If you can make changes and take steps to avoid uncertainty, change can be great.

So, we tackle this problem from two directions: first, socially, by reforming the culture of the movement to welcome contributions and opinions from women every bit as much as we welcome those from men. And second, individually, by admitting our vulnerability, armoring ourselves emotionally so we can withstand the unpleasantness of both men and women (and debate moderators!) toward us, at some point. The competence and confidence of women in the movement isn't a threat to anything but the dying paternalistic power structure.

Aspire to it, rather than fearing or competing with it. Build each other up and embrace one another. Amplify the voices of women who are ready to lead, and who blaze a path for more women to follow into leadership and outreach. Getting involved in the movement can be as simple as joining your state party, attending their convention, and supporting quality candidates. Or it might be showing up to a Tax Day protest at your local post office in April. You might choose to do nonpartisan issue advocacy around something you really care about, like the second amendment, criminal justice reform, school alternatives, or environmental conservation. You might invest yourself in alternatives to government control, like joining a microschool, or supporting a health co-op, or growing your own food, or starting a wetland cleanup group. If you're pushing back against top-down control and helping people reclaim power in their own lives, it's libertarian.

To borrow from Howard Thurman, don't ask yourself what the movement needs and try to do that. Figure out what makes you come alive and do *that*...because what the movement actually needs is more people who have come alive.

A Greek proverb says, *"A society grows great when old [wo]men plant trees in whose shade they shall never sit."*

I'm not sure what's next for the liberty movement, nor my place in it. I think this year I'll start with tomatoes and kohlrabi and see my grandchildren and visit my sister up north and watch this latest season of the Party unfold. I know I'll continue to be active in the movement, our nonprofits and our party, though how I might be most useful will change, as it has already and must. I'm open to the right opportunity when it comes. You can't hurry a garden. You can only support and nurture it, providing the best conditions for the growth that comes of its own accord. The seed holds the potential of the whole plant hidden inside, shyly waiting for the right conditions to burst forth into productive beauty. Each time I go out to events or open my social inboxes, I see these seeds, packed with potential, all over the country. Young women of character and conviction, driven to create change and to challenge authority. They contain the revolution of American life inside them, but it needs the right conditions to explode into action. That's where I see my role in the liberty movement, if I get to choose it. I want to provide the rich soil for those seeds and replenish it. I want to understand the patterns of sun and shade that encourage young things to grow, not only the showy foliage of professional success and popularity, but within themselves, the core, the strength, the roots that will sustain them.

Encouraging new growth in your garden often means pulling out older plants that are draining resources without producing fruit. Some long-rooted plants deplete the soil and block the sun, stunting the seedlings; these must be pulled out, so they don't interfere with future productivity. The long-established patterns of watering and fertilizing may have lost their effectiveness. We can reroute water from old growth to new shoots. Healthy older plants can provide trellises as the new vines climb, but we must be ready to be replaced when our season is passed. We teach the garden to tend itself, and to weed itself, and the seeds to nourish themselves and each other. That is what this book aims to do.

This is how we ensure the garden of the liberty movement produces rich harvests of healthy fruit long into the future.

Grow strong.

Be Optimistic

(But Not Too Much)

"Both optimists and pessimists contribute to society. The optimist invents the aeroplane, the pessimist, the parachute." - George Bernard Shaw

One of my favorite things about living downtown in Greenville is that I can walk to the grocery store in about fifteen minutes. No gas, no parking, just walk over there and back. And it's great exercise. Several years ago, in the very early summer, I did just that. I enjoyed my stroll on the way over, and while browsing for whatever I'd actually needed, I discovered they had just gotten in the first watermelons of the season. And not those worthless, round, personal-sized ones! No, these were the large, oblong ones that looked perfect. The absolute hallmark of summer. After being deprived of watermelon for months and months at this point, and considering the weather, watermelon sounded perfect. Of course, the thought immediately entered my mind that I'd have to carry this very large watermelon home, about a mile-long walk. And that was in addition to the groceries I had come for.

But as I often do, I simply ignored the fact that I'd have to carry this full-sized watermelon, along with juggling my actually needed groceries, back home. In my mind, it didn't even feel like there was a choice — it was summer, and there were watermelons to be had. So, I lugged it, in fast-fatiguing arms, all the way back past Main Street. Yes — Main Street — the trendy main street through downtown, complete with the cute shops and nice restaurants that travel magazines keep telling the world about. Definitely not watermelon-lugging country. I didn't learn until later that my daughter was on a date on Main Street that day, and I had missed her by only a block or so. I can't imagine how embarrassed she would have been to see her mother struggling up the street, out of breath, lugging this enormous melon she'd optimistically, irrationally, decided to bring home. I don't have it in me to be embarrassed by much anymore, but my daughter was, inexplicably, born normal. She'd have been mortified. But I didn't think of that either. I was focused on getting that watermelon home.

(Did I make it? No. After more than half a mile I was exhausted, and called my then-husband to ask him to come get me — and the watermelon — in his car.)

Several years ago, I found a copy of Martin Seligman's classic *Learned Optimism* at a charity book sale. It's a psychology book written for the general public by a respected researcher, which is generally the best kind of book to read in fields outside your own specialty. In Chapter 3, Seligman includes a 48-item quiz to rate your own level of general optimism. I scored off the charts optimistic — which may sound like a positive. But to be the most optimistic isn't necessarily a good thing. It's possible to be so optimistic you're clinically delusional. I tested as high as you could score, so I didn't finish the book, because Seligman promised it would make me more optimistic, and I didn't want to enter the delusional range. Besides, research shows that the optimal level of optimism is around an "8" on a 10-point scale, for both happiness and success. Those who score a "10" tend to beat their heads against the wall or continue a losing strategy such as buying stock that keeps going down or turn down life-saving surgery from optimism they can "beat this" on their own. But I have read quite a bit more of Seligman's work since then.

As Seligman tells it, he was driving in the car with his granddaughter, who turned to ask him, "Why are you always so grumpy?" The thought possessed Seligman, who did indeed find himself irritable and grumpy at home. At work, not coincidentally, he'd been researching depression, including managing animal behavioral studies where they would apply electric shocks to dogs.

The studies that Seligman and his colleagues ran on dogs were, I feel compelled to mention, quite sad. The experiments have already been done, though, so I think it's good to learn from them.

One of his experiments might look like this. Imagine putting a dog in a room with half the floor painted red and the other half concrete. The red half of the room has an electrical current running underneath it, so the dog receives a mild shock anytime he steps on that side. Needless to say, the dog would settle in on the concrete side. Then shut off the electrical current on the red side of the room while running a current under the concrete side. The dog would quickly learn to now stay in the red half of the room.

Now for the saddest part. Run the electrical current underneath the entire room, so no matter where the dog lies down, he's unable to escape the shock. Typically, you'd find the dog would just lie in the corner, defeated.

The last part of the experiment returned to the original setup, in which the red half had an electrical current and the other side did not. If the dog had been lying down on the red side, the part that still had the current, he would continue to just lie there, still defeated. All the dog has to do is to get up and walk a few feet to the other side of the room, as he did in the beginning of the experiment, and he wouldn't get shocked at all. Yet he would continue to just lie there, resigned to his suffering.

Seligman called this resignation "learned helplessness."

Unfortunately, humans sometimes succumb to learned helplessness the same way the dogs did. If we find ourselves in a harmful or unpleasant situation, we can sometimes feel helpless to do anything about it. When going over this concept in class, I always ask students if they have found themselves in this situation with grades in their classes. Have they tried studying one way, and then another way, and then finally feel like it doesn't matter what they do – that they're just stuck getting bad grades and it's useless to even try?

Of course this extends far beyond the classroom. If you've had ten job applications rejected in a row, you might start to wonder if there's something wrong with you — not just your resume, or the fit with those particular roles, but you, on a deeper level. You start to wonder if there's any point in applying for the eleventh or twelfth listing. And in our insulated worlds, in which our computers have taken over as the way to find dates, it can be discouraging to either get rejected by those you are interested in, or wind up going on a long string of dates without a match in sight. Inviting strangers to pass judgment on your worthiness is not without consequences. It can wear you down.

This can affect so many areas of our lives. In addition to a job and a romantic life, you can feel helpless and hopeless over losing weight, being able to afford to buy a house, living in the part of the country you dream about, or anything else you value. Have you thrown your hands in the air and said, "I give up?"

If that sounds close to where you are, I'd like to caution you that this can become serious. Right now it might just seem like things aren't going your way, but unaddressed, those feelings can lead to a general perception that "life is against me and there's nothing I can do about it." That, in turn, can lead to more serious problems like depression. After all, Seligman's study on dogs was an investigation of depression.

While it's more familiar now, fifty years ago this idea was quite revolutionary. Scientists had assumed that an animal in a bad or dangerous situation would do anything it could to escape. Learned helplessness occurs in animals, including people, who are so discouraged about their situations that they see no possible escape, whose sense of self has been so pummeled by loss of control that resistance seems futile.

But as we discussed, being overly optimistic and confident things will go well for you can also have detrimental consequences. People like me, at the far end of Seligman's spectrum, may end up knocking their heads against the wall because they persevere when they should be re-evaluating their previous choices. They might rush into a marriage or a business proposal, certain that what seems right cannot fail, without having the skills or forethought to navigate it successfully. They might assume that they can master a semester's worth of content in a single all-night binge and find out on test-day that their optimism was overblown. They might fail to correct their choices, sure it will somehow work out. Having a realistic view of the risks while making decisions is valuable.

If we're consistently optimistic that things will turn out just fine, we may fail to take necessary precautions or take on more than we can manage. You might have people who don't give a second thought to walking a mile while lugging a large watermelon and bags of groceries. Those who decide to run for vice-president and later president of the United States, as an act of self-defense against power-hungry politicians.

After I decided to run for VP, I called my mom and told her over the phone, "*Guess what – I'm going to run for vice-president!*"

Her reply – "*Vice president of what?*"

"Of the country!"

She turns from the phone, and I hear her tell my dad: *"You'll never believe what Jo's going to do – she's going to run for vice-president!"*

His reply? You guessed it – *"Vice president of what?"*

My mom: *"The country!"*

That would be me, the eternal optimist.

Seligman had the self-awareness to realize he was definitely grumpier than he wanted to be, and he had the training and skills to actually look into root causes and possible treatments. Crucially, he realized ninety-nine percent of all psychological research up to that date had been on negative things: disorders, diseases, negative social behaviors like stealing. His personal investment in learning how to make himself happy aligned with a research gap in his field and he was in business. Seligman began building what became the field of "positive psychology," the study of happiness.

If the poor tortured dogs in Seligman's lab learned helplessness, could we *learn optimism*?

Optimism, broadly, is your level of confidence that things will turn out positively. Any task worth pursuing will require you to overcome some obstacles, navigate some challenges. How you feel, and how much control you think you have over the outcome of your situation, plays a big role in your success.

There is a genetic component to where you fall on the optimism/pessimism scale, too, but you can learn to be optimistic. Most people would benefit from being more optimistic than they are (if they're not, like me, teetering at the tipsy end of the top scale). Optimistic people tend to be more successful. Believing you can succeed turns out to be a key predictor of whether you can. Optimistic people not only get more jobs and promotions, but also enjoy better mental and physical health. Optimists are happier at work, they recover more quickly from falls and injuries, they have lower rates of hypertension and less fear of aging.

Because a moderate level of optimism encourages us to maintain a healthier diet, exercise, and seek medical advice when we're sick, optimism is correlated with a lower risk of death. But too much optimism can be hazardous to health.

So, if you find yourself often drawn to negative, shakable beliefs about yourself, there's value in training yourself to be more optimistic.

Depending on where you fall on Seligman's scale, there is also value in tempering or tamping down your optimism, to be more in line with reality. Unrealistic optimists underestimate their own likelihood of heart attack, divorce, alcoholism, and early death. Some optimistic people continue to smoke, thinking they won't be one of the unlucky ones who gets cancer, or delay getting medical tests or treatment, because they assume ailments will go away on their own.

The kind of person who believes they can succeed, and in fact finds success, may risk the downside of confidence: over-optimism. A well-known case of a Fortune 500 CEO delayed treatment for his pancreatic cancer, and opted out of life-saving surgeries, optimistic that he could cure himself with an extreme vegetarian diet. He was wrong, leading to deadly consequences.

Doctors said he'd still be alive, and that his prognosis would have been good had he had tumors removed. Far more Californians buy lottery tickets than buy earthquake insurance. Which is to say, the balance between optimism and pessimism can have a big impact on our choices.

When I think back, there were many metaphorical watermelons I impulsively decided to carry home, because I was excited about the outcome and didn't think through the mechanisms that would actually bring that about. Sometimes, my optimism outpaces my pragmatism, and I look before I leap. More about that in another section.

When I get in my car to run errands, I am often quite confident I can stop quickly at the post office and still get to the appointment across town in eighteen minutes. But traffic doesn't respond to my optimism, and that might mean I'm late for something important. I've run out of gas at least once, stubbornly sure I could make it to the next exit before stopping. An overly optimistic brain isn't always an asset. But often, it is.

Because I tend to expect favorable outcomes, I "go for it" in situations where people who envision more barriers would slow down, or not even attempt it at all. When I was finishing my undergraduate degree, I was missing a specific credit but had a similar one that could be applied. I walked into the registrar's office with confidence that I could make my case compellingly and win them over (and I did).

My brain simply doesn't generate the worst-case scenarios, so I don't let the perceived barriers slow me down, even if perhaps I should. I don't think about the distance from the store to home, or how sore my arms will be; I'm hungry for watermelon and it sounds delicious. I never say, "I just can't." My (overly?) optimistic brain is certain that I can. In fact, I think I had a total of four petitions in order to graduate: one involving a calculus credit, another involving getting permission for senior-level economics courses (I hadn't taken any economics classes at this point), and another using a graduate statistics course for a required undergrad course (technically, the grad course I took was much more difficult than the required undergrad course, but for me and my love of numbers, I breezed through the graduate statistics course). I don't remember what the fourth petition was about, but I'm pretty sure I had four. I would like to point out, though, that most of my petitions weren't about getting out of work. In some cases, the courses were more difficult. But I didn't follow the cookie-cutter degree plan.

Seligman and his successors did significant research on athletes, comparing patterns among optimists and pessimists.

Experimenters put runners on a timed trial. Each was told his performance was slightly below expectations.

Those Seligman identified as optimists pushed themselves on a second attempt and performed somewhat better in the next trial. Pessimists ran slower in the second trial. What accounts for the difference in reactions?

Natural disposition matters, but to a shocking extent, researchers discovered. Explanatory styles were key predictors. When things happen, our explanatory styles guide the story we tell ourselves about why they happened.

Optimistic runners were likely to say, for instance, "I got a cramp at the end of the third lap and slowed down," or "That was really not my best time. I must have been distracted." Pessimistic runners blamed it on themselves, on lasting characteristics s. "I'm just not very good at this," or "I'm one of the slow ones."

Any time we don't get something we value, we tell ourselves a story about why. You can use this to your advantage. If you're not a runner, apply this explanatory framework to any pursuit in which you might end up "losing." So, if you're passed over for promotion, or don't get hired after an interview, don't reinforce any negative feelings you might have by telling yourself "I'm no good at this." You have the choice to tell yourself, "*Today*, I wasn't at my best, but next time I will do better!"

When you DO get the job, or the promotion, or the marriage proposal, a strange thing happens. When we get what we want and value, when we win, those explanatory styles actually reverse. When an athlete has a particularly good day, a pessimist will attribute his success to fleeting, incidental, and external causes. He won't be able to take credit for what he does well. A victorious pessimist does not conclude he is fast, or skilled; he concludes that his opponent was not very good. The victory doesn't seem earned, but incidental, and he takes no improved sense of self away from the accomplishment.

That pessimistic bias discourages you from trying to find a way out of the dog-cage of pain.

What Motivates Us

So, what does it take to transcend and change your circumstances? A Canadian researcher of organizational behavior, Victor Vroom, developed a theory that motivation to reach an outcome consists of three factors: expectancy, instrumentality, and valence.

Expectancy: your belief that the efforts you make will get you closer to that goal, for example, that taking good notes and studying hard will lead you to perform better on a test. Do you believe that you can successfully complete the task to reach your goal? In my case, did I believe I could tour the country, attend state conventions, and successfully compete in the pre-nomination debates with other candidates? Why, yes, I did! Someone else might think "No, I'm not good at thinking on my feet" or "No, I don't have the stamina to attend two or three different state conventions (in different states!) in one weekend." (While I had the stamina and had attended multiple conventions in one weekend, COVID stepped in and allowed much of the debating to be done, later on, from the comfort of my home.)

Instrumentality: your belief that better performance on the test will get you the outcome you want. Do you expect that your work will lead to the outcome you want? In my case, did I believe that by doing a good job in the debates and campaigning at state conventions, that delegates would vote for me to win the nomination?

Well, this one got to be tough at times. In the very beginning, I was very optimistic. The straw polls that had me in 3rd or 4th place in some states were very disheartening. Someone else might think "No, the system is rigged," or "No, I could be the best candidate, and it wouldn't matter, because delegates will just vote for their friends, even if their friends are horrible candidates," but I stuck with it.

Valence: the degree to which you desire or prefer a particular outcome. If getting an A on a test is really important to you, you're likely to be motivated to get that good grade. In my case, absolutely, I valued the outcome! I couldn't wait to go out and spread the message of why our country would be so much better if we got to make our own decisions and spend our own money, instead of having the government make decisions on how we should live and how our money should be spent. Others might say, "Well, I enjoy spreading libertarian philosophy, but I already get to do that on my podcast, so it's not worth it for me to give up my podcast and speaking fees to get the nomination." Or, even, "I enjoy debating the free market with radio talk show hosts, but it's not worth traveling around the country for," or "I have too many skeletons in the closet that it's really not worthwhile."

A note on valence. It's called "valence" instead of "value," because it takes into account that worth is subjective to each person. The example I give in class is finding a $100 bill on the sidewalk. Economists assume that $100 is worth $100. Well, it may not be worth it for Bill Gates to pick up that $100 bill (according to one estimate, he would have earned

$500 in the time it takes him to pick it up), but it's certainly worth my time to pick it up! So, valence (and not value), considers how much $100 is worth to each person. In my campaign example, it was priceless to me to get the nomination.

If any one of the legs on that three-legged stool is wobbly, your motivation will falter. If you believe that no matter how hard you study, your performance on the test won't improve, perhaps because you just aren't a good test taker, then expectancy is missing. If you believe that no matter how hard you study or how well you do on the test, your teacher won't give you an A because of some personal bias or animus, then that instrumentality piece is missing. If you don't really care about the outcome, because a sport or a romantic relationship has become more important to you than your grades, and even getting an A is unlikely to be personally satisfying, then valence is missing. When all three factors are present, you're likely to be motivated to do the hard work in pursuit of your goal.

A big factor in expectancy is *perceived control*, or your belief about how much control you have over the outcome. If you believe that you can change what's happening to you through your own efforts, you keep that sense of control close to you, and you feel less at the mercy of larger forces. This increases self-efficacy, or your belief in your own capability to bring about the results you prefer. Entrepreneurs, leaders, organizers, and effective folks in any field must believe they can make a difference and direct their efforts toward where they can successfully create change.

When people succeed, other people notice them succeed. We build up optimism and self-efficacy by learning from role models. When someone whom we perceive to be like us accomplishes something wonderful, we integrate the knowledge of that success into our own self-perception. When the role model teaches us directly from the mastery they've achieved, the self-perception can become part of our self-identity.

I watched my father build our house. I also watched my grandfather plaster the crown molding in our living room. Watching them not only taught me the skills but gave me the confidence to tackle home repair projects, even before YouTube videos and HGTV made it trendy to "DIY." Being "handy" is a form of self-efficacy and any "handy" person will tell you they've made mistakes and pushed through them. Later, I would remodel properties

I lived in. I never shied away from making repairs on my home, except for plumbing and electricity.

Because it's important to push yourself and also to know your limits!

When we see someone who looks like us, or speaks like us, excel, we gain confidence and self-worth. We begin to believe that we, too, can achieve that greatness. The more closely you can relate to a particular role model, the more you will be motivated to achieve what they've achieved. We see this in deliberate empowerment campaigns, but also with the gradual inclusion of women, ethnic minorities, people with disabilities, and other historically underrepresented people in highly visible positions. Such visibility in real positions of influence — not just in media portrayals — speaks to the self-efficacy in each of us: "She's like me and look at what she's accomplished." (My daughter and I loved to watch *Gilmore Girls* together when she was in high school, because the mother and daughter team in that show had personalities so similar to ours — and different from each other — that it was easy to imagine ourselves in the scenes and situations. Yes, like Lorelai, I was the impulsive one, while my daughter was the responsible Rory.)

I'm not exactly sure what part of me is a "woman" doing the things I do, because I've not had the opportunity to experience anything else. (I was often asked by reporters if running for president was different for me, because I'm a woman. My reply: "*I don't know. I've never run as a man!*") I've only ever had the chance to inhabit my own body and brain, and I happen to be a woman, but I'd like to think I would be very substantially like myself, even as a man. So, it's taken some patient conversation with campaign staff and other people I trust to encourage me to engage "woman" as part of what I want to model. The research on inclusion shows me why seeing a woman's name appear on ballots and on television would maybe connect with girls and young women who'd never seen someone they see as 'like them' in the nation's top spot. I recall those paper placemats we used to get in greasy-spoon breakfast spots, with pictures of the presidents in their little embellished ovals. It didn't seem strange to me as a kid how similar all those faces were. Now that Barack Obama appears in that sequence, something feels notably different, broader, more inclusive and representative. Adding a woman's face to those placemats, no matter who she may be, will help people who feel excluded to imagine themselves helping to shape solutions.

Self-efficacy is not witnessed, though. It is built. Dozens of times over our years on earth, we set a goal, persevere through challenges, achieve that goal, and enjoy the positive results. The more often we do this, social science research says, the more we understand that outcomes are reflections of our efforts. We learn that we can succeed, and that we have the skills to overcome adversity. That increases our willingness to do the hard work when it is required. We might think we want to achieve quickly, without struggle or sustained effort, but that can train us to avoid adversity and actually hurt us long term. Overcoming challenges and disappointments build up muscles of resilience. If we don't build those muscles, we may become easily discouraged.

The Tempered Optimism of American Politics

When reporters asked me, "*Do you think you can win?*" I used Ed Clark's brilliant response from 1980, which is that if I had the chance to sit with every American family around their kitchen table and explain libertarianism to them, I would win in a landslide. But in a nation of 332 million people, the defining characteristic of the election outcome wasn't going to be the soundness of libertarian ideas. That just wasn't within my control.

The disparate campaign budgets and levels of media attention, as well as all the legal impediments placed in front of third-party candidates, were going to have much more salience in determining the outcome. In 2016, when Gary Johnson made it to the polling threshold to be included in presidential debates, the debate commission changed the rules to exclude him. My expectation was never that I would be allowed to debate, so I wasn't terribly disappointed. Nor did I spend a lot of resources lobbying to change those rules (though the grassroots *Let Her Speak* campaign made a stunning effort on my behalf, which I so appreciated).

The likelihood that any third-party candidate for president would win the office was so remote, and the factors so far from my control as a third-party candidate, that I didn't lose much sleep over it. I didn't grow up wanting to be president, and I'm sure I love my current job 100 times more than I would enjoy being president. I've always been suspicious of those who've had a life goal of going into politics — I think people who do want that power disqualify themselves. I much prefer to see, for instance, mothers fed up with the local schools decide to run for the school board in their 30s, never having considered running for any office before then. Or a business owner who gets fed up with local licensing laws, so decides to run for city council or statehouse.

Vroom's three criteria can act as a filter, letting you know what's worth your time and energy. To keep from going crazy, I chose to manage our campaign goals and apply our efforts to the things we could control, and where applying effort was likely to make a difference in getting our message out to people. My definition of 'winning' wasn't what the reporters were asking about, what people thought I should want. My goal throughout was to do the things that were within my control as well as I possibly could. That kind of locus-of-control realism kept me motivated and kept me encouraged, by focusing optimism toward where my efforts mattered. I wanted to be a good messenger for the party, wherever the position of candidate would allow me to speak, and to make people genuinely wonder if there weren't choices, they were better off making for themselves. Holding their attention long enough to change their minds. That's the win.

Reclaiming Your Control

I also made it a point in our campaign materials and messaging to be realistic about what choices a president could or should try to make for people. It's unethical to say, "if you elect me, I'll guarantee to lower your price at the pump," because the President doesn't have much influence over gasoline prices. Nor should they! But making impossible promises of hope and change, lower healthcare prices or better educational outcomes, whether they're running for a position that could influence those outcomes, or not -- that's the stuff of campaigns, politics as usual. We were out there telling people they could take back the power from politicians who were abusing it and make choices for themselves. I wanted to call out to self-efficacy, and optimism.

The ever-expanding reach of government into daily life damages our self-efficacy. When you feel like your efforts make a big difference to outcomes, you try harder and strive more. But when you see your choices taxed and penalized, you start to feel your feet being shocked by the floor. If you start a business, you'll find a little cage closing around you. Now and then you get zapped, just like in Seligman's lab. A late fee from the licensing committee, and the second visit from the code inspector, and the parking usage waiver extension, and the form 897B that was supposed to be filed last week. Really successful entrepreneurs and innovators will be called before Congress, accused of bad action, slapped with burdensome regulation, or otherwise brought back in line with the herd. Each time you feel a shock, self-efficacy fades a little. Self-efficacy is undermined.

When big coercive governments interfere too much, each leg of the Valence-Instrumentality-Motivation triad is disrupted. Among the governed, the perceived incentive to achieve is reduced. We put in a staircase for an elderly neighbor to visit the park, and have it torn out by city builders who hadn't approved it. We want to open a business but get cease-and-desist notices, the barriers of some expensive training and licensing class. Our motivation to build and create is weighed down by red tape, blocked by special interests and distant regulators.

We learn that outcomes are tied to the whims of bureaucrats and lawmakers, not to our own dedication or ingenuity. We no longer expect that our efforts will be enough to change our circumstances. Or we become so discouraged that we believe circumstances will never change, regardless. And when that sense of being able to change your own life breaks down, you try less often to change or escape, creating a self-reinforcing downward spiral toward learned helplessness.

Career politicians strategically appeal to your dwindling optimism by saying they're going to save you, protect you, or provide for you. They want you to cede more control of your choices to them, so they promise you the outcome can be accomplished without your efforts. The ultimate form of this wish-thinking is in bill titles: if you call it *"No Child Left Behind,"* then everyone's kid is left at the starting line. Or if you call it the *"Inflation Reduction Act"* it won't matter that its impact is actually to vastly increase inflation. We are called on to believe that someone else has control, and to welcome the surrender of self-efficacy. Being too optimistic about what politicians can offer you leads you to believing false promises, being easily manipulated, losing control of your own life. Skepticism is healthy, especially if it convinces you to keep the locus of control in your own hands.

"Vote for me" is a poor substitute for instrumental change.

On the other hand, despair about the state of your life, the nation, or the world is both unwarranted and unhelpful. You can't live in constant fear and depression and have a healthy or meaningful life. American young people (the much-maligned Gen Z) say they're pessimistic about the fate of the country, although they vote in record numbers. They are reportedly fearful about the economy, employment, and the climate fate of the planet itself. But these grandiose and distant fears, most specifically climate, requires action to address that is so far removed from our control that as worries, they mostly serve to make us miserable, not active. So much of this generation, mired in debt and unappreciated in the workforce, saturated with doom-scrolling and predictions of climate disaster. Solutions seem so distant and problems so insurmountable, they don't take even the smallest of steps toward actual change. Overwhelmed with anxiety and the pressure of "adulting," they float in learned helplessness, awaiting disaster.

So, take heart. People can overcome barriers. A key step is realistic understanding of what you can change and how to make things better for yourself and those close to you. You shouldn't believe that inflation or currency devaluation will magically end tomorrow, or that its impacts will never be felt. But you can cultivate optimism necessary to get another job or a better job, or grow a garden, or learn how to cook at home, or whatever you're going to do that will make you flexible and able to persevere. Believe in yourself. Prepare *yourself*.

Not just individuals, but as a people and a nation, we have a lot to offer. American exceptionalism is a balancing act. There is much in our national character that's unique and special, but we shouldn't confuse that with having the right to tell other nations what they can and cannot do. We can't assume that progress will be in a straight line, that things always keep getting better. Material conditions sometimes get worse. Civil rights are eroded or erased. Moral progress backslides. But as a people, we are industrious and kind. We have an energy for innovation that other parts of the world just don't seem to have. We have endured truly harrowing periods and emerged from them stronger than we went in. Optimism in the American experiment, even when it is sometimes overblown, is not ill-founded. What people can do for themselves is so much, much more powerful than what any politician or national government can do for them, in part because we all define our success and good outcomes differently. We maintain internal locus of control.

We exercise freedom. We amend and evolve. Keep your eyes on the things you can actually change and do what must be done to change them.

How to Be More Optimistic

If you realize that you tend to be pessimistic and grumpy, know that this is changeable and probably worth changing. There are exercises you can do to help yourself become more optimistic. Statistically and anecdotally, pessimism is likely to hold you back. If you don't believe in yourself, you may be easily discouraged by setbacks and obstacles, which are inevitable. Additionally, optimists tend to be happier, can handle stress better, and are more creative when needing to solve a problem, so there are many reasons to increase optimism.

Fortunately, there are strategies to improve your outlook and access the improved outcomes, health, success, and benefits of optimistic thinking.

To make a difference in how you see yourself and your life, Seligman recommends imagining your best possible self. Write out, in present tense and in detail, the experience of a life where you've accomplished your goals, where everything has worked out. Reflect on that "Best Possible Self," and see what lessons, motivation, or inspiration you can take from envisioning it.

When something happens, good or bad, be aware of and challenge your explanatory frame. Savor the control you have over your environment, which, if you believe you can, you can change again and again. Enjoy what you've achieved, and remind yourself that you are capable of change, and deserving of good things.

Listen to music, podcasts, books, or lectures that make you feel energized and competent. Document the things that give you a sense of positive control. Create accountability mechanisms that keep you focused on achievable goals. Cultivate the belief that you can change your circumstances.

On a national scale, we should be doing all of those same things. Elevate and listen to voices that inspire us to be hopeful. Take responsibility for creating change close to you. Document your success and tell others how you did it. Stay accountable to the Constitution and the duties we have to each other, not to lobbyists and legislators.

Cultivate the radical idea that civic virtue matters and action toward reclaiming control over our own lives is inherently virtuous. You CAN be trusted with freedom.

Create Meaningful Goals

My dad ran away from home when he was 14 years old to join the Navy. Of course, the Navy doesn't accept 14-year-olds, but he had a plan for that, as well: he would simply lie and tell them he was 16. While the military has had problems over the years, the recruiting officers had no problem identifying a minor, and promptly delivered him back to his parents. When he was 16, still too young to enlist on his own, my grandparents signed paperwork allowing him to join.

He didn't complete his high school degree, since he was in the Navy, although he did earn his GED. His sister was two years younger than he was, and the school allowed him to walk for the high school graduation with her, GED in hand. The local paper even printed a picture of the two of them. After that, he enrolled in one semester at college to learn accounting for his business, and that was the end of his formal education. He took over the cement contracting business from my grandfather, pouring basements and sidewalks. (Many jokes were made to me about the kind of guy who ran a concrete business near Chicago in the 1960s and 70s!) My dad had no problem setting goals and sticking to them, and he expected the same from his children.

My dad was not what you'd call a believer in higher education. He often told me that the amount of education someone had was inversely proportional to the amount of common sense they had. You go off to college and get your brain scrambled.

Despite his strong feelings about that, he was fine with my going to college, but only because I was certain I wanted to be a medical doctor. This was one of the few professions that he thought was a legitimate reason to go to college. Neither of my parents had REALLY gone to college. In those days you didn't just go to college, especially women.

My mother wasn't ashamed to admit that she had scraped through high school with a C average, which she maintained only to stay eligible for the cheer squad. I think if I had wanted to be an accountant, my dad would have pushed hard for trade school. Only about five percent of doctors were women in 1970, so my mom was very much in the mainstream when she asked me, *"are you sure you don't just want to be a nurse? Then it's not all that responsibility."* And my dad said, *"No, she's like me. She wants to be in charge."* (And yes, much of my stubbornness does come from him, although I also received a healthy dose from my mom.)

One big reason I chose Baylor was that they had a great pre-med program and a strong record of getting people into medical school. I had never heard of Baylor, but my dad's friend had a daughter already attending, and he learned that somehow, going to this private college in Texas was much cheaper than going to an in-state public school in Illinois. My dad was willing to pay for college, but in those days, Baylor was less expensive than U of I.

I was also pretty hungry for independence, like lots of young adults back then, and Baylor had the advantage of being far away. I wanted to be at least one day's drive from home, so that I couldn't claim to be going off to college, and then just be able to run home when things got tough or go home for the weekend and see friends I already had. Or even just do the laundry. I wanted total immersion. A completely new world. Texas was a sixteen-hour drive away from Chicago, and more than met my goal.

Within the pre-med biology program at Baylor, I reluctantly signed up for a psychology course to fill some particular requirement. My view of psychology in those days was not positive. It didn't seem like a very rigorous science, and I thought of it more like astrology. In fact, back in those days, bookstores would have sections labeled "psychology/astrology," and one bookstore had the nerve to give astrology top billing! I bought my roommate's old textbook, even though textbooks were reasonably priced back then (I think this was one of only two used textbooks I bought during the four years). After all, I wasn't about to hang on to the book after the end of the semester anyway. And I certainly wasn't going to use it as any type of reference! In the end, I thought, *"Okay — fine, I'll take your little psychology/astrology class — whatever it takes to get my M.D."* But in that course, I learned of a study conducted in a hospice setting with people at the very end of their lives.

Doctors and nurses were asked to make predictions of who would live, and for how long, who would die, and when. The doctors used medical tests, such as EKGs and blood tests. The nurses' predictions were based almost entirely on the patients' demeanor — how optimistic and cheerful they were. The nurses' estimates were considerably more accurate than the doctors'.

All these years later it still gives me goosebumps. I felt the realization crash in on me. If the mind is that powerful, if the mind has that much control, then *that* is what I wanted to study. My goal was to improve people's lives, and it turned out that practicing medicine wasn't my best route to doing that. There was a better way to reach the goal.

I changed my major from biology to psychology and of course, my dad wasn't too happy about that. He shared my initial impression that psychology was about as credible as astrology, and I failed to change his mind.

Once I was immersed in psychology courses, I discovered a subfield that was even more exciting to me. I took a statistics class in the psychology department taught by a well-known statistician, who consulted with companies all over the country. When he explained to us how he saved a company in Ohio a million dollars a year by simply giving dexterity tests to predict which employees would be best qualified to work with specialty machinery, my budding capitalist ears perked up (I had just finished *"Atlas Shrugged"*). I came very close to joining the doctoral Behavioral Statistics program under that professor (I took the first class in the program as an undergrad, and outperformed some of the grad students), but then, to loosely quote John Lennon, life happened.

Only more than twenty years later did I earn a Ph.D., and in Industrial/Organizational Psychology, a field that wasn't even around to be studied when I was an undergrad. What my stats professor was doing, along with his colleagues, had bloomed into a fully developed field of study. I was hooked.

To invoke John Lennon a second time, my Industrial/Organizational Psychology Ph.D. hasn't gone primarily toward helping companies. Instead, I was lucky enough to find a passion in a profession I had never considered — teaching. More on how I fell into that profession in a later chapter. I've come full circle, though: I now describe the hospice study to my students on the first day of class to give them an idea about how amazing and powerful the mind is.

What We Know Doesn't Work

Before we dive into strategies for setting and meeting goals, let's first dispel some myths, and clear out any roadblocks that might be holding you back. One of the most pervasive myths is the idea that some people have a "fear of success," and don't actually want to be happy or successful. Research has shown that the problem isn't this so-called fear, but that people lack the knowledge of how to implement their goals, and so fail to reach them. It's not some deep-seated fear that's out to sabotage you. That misconception can derail otherwise successful people, especially women, since such psychobabble is often aimed specifically at us. The "fear of success" is difficult to understand (as it would be, if it doesn't really exist) and leads some people to believe there's something deep inside us that can't be fixed. That's not the case.

Another myth isn't quite as destructive, but if you solely rely on it, won't get you very far. That's the Tony Robbins-esq rah-rah, positive goal-setting approach. Unfortunately, relying on just energy and enthusiasm isn't sustainable, and it doesn't give you the skills or supports you'll need to get through the inevitable difficulties.

The sky-high feeling you had at a weekend seminar five months ago will not only have left you by this point, but also won't tell you what to do when you're starting your business and facing a cash crunch and a dispute with your business partner. Any residual positive feelings you still have won't help you push through a rigorous workout or give you direction when things get hard.

Some myths come with a kernel of truth. In the mid-2000s, shortly before I started teaching, I happened to catch a segment on Oprah Winfrey's eponymous talk show about a self-help book called *"The Secret."* The book, by Australian Rhonda Byrne, focuses on The Law of Attraction (borrowed, badly, from the law of physics), the idea that your thoughts and feelings attract similarly attuned results from the universe. Think about positive things, and that positive energy will attract those positive things into your life, the book claims. So, the recipe for success is to banish negative thoughts and worst-case-scenario thinking (benign advice, especially if you are prone to anxiety) and focus on the things you want.

If you want a Ferrari, The Secret's system suggests, put a picture of one on the fridge, or on your vision board, and imagine yourself driving it to work. Perhaps build a garage, with the confidence that a car worthy of its care will eventually appear. Show the universe you are confident you'll get it, and it will come to you.

Like most self-help sales pitches, The Secret contains just enough psychological truth to *feel* valuable, and more than enough nonsense to be dangerous. It's true enough that many of our life circumstances are a result of thoughts we've had, and the choices we've made based on those thoughts. But many aren't. Some problems can be solved by reframing the issue and choosing differently, but many can't. It was reported that even Oprah, after decades of promoting the book, pumped the brakes briefly when a viewer named Kim wrote in to say she'd decided to stop breast-cancer treatments and heal herself with positive thinking.

As powerful as our minds may be (and the patient's mental outlook does have a surprisingly large impact on survival rates and recovery times, as shown in my Psychology Intro class), positive thinking cannot cure cancer.

It would be equally unfair to preach "you create your life circumstances with thoughts, and your world is a result of your choices" to kids born into extreme poverty, victims of crime, and others who are truly beset by forces outside their control. And if someone's getting rich themselves by telling you to "think positive" and "trust the universe," keep in mind that this has strong echoes of confidence men and other run-of-the-mill swindlers.

But can visualizing help? Most certainly! Psychological research shows us, though, that The Secret has everyone focusing on the wrong thing. It's not the end result that you should focus on, but the process. One study clearly demonstrates the difference between focusing on the goal and focusing on the steps to achieve it.

Study participants — the proper term is participants ("rats are subjects/people are participants") — were groups of students, as psychology participants often are. Undergraduates are a very popular pool for researchers to pull from, because they are generally close by, have free time, and will complete seemingly nonsensical tasks for very little pay and sometimes just pizza or class credit. (Psychologists sometimes say that we don't know much about how people in general act; we just know how college sophomores act, because all psychological research has been done on them.)

In one study, students were asked to imagine doing well on an exam coming up, but also to imagine themselves studying hard to prepare. Other students were asked to simply keep track of how long they studied for the exam.

The students who imagined studying hard scored 10 points higher than the other students, most likely because they did study more than the others.

In another part of the study, students were told to imagine the outcome, (getting a good grade) in a very visual, emotional way. They were told to imagine walking up to the posted grades hanging on a wall (this was common in the 1960s, before privacy laws, when the study was done), finding their assigned number, and with a fingertip, following the line across the paper to see a good grade listed. Once again, the other students were not given instructions to imagine the outcome. In this situation, grades of the imaginers were only two points higher than the others.

So, while students who focused on the results (the Ferrari in the garage) scored two points higher, the students who focused on the actual steps needed to obtain the goal outcome scored 10 points higher.

According to the research, in the case of the Ferrari, you're more likely to get it if you picture yourself doing the work necessary to achieve it, not simply popping a photo of the car on your fridge. Focusing on the goal you want to achieve is only useful if you're also working on the actual methods to obtain it — the ones that get real-world results. Without attention to the method and incremental steps, positive thinking is just daydreaming. It may make you more cheerful, but it won't change your fate.

As mentioned earlier, people mistakenly think that "change is painful," according to psychologists. When making changes, take steps to avoid uncertainty to help bring you closer to your goals.

So, let's turn to what research tells us we should be doing to achieve our goals.

What Research Tells Us about Goal-Setting

Research has shown that people tend to set realistic goals (such as "I'll get a bachelor's degree in four years) but tend to be too optimistic when actually pursuing those goals ("No problem - I'll just pull an all-nighter for the final exam that's worth half of my course grade!"). When you set goals, there's a good chance you are setting some pretty realistic ones. The trap lies in pursuing them.

Most managers and workplaces use some form of the "SMART" goal model. The logic is that successful goal-setting should have five characteristics, corresponding to the letters in SMART: goals should be Specific,

Measurable, Achievable, Relevant, and Time-bound. Clearly defining goals this way forces you to think about your priorities, and what you'll need to get things done.

I have two big problems with the SMART goal model. The first is that it doesn't account for feedback.

Feedback is one of the most, if not the most, important ingredient in achieving your goal. During the pursuit, you need to compare where you are now with where you've been and where you're heading. Whether you're doing the necessary things to achieve the goals, and whether you're on the right track. Just because you're working toward a goal, even if you're working hard, your efforts are not necessarily getting you closer to your goal.

My other major gripe about this popular method is that "achievable" bit. Yes, achievable goals do work, but research shows even impossible goals can be effective motivators, if you accept the goal and it involves tasks you want to do. A great example is the Apollo program. When President Kennedy announced that we'd have a man on the moon by the end of the decade (1969), the reaction of the engineers was basically, "BS." They all thought, given the technology on hand, that this was an impossible, or nearly impossible, goal.

But it was something they valued and something they wanted to work towards, and they made it a reality. Think of where we'd be if the engineers were given only what they believed was an "achievable" goal.

According to work done in behavior modification (a system to achieve behavioral goals such as losing weight, quitting smoking, or changing habits at work) a key element is establishing a baseline. Even if you have a really good map, you have no hope of finding your path to the destination without knowing where you are now. This means you start with a diary of your behaviors, without any thought to how you're going to change, for about two weeks. You need to know where the starting line is before you start. So, for instance, if you want to lose weight, you write down everything you eat for two weeks. Yes, everything!

While the purpose is to establish a baseline, sometimes this is actually all you need to do to change your behavior. For instance, just the thought of having to write down, "I ate an entire pint of ice cream tonight" might be enough to keep you from eating that pint (or quart or half gallon!). Even if you do end up eating it, writing it down might cause enough inner pain to help you to make a different choice next time. Viewing the choices you're making now more objectively, you may realize they aren't the choices that you want to be making. It draws your attention to what you're actually doing, instead of the story you're telling yourself. If you record what you're doing, every ten minutes of a three-hour study session, you'll find quite a bit of the time is spent on social media or fixing a snack or chatting with your study-buddy. Sometimes more realistic awareness is enough to help guide you toward better choices.

Once the baseline is established, the next step is to write out the plan, including rewards. And, as with the studying example above, you need to reward the process, not the out-come. That might seem a bit counterintuitive. After all, shouldn't you wait until you get that promotion or lose those extra 20 pounds?

Rewarding yourself in the end is fine, but from work in behavior modification, we know it's more important to reward what you're actually doing along the way instead of the result.

First, you want to "keep your motivation up" (in quotes, because technically that's an incorrect use of the term motivation). Second, you really can't control the outcomes, and it would be very frustrating to do everything right, but not quite meet your goals. For instance, you might have a goal of losing two pounds a week, but after a week of healthy exercise and eating, you don't have control over whether your body loses one-and-a-half pounds or two-and-a-quarter pounds. So, your goals (and your rewards) should focus on the things you can control what you eat, how much you eat, how much you exercise, and how much you sleep (which is totally underappreciated as a cause of obesity). While the overall focus may be on an end result, your rewards need to be on the behavior, or process. Periodically check whether you're heading in the right direction to reach your goal (the feedback element) to make sure your process goals are leading you closer to the outcome goal.

Many people think of goals in terms of willpower. Willpower is a renewable, but not unlimited, resource. You have a certain reserve of emotional energy each day that you can commit to bullying yourself into doing things you'd rather not. In one famous psychological study, subjects were seated at a table which had both radishes and freshly baked chocolate chip cookies. Each participant was then told they were assigned to eat either a cookie or a radish, which they did (and yes, the cookies were freshly baked enough for the radish eaters to smell them!).

All participants were then asked to work on difficult problems that, unbeknownst to them, were impossible to solve. Those who were relegated to eating radishes worked on the problems for only half as long as the chocolate chip cookie eaters did. Having used up their willpower to fight off the cookie urge, they gave up easily after when faced with the puzzle challenge. Moral of the story? Willpower can be transferred from one realm to the other, and there's only so much of it to go around.

If willpower is finite, it's important to spend it wisely. I tell my students that yes, they need to have fairly healthy habits during finals, to fuel the body and ward off illness, but that is not the time to go on a diet.

Students are already under pressure and there are more important priorities during exam week than calorie control. So, if a friend brings over a pizza and they really want some, perhaps during finals would be the time to indulge, so that willpower can go towards studying. There are real world implications, as well. If you're working on an important project at work, it's probably not the time to hold back from eating the donuts that appear every morning in the breakroom.

By now you're probably thinking "Wow - this is a great excuse to eat pizza, with chocolate chip cookies for dessert!" After all, I need all that willpower for my job, my kids, getting stuff done around the home. But it doesn't work that way. There was a third group in the study — participants who didn't eat anything. Their results were close to the chocolate-chip-cookie-eating group, which means that eating the pizza won't give you extra willpower; it's just that resisting it costs you willpower.

Conversely, research also shows that it's possible to train your willpower, like lifting weights to build strength. Go to the store and take the ice cream treat out of the freezer case, stare at it longingly for a few seconds, and then put it back. Think of your arm lifting up that carton of ice cream as lifting a weight.

Even though I hadn't yet received my Ph.D. when I ran with Harry Browne in 1996, and hadn't yet learned all these goal-setting techniques, I didn't spend much time visualizing what it would be like to actually be Vice President. I went straight for the process and set actionable steps. The formidably clever Michael Cloud, who helped us on the Browne campaign and would go on to co-found the Center For Small Government, put me on a crash course reading quota. For one hour every day I would read books he assigned me, mostly on policy, with a healthy dose of libertarian solutions. It was amazing how all those one-hour reading sessions added up, and it didn't take long before I had a large arsenal of policy knowledge, potential solutions, and poignant examples at my disposal.

My goal was to bring libertarian messaging to more people who hadn't heard it before, and to be a good steward of that brand. I wanted to support my top-of-ticket candidate effectively, when that was my job, and to be a good representative of the ideas, as well as the delegates who chose me for the spot. That made it exceptionally easy to focus on the steps I needed to take, instead of the end goal.

The same was true twenty-four years later, when I ran for the presidential nomination. Whether I was elected president or even nominated as the LP presidential candidate wasn't really within my control, and I was well aware of the big systemic factors working against that outcome. What was in my control, however, was the opportunity to spread libertarian messaging, and to make that message both comprehensible and inviting. I don't doubt that some candidates for president fall asleep at night staring at vision-board photos of the White House and Air Force One, visualizing themselves at the Resolute desk or taking the oath of office. Probably relatively fewer are imagining Super Tuesday vote totals and district maps turning their preferred color. And fewer still are diligently reflecting on how they can conduct themselves in order to be worthy of the power that might be entrusted to them.

Goal-Setting for the Libertarian Party

When the Libertarian Party was being founded, the small group of activists couldn't agree on whether we should even run candidates in elections. The desire was to spread the word about libertarian ideas. What works for winning elections — like a billboard featuring a single candidate's face and name — doesn't educate voters about our ideas. And the candidates seemed unlikely to win, back then, anyway. If we were spreading ideas, perhaps that money should be spent putting out philosophical pamphlets. It was difficult to decide which mattered more, and where it was proper to spend members' resources.

But now, fifty years later, it's no longer a reasonable debate, since we have many educational organizations. That niche is being filled by Reason, Cato, the Advocates for Self-Government, the Foundation for Economic

Education, the Future of Freedom Foundation, the Atlas Society, and a dozen other focused, purpose-driven organizations. Some of them predate the party and some have grown since, but the goal of educating the public is being well served by others.

So the goal of the Libertarian Party, as the political arm of the movement, must be to run candidates and win elections. That means focusing on the incremental goals that get us toward electability. Running for state and local offices, including school board and city council, is a challenge for many libertarians. First, libertarians need to run for positions that, in many cases, they don't believe should even exist (such as running for school board, making decisions for other people's children, when they believe that parents should be making their own decisions). Second, libertarians just tend to find the national issues to be the sexy ones. Get into a debate with a libertarian, and it will quickly go toward national issues, such as the military and healthcare. Local and attainable just isn't as exciting.

For me, those incremental steps were developing strong messaging, and then taking it to people who might be ready to listen. The goal of self-government, like every other higher-level goal, required focusing on the process, on the small, achievable steps. We could prompt people to think, just a little bit, about how much power they'd given away, or had taken from them, and what they would be willing to take back. We were reminding people, "You know better how to educate your child, how to farm your land, and how to spend your money, than some distant bureaucrat possibly could."

One of the essential arguments that eventually made me a libertarian had to do with goals: how do you get resources to those who need them most? In grade school, I was taught that the Soviet Union, through central planning, had no idea about whether certain amounts of steel should go towards making cars or making refrigerators. How could a handful of people in one city plan adequately for millions of people in a very large country? The answer, of course, is that they couldn't. As explained to me, the beauty of capitalism is that money is information — if there is a shortage of cars and the citizens can't find the kind of cars they want, then car manufacturers will be willing to pay more money for that steel than those making the refrigerators. Same if there's a shortage of refrigerators — they'll be willing to pay more for the steel than auto manufacturers. Our goals are so individual, and so varied, that it's impossible to centrally plan what will make a whole population happy.

Even with the lofty goals the Soviet Union espoused in those days, including equality and improved living conditions for all people, they couldn't get the incremental steps right. It was impossible for central planners to know what people would want: more refrigerators, or more cars? More washing machines, or more stop lights? Even if central planners could see the rosy end-goal, the lack of a functioning market, with its transfer of information through prices, stumped planners. Envisioning the final goal didn't reveal the incremental steps toward greater happiness, not even the first step.

How To Set (And Achieve!) Your Own Goals

<u>Choose a goal</u>

Think of all the possible goals you might have right now and narrow yourself down to a few. You'll most likely have some that relate to work, others that relate to personal relationships, some related to leisure, and others to just getting a few things done around the house. You'll have some short-term goals as well as long-term goals. If you want to build up some confidence, try getting a few short-term goals out of the way: The feeling of conquering a task helps build an appetite for the next one. One study showed that the average person has about 15 total goals at any one time, so you should have plenty to choose from. For right now, just pick one.

<u>Ask yourself why</u>

Are your goals really your goals, or someone else's? Why do you want to pursue your chosen goal? Be honest! Why do you *really* want a McMansion or a big SUV? Is it because it's something that you really want and will serve you well? Or is it because you want a bigger SUV than your neighbors'? Or a house that will be the envy of your family members. (H.L. Mencken quipped that wealth is making at least $100 more than your brother-in-law.)

Unfortunately, there's a good chance that your neighbor's opinions are driving (no pun intended) your choices for a more expensive car or bigger house. Humans are social animals. We care what others think of us. We are hardwired to read subtle cues in other humans' faces, letting us know what they're thinking. Just as dogs are equipped to hear high sounds that we can't hear (detection), we are equipped to understand minute facial expressions (resolution). We're built that way to get information from other humans. A classic social psychology experiment involves judging other people's behavior to determine whether smoke coming into an office is a danger — if other people shrug it off, we don't take action either. Animals are more likely to get information directly from nature; You may have heard of animals being aware of tsunamis and tornadoes before people.

It goes even deeper than that — over 50,000 years deeper. We have a drive to have children, to keep the species going. Male animals often have behaviors and displays that make them appear larger and more attractive to females. Think peacocks. Males strut around showing impressive tails, even turning towards a certain angle of the sun during courtship to emphasize their tail's iridescence. Showy plumage means health, status, and good genes to be passed on. So, what do human males do? Buy big trucks and big houses to impress their females, sending the message that they are capable of financially supporting offspring. Yes, we women are perfectly capable of supporting our own offspring now, but 20,000 years ago it wasn't so easy. Law school was not an option. Someone had to watch the children while the physically stronger men went out on hunts.

If it's the male's role to show off assets, why do women also have that deep-seated need to show off their large SUVs and remodeled kitchens with granite countertops? To send a message to others, and possibly to reaffirm to ourselves, that yes, we are taken care of and our offspring will be well provided for. Yes, my husband loves me and can take care of our children so well that he bought me granite countertops. How much does your husband love you? Can he take care of your children? It's our peacock plumage.

This isn't unconscious in the Freudian, your-mother-potty-trained-you-horribly sense, but something that is unacknowledged. Men will select a sports car from an ad with a scantily clad woman in it, while insisting it was the price or horsepower that convinced him. Sigmund Freud wasn't even a psychologist — he was a medical doctor! We don't claim him. But there's truth in the idea of being motivated by desires of which we aren't fully aware.

While these displays may have been useful in the past (just as animals in the wild still display them), they are unnecessary in modern society. A quick trip to the grocery store (without the threat of wild animals or terrain) replaces the dangerous hunt. Unfortunately, most people don't question the roots of their desires to keep up with (and surpass!) the Joneses. Women will insist that safety is at the core of their decision for that newer, nicer car, but there are some old sections of our brains that are still influencing us today in ways we never imagined.

Our desire to look to other people for approval helps in some situations, especially survival, but it works against you when setting your goals. To get around this, consider framing your more dubious goal as a fear, and work your way through it. You don't want to drive a 20-year-old car because you think your neighbors, all sporting brand new cars (and better makes, at that) are judging you. Okay, so what? So they judge you. Do their opinions cost you money? Cause you physical pain? Decrease your gas mileage? Of course not! Your pain is self-inflicted and will not serve you well. Besides, will your neighbors help pay your exorbitant car payments or credit card bills from going into debt to impress them?

Another reason we care about what others think is that we do live in a civilized society. You feel bad if people see you run a red light, and you should. Some social rules and social norms are needed and to be followed to live harmoniously.

Last, going after someone who is physically attractive may seem very shallow, but it's built into our genes. We want our children to have the best chance of survival, and attractiveness in our mating partner (symmetry, lack of sores from diseases, etc.) historically meant a healthier partner. Healthier partner genes equal healthier genes in our children. Not only do we look for physical symmetry, such as the symmetry found in the faces of supermodels, we look for other symmetry, such as women preferring men who can dance. As Roy Baumeister and Brad Bushman point out, having two left feet is not very symmetrical!

<u>Look at the timeline</u>

Can you reasonably finish this goal by the time it needs to be finished (if there is some kind of deadline)? Keep in mind that people tend to pick reasonable goals but are way too optimistic when planning how to reach them.

Like a home renovation, any project worthy of your long-term attention is likely to take longer, and cost more than you expect.

<u>Set up regular reflection and feedback</u>

For the most part, SMART goals work well (just be sure to add the feedback step to it, and don't be afraid of goals that seem unreachable). If it's a behavior you want to change, think carefully about what we know about changing behaviors, so you can set yourself up for success.

<u>Identify any barriers</u>

Understand the things that might be getting in your way, physical or psychological, and try to get rid of them, or at least reduce them a bit. For a long time, I neglected one portion of my sunny garden because there wasn't a water spigot where I needed to be, and it was a lot of trouble to wrap the hose around the length of the house to make sure those plants were cared for. After killing a few seasons' worth of investment in that corner, I invested in adding an extra spigot, and put raised beds really close to the house (on cement from an old carriage house that had burned down). I know it doesn't sound like a big deal, but getting rid of that barrier made gardening much easier and enjoyable. Sometimes you have to stop and really think about what could be in the way of making your goal easier to reach - barriers can often be unconscious (not in the Freudian sense, but something you don't realize).

<u>Tell others</u>

Unfortunately, we don't honor the promises we make to ourselves as well as those we make to others, so go ahead and tell someone. Make a commitment if it's possible. One goal that I've had for about 40 years is to take racing lessons, but either lack of time or lack of money always got in the way. I finally did take a performance driving class at the BMW plant (near my city) and had a blast, but now I need to take it to the next level. My business partner (who got into racing after I let him drive my "new" 1973 Triumph Spitfire a while back) said a lot of the guys at the track want to meet me, since I was the LP presidential candidate. I've already told him that

I plan to meet his buddies this summer by signing up for racing lessons at Road Atlanta. Once I get involved in day-to-day activities that make me think I'm too busy to take racing lessons, I'm more likely to figure out a way to make it work, because I've committed to him, not just myself.

<u>Just get started</u>

Despite your best intentions and telling others, you're probably not going to feel like doing what you need to do.

You might be tempted to wait until you "feel like it," or are "in the mood" to tackle your goal-oriented steps.

Instead, just start. Tell yourself you'll do it for 15 minutes, and after 15 minutes you're allowed to stop and go back to being a couch potato. There's a good chance that by the 15-minute mark, you'll get into the activity and want to keep going. Even if you don't, you've strengthened the "getting started" muscle of your brain. To put it in psychological terms, you don't always need the right attitude in order to perform the behavior. Sometimes doing the behavior brings about the attitude. You may have experienced this if you finally got around to cleaning out a closet because you had to, and then you got into a rhythm and somewhat enjoyed it (at least as much as you can enjoy cleaning out a closet).

<u>Reevaluate often</u>

Regardless of the commitment you make, you may find halfway through that this goal is not what you thought at all. While using commitment is a great way to get a few steps completed, it doesn't mean you have to continue for the rest of your life. Yes, my commitment will get me to the racetrack at least once, if not a few more times. But if next year I explain to everyone that the weekly (or whatever) drive is just too much for my schedule, I know everyone will understand my short-lived foray into racing cars, and then I'll move on to another goal I've been meaning to get to.

<u>Enjoy!</u>

Humans thrive when they have goals. We have unconscious mechanisms that are like a tap on the shoulder that reminds us of what we need to do. (You may have felt that tap while at a party the night before an exam!) We unconsciously juggle different goals, with reminders to get back to important goals. Yes, being a couch potato for a short time can be a lot of fun, but that's not how we're designed. We're designed to get stuff done.

Set Meaningful Goals, Whether You Fulfill Them or Not

I hope this chapter has encouraged you to be very deliberate in how you set and pursue your goals.

Unfortunately, there are lots of cultural and social forces that want to give you goals, instead of letting you choose them. Advertising is one obvious example, where companies are motivated to sell you the outcome that benefits them (bigger house, fancier car, college education) whether that's really a goal that would benefit you, or not. Parents also have a way of imposing goals on their children, either because they want the absolute best for us, or as a way of fulfilling some goal they didn't get to (the number of little kids in Future Ivy League sweatshirts is a good indicator). The people you spend time with will also influence the goals you set for yourself, so choose them wisely. The friend whose top goal is to break his beer-funnel record is not going to spur your work ethic like the friend who's determined to graduate with honors. Choose your goals consciously and pursue them deliberately.

Persevering in pursuit of your goals doesn't mean holding onto them no matter what. Your goals will change over time. Very few of us know exactly what we want, and never change our minds. I might even argue that would be a sign of not having grown very much, if what you want out of life never shifts. When you were very young, perhaps you wanted to be an astronaut, or a veterinarian. (I wanted to be a medical doctor.) Then as you got older, your interests and priorities shifted. Maybe you considered being a concert violinist, or a famous surgeon. You aren't obligated to keep the same goals over decades and decades. Either you might shift your goals toward something that suits the person you're becoming, or you might fulfill certain goals (like running your first 10K or running for state house) and move on to bigger ones (like running your first half-marathon or running for governor).

Not all of your goals need to be grand, long-term quests. At any one time, people have short-, medium-, and long-term goals. Imagining the life you want can be inspiring. But real progress lies in taking action to create a better future for yourself, whatever you believe that to be.

And if you don't reach your goals? That's okay, too. Research tells us that merely pursuing goals makes us happy. As Harry Chapin's song reminds us, "*It's got to be the going, not the getting there, that's good.*

Set Up Systems that Empower YOU

Change Those That Don't

When I was in sixth grade, we were required to read at least one book a month. And in the back of the classroom, the teacher had a chart of all of our names, followed by empty boxes [mentioning the empty boxes seems confusing, since that's not explained (it doesn't say that the stars are put in the boxes, and I'm not even sure there were boxes) – maybe delete that phrase]. After each book, we'd do a little written report to prove we'd read it, and then we got a star sticker placed on the line with our name.

This was a system seemingly perfectly designed for me. I have always been fiercely competitive — give me any game or task where I can get a score and I want to get a higher one than anyone else — but also I loved to read. My social, athletic, well-adjusted mom didn't quite know what to do with her daughter who would spend the entire summer vacation reading alone in the living room. Most parents are hounding their ten-year-olds to do more reading; I, on the other hand, was told to, "go outside and play — you spent too much time inside reading!"

I even got my library card in secret. In the very small town where I grew up, the town library was within bike-riding distance. It's not that my mom didn't want me to have access to all those books, but she thought of it almost like a line of credit: if you check a book out, you're responsible for it, and if you don't bring it back, there are penalties. I'm not sure she thought I was ready for the responsibility.

The librarian, fortunately, had no such concerns. My friends, after being surprised to learn I didn't have one, rode their bikes up to the library with me to show me how to get one. So I got a library card, essentially behind my mother's back, and in no small part so that I could keep getting these gold stars for new books. I was consistently reading more books than was required, because I like reading anyway. (For the record, I did show my mom the library card the same day I got it. She was beyond surprised that a library would give a little kid such a responsibility, without a parent's signature.)

My name, just by happenstance, appeared on the chart right next to a kid with the last name of Johnson. And I guess he either liked to read or was competitive, or both, so by the time we were halfway through the academic year, most kids had five or six stars next to their names, and the lines for Johnson and Jorgensen extended right off the bulletin board and onto the painted cinder block wall. (Keep in mind - J appears in about the middle of the alphabet, so our names were front and center on this board!) The stars were starting to get zigzaggy, and I can promise you that any given day of the week Wayne Johnson and I knew who had the lead.

The teacher kept us after school one day. She told us that, apparently, we were having a competition with each other and that we had the wrong attitude toward the process. She thought we should be reading books because we love learning and because we enjoy reading, and that we shouldn't do it to be in competition.

And in my little sixth-grade mind I'm thinking, well, then why did you put up stars next to our names on a public bulletin board if you didn't mean for us to compete with each other? Check your premises, as Ayn Rand always said. The teacher set up a system of rewards and behaviors that turned out not to be what she meant to reward. (For the record, I was the "winner" in this contest!)

What's remarkable is that almost exactly the same process played out in my fifties, when I started going to a yoga studio. On the wall was a very similar board where you could track your progress, and you would put one sticker by your name for each class you attended. It was supposed to be healthy, to give you reasons to prioritize self-care. It wasn't intended to be a competition, but on some level, I couldn't help viewing it that way.

They had all sorts of stickers to choose from, little plants, animals, shapes, some with sparkles.

But I was pretty well-versed in Gestalt psychology, and I knew that if I used the same sticker each time instead of all different kinds, the consistency would be more noticeable. My "progress bar" would stand out amongst the others. So, I chose an orange paw print that looked surprisingly similar to the paw print logo for Clemson, the university where I received my Ph.D. and now teach. And I added them. Day by day, week by week.

I later heard that there had been a discussion between the husband-and-wife team who owned the place, and a few of the instructors, about whether the externally motivated rewards would be appropriate for yoga, a process that was designed to be very individual and internal. And it was my endless line of orange pawprints, each perfectly straight, that had proved the critics right.

The extrinsic rewards made what was supposed to be self-care for your own reasons look like a competition. I did more of exactly what was asked of me, modifying my behavior in a positive way (doing yoga five times a week instead of two) and suddenly I was back in sixth grade all over again (reading more books). "Do more of this, but not like that, or not for that reason." Ridiculous.

Both of these are perfect examples of the classic article I was asked to read in my Industrial/Organizational Psychology doctoral program, called *On the Folly of Rewarding A, While Hoping for B,* from the Academy of Management. This problem is remarkably widespread.

For much of the 1990s, companies were trying to brand for, and outdo each other on, "quality," but paying their employees for "quantity." And we're still doing it. Companies will say, "quality is our number one priority," but then set up departmental goals and bonuses to reward quantity.

Do you think, perhaps, that employees might cut a few quality corners on the way to a bonus for producing high quantities? Sometimes managers say they want to reward seniority and loyalty to the company, but the budget for new hiring is larger than the budget for promotion and retention. The result? Newer people are generally paid more than long-time employees, and top performers only get raises by leaving the company. We have certain ideas of how we want people to behave, and we try to set up systems that reward those behaviors. And we're remarkably, astoundingly, bad at it.

The whole impact of extrinsic rewards is psychologically questionable. We tend to reward kids for doing chores with gold stars or treats. We reward getting good grades, which is an extrinsic motivator stacked on an extrinsic motivator (an "A" is just a different kind of gold star and has only a tangential tie to having actually learned the material).

You may be surprised to hear that I do advocate communism — but only in the context of family. First, another psychological term: reciprocity. Reciprocity means pretty much the same thing in psychology as it does in lay terms (the feeling of indebtedness after someone does something for you, along with the sense that you need to repay that favor), and psychologists discuss it as a powerful motivator for humans.

Reciprocity is part of how we structure societies. Getting rid of reciprocity, and the accompanying emotional motivation, can have unintended consequences. Famously, a daycare center was having problems with parents picking their children up late. The parents were sincerely apologetic when they finally arrived, explaining that something critical had happened at work or an accident had held up traffic along the way, but, nonetheless, the daycare workers couldn't get home to their own families until all the children under their care had been picked up.

The daycare instituted a penalty system — one dollar per minute for every minute after 6 p.m. that a parent showed up late.

To the surprise of the daycare center (but perhaps not to psychologists watching this unfold), parents started picking their children up even later than before the penalties! This was reciprocity in play. In the past, parents were aware they were imposing on the workers when they picked up their kids late. And they were very grateful for the favor and tried to avoid being indebted. (That's the flip side of reciprocity — we don't like being indebted to others, because then we have that favor hanging over our heads. For a hilarious example of this, watch the episode of *The Office* in which Dwight and Andy keep trying to outdo each other so they're not in debt to one another.) When the daycare instituted a penalty system, though, the policy replaced the emotional obligation with a fee-for-service exchange. The parents figured, "Well, I'm paying for them to stay late, so I'll just make one more stop on the way there."

Yes, from the start, daycare is an exchange relationship, but given the nature of the business and how close the parents were to the caregivers, there was a strong communal relationship mixed in there.

This also brings into play the difference between communal and exchange relationships. Communal relationships are those, as the word might predict, with communist-type ideals — those of mutual concern. Which brings us back to communist families. Families are most functional when there is give and take — when family members help each other because they love and care about each other. They help because they want to, for intrinsic reasons, not extrinsic rewards.

Research shows that married couples who have a joint bank account, where they don't keep explicit track of who pays in or spends what, tend to stay together longer and have a more mature relationship. People who have joint bank accounts while they are dating and living together are more likely to go on to get married. Working together without keeping score deepens the relationship, as you each work for the other's wellbeing. There is a long list of benefits from being in such a relationship. In my own life, it didn't even occur to me to have separate bank accounts when I got married, but I realize I was raised in a time when merging bank accounts was the norm for marriage.

Now consider how we try to motivate children within families. Many people rely on allowance and gold stars on chore charts. But by paying for chores and grades, you've inserted an exchange relationship into your family. You've reduced the child's intrinsic motivation to be helpful because they are part of the family unit and replaced it with an extrinsic motivator. Sometime later you might ask your child to help with some out-of-the-ordinary chore, like helping you to take down the curtains for spring cleaning. Your child then whips out his iPad, and says, "Hmm...our allowance contract doesn't include curtains or spring cleaning. I'll get an estimate back to you within the hour. Any other services you're interested in today, ma'am?" The emotional import of being helpful has been displaced by the reward system.

It's also common for parents to pay children money for grades. Children are naturally curious and enjoy learning. By paying money for grades, the parent gets the child thinking, "I'm getting paid for this, so it must be work (like chores) so I must not enjoy it." You certainly don't want to destroy any love of learning for your children. I must quickly add, though, that there is some research showing that if the rewards are framed correctly, it's possible to not destroy the child's love of learning — but it takes a deeper understanding of the system, and kids are very good at coming up with their own explanations for things! So I think it's best to steer clear, unless it becomes necessary. (If it's a task that you don't have intrinsic motivation for, then, yes, being paid to do it will increase your motivation. There are other ways to avoid this problem, but it's easier to just not do it.) Luckily for me, when I was the parent of two young children, I wasn't organized enough to keep extensive gold star charts, so I didn't have to make the decision of charts or no charts. My ADHD brain settled that for me. Either way, I didn't inadvertently destroy any intrinsic motivation my children had. I think.

Adding an external incentive really can kill motivation, especially in our "work hard/play hard" culture. Lately, we're under a lot of pressure to turn passion into employment, and hobbies into "side hustles" or marketable skills. And there are more and more platforms that allow you to monetize your talents. Maybe you really like making little succulent arrangements, or crocheting baby booties. A friend just loves your baby booties and points out that you could make some good money selling them. So, you set up an Etsy store or a craft fair booth and you start producing more of those things you enjoy making. And suddenly your feelings about that process of creation start to change. As you observe yourself crocheting, your brain is telling you, "I'm getting paid for this, therefore, this must be work, and work is, well, work!" And you start to enjoy it less. You are now the victim of what's called the overjustification effect, in which your intrinsic motivation, which involves enjoyment, goes down because you're being extrinsically rewarded. (And don't forget the other random tasks that go with selling crocheted booties, such as filling orders, keeping track of customers, and getting things shipped out on time...now it's a real job.)

American society will tell you that producing 100 pairs of baby booties every week is success.

Making money is often confused with success. But if you're making plenty of money, and you're miserable, are you really successful? I'd say happiness is the ultimate form of success. And you may have bad days or parts of the task you hate (standing in line at the post office, as opposed to the actual crafting), but overall, how you spend your time shouldn't just make you money, but to some extent, make you happy. The research is overwhelming that intrinsic motivation and rewards bring about a lot more happiness than extrinsic motivation and rewards.

Perhaps this is what my sixth-grade teacher was trying to get across to us: that we should be reading books because we enjoy them, not just because we're rewarded for reading. And I did, and still do, love reading. But what truly made me happy was crushing the competition, so, I figure, I won either way.

Systems That Shape Us

To say I'm not a morning person is an understatement. I catch my second wind about 10 p.m., and become very productive, reluctantly going to bed around 2-3 a.m. (Another reason I'm thrilled to have found the job I have, with very flexible hours. The students don't mind either, since I answer questions about upcoming exams the next day until well past midnight.)

In college, I ran at night – 11:05 p.m. during my first year, to be exact. Curfew was at 11:30 p.m. (they locked the doors of the women's dorm at the Southern Baptist college I attended), so I left at a very motivating time to make sure I didn't give up along the way. I kept my pace up because I absolutely had to. That, and my night-owl tendencies, set a preference for running at night that I've held onto for years. I've gone "running" (in quotes, since it's very slow, or "kind of a walk-run thing" in the words of my mom's best friend) several times a week for my whole adult life, including right up until my due date while pregnant with my daughter. I find it's a great way to destress and calm my mind after giving my mind a workout, just allowing my thoughts to flow freely. And it keeps me in reasonable shape.

On the first presidential campaign bus trip, the logistics people would have us up and on the road by around 8 a.m., drive hours to the next event, set up the stage and podium and tents and tables, and then I would give my speech, often in the afternoon. Then we'd have some dinner and perhaps another event. By 10 p.m. everyone else was exhausted, but being a night owl, I'd just be beginning to get my second wind. I would finish up some work at the hotel. Then I'd go to bed sometime after midnight, so I could get up early in the morning for our next trip.

I asked the logistics people if it'd be possible on the next trip to reverse things – could I do the event (even a late afternoon event) and then we all get on the bus to drive to our next destination? I was surprised at how willing they were to go along with it, and within a short time, the team realized that this schedule worked better for just about everyone. Instead of arriving in a city and setting everything up after a long drive, we'd already be there, waking up in a new city, so we'd be full of energy. Crucially, this allowed me to run at night. I often ran at 11 p.m. or midnight, after arriving in a city. (I think the latest I ran was 2:30 a.m., but I made sure it was well-lit. Or I'd call the campaign Media Managing Director who was in California — earlier time zone — to go over a few things. I'd always give her my exact location, with instructions to call 911 immediately if she heard a scream and I was no longer there. A few times I had to restrict my run to many laps around a hotel parking lot, but most of the time I could run safely by myself on actual roads where we stayed.) Deputy Campaign manager Jess Mears and whichever main staffer was on that leg of the trip also took to walking late at night, discussing the next day's campaign event.

No one had bothered to question the drive-in-the-morning schedule for most of the campaigns any of us had ever worked on. I wanted to feel less tired and have time for a run. I wanted the system to work better for me, personally. Once we questioned the system and changed things around, people discovered all kinds of unanticipated benefits that worked for them. In my profession of I/O psychology, I can't tell you how many times I've heard from people that the reason they follow a certain process at work is "that's the way we've always done it." That's a sure-fire way for a company, and an individual, to remain stagnant.

I'm still a night owl. (Research has shown there's a strong genetic component for that.) As I write this section of the book right now, it's almost 2 a.m. And, yes, I teach tomorrow.

It's great having a job where I can request afternoon-only classes, and they go through the trouble to make it fit. One of the best parts of adulthood is letting go of how things "should" be done and figuring out what actually works for you. Building a career that gives you the kind of flexibility and outcomes you value comes from hard work, but first, from knowing what you value and seeking systems that reward it.

Systems We Shape

When I took Latin in college, given my schedule, I had no choice but to take the 8 a.m. section. Whenever we had a test, I simply stayed up all night to study and took the test first thing, which was actually 'last thing.' Then I'd go back to my dorm room and crash before the next class (Luckily, I could fit in a couple of hours of sleep). It isn't what you're "supposed" to do, and I advise my students to not do such things, but it worked for me. It was just unrealistic for me to stay up late and study (perhaps "cram" is a better term!), then go to bed and try to get up at that ungodly hour. Not everything works for every person, and what works for you will change over time and in different circumstances. Knowing yourself and setting up your life so that it suits you, is both freeing and empowering.

The systems we design for ourselves are most noticeable in time management, and in how we keep our homes. How do you feel about the space you're living in? A home can be a "sanctuary," as those home designers on TV call it, or it can be a constant source of frustration. My home is a bit of both, a kind of testament to my ADHD, full of half-finished projects and things I purchased two of because I couldn't find one (I currently own at least four curling irons, because when I owned three, I couldn't tell you where a single one of them was). I freely admit that this is a work in progress for me, and I am working towards a more organized environment.

At the moment, I can tell you where (at least!) three curling irons are.

We are products of our experiences, in addition to our genetic make-up, and we tend to repeat behaviors that work for us. Unfortunately, I've been rewarded many times for my disorganization. In one peculiar instance, I needed a hammer for a project. Luckily for me, there was a hammer sitting within a few feet from me, on my living room coffee table, left there from a recent previous project. I can't remember which projects required a hammer(!), but in an old house, it's not that unusual. Yes, the downside of losing curling irons greatly outweighs the benefits of simply reaching for a hammer, but my optimistic brain seems to remember all the times I've come out ahead.

I did adopt one great habit early on. Before the home office came about, people always seemed to have paperwork in their kitchen, and many still do. This is something I've never done. While working at IBM, I became friends with this super-competent woman who was Rookie of the Year, a real go-getter. And I noticed that she didn't have any papers at all in her kitchen. No mail, nothing. This was the early 1980s and because there weren't home computers, and homes were smaller in general, it was very unusual for people to have home offices. But she had a little rolltop desk just outside her kitchen. And she said, *"Oh, my god, I would never bring paperwork or mail into the kitchen,"* even though that was the practice in pretty much every home I'd ever been in since the 1960s. And I thought, you know, she's right. It makes no sense to have your mail sitting on the counter next to where you're cooking. I decided at 24 to emulate that. I cleared all the mail and paperwork out of my kitchen, and I've stuck to it ever since. In fact, I tend to keep a clean kitchen (I'm disorganized, not dirty!), and sometimes total chaos in the kitchen erupts, but there's no mail in the mix. I highly recommend it.

That said, it takes me forever to get around to opening mail. I'll let it sit in an envelope for weeks, which as you can imagine has the potential to cause all kinds of unnecessary problems. So, I'm able to put a hard-and-fast rule about mail in place when it makes sense to me, and stick to it for decades, even when it's the opposite of what most people do, but then a seemingly easy thing, like opening the mail every day, I just haven't managed to make it stick. I wouldn't say that's a system that's exactly working for me, but hey, I'm nothing if not a work in progress.

We spoke in the goals chapter about how to set good habits if you're trying to modify your own behavior. While there are some general principles that seem to work for most people, individual psychology plays a large role. Someone who wasn't as naturally competitive as I am might have been uncomfortable with the gold-star reading chart stretching off the board, or might have been discouraged in meeting their own, more modest reading goals because they couldn't catch up to me and the young Mister Johnson.

The systems we design — or that others design, and we have to live with — have tangible impacts on our behavior. We get more from ourselves of what we reward, generally, but not always the way we imagine. Sometimes small changes have more positive — or negative — side effects. Unintended consequences come in all flavors and sizes.

My consistent string of orange paw print stickers for yoga classes was one simple system, and probably the one the studio organizers had hoped to engage: I wanted to keep my streak going. I like to beat my personal records in just about every area, so I have fun keeping a streak going.

There is a downside, though, which is you can beat yourself up too much when the streak gets broken. That can even happen from events beyond your control, but regardless of why you break your streak, just make sure it's not counterproductive. Don't let a slip become a slide.

Whatever you find "works" for you, try to acquire positive mental habits. Priming yourself to repeat a behavior helps to make it automatic and sets the conditions to make it easier to continue with a behavior, even when it's not the one you most enjoy. You're exercising the muscles of your brain, slowly reshaping your perception of normal, and eventually your sense of self, to include the behavior. Repeating a behavior reinforces your commitment to it. Some research has shown that about half of our behaviors are habits (which is a great time-saver!), so if you can move a desired behavior from conscious to automatic, you're in good shape.

Changing A System That's Sucking the Life Out of You   and Everyone Else

Like the sixth-grade gold-star reading chart, and the campaign travel schedule, every system tends to encourage or discourage certain kinds of behavior by creating external incentives. These external incentives can be powerful – think of the term "chasing the dollar." You've probably known people who almost ruin their lives going after unimportant things.

Earlier I mentioned that communal relationships work well within families. So why not for countries or governments? Currently, many politicians and Americans are advocating for socialism, regardless of the fact that it's never worked anywhere in the world for any length of time, and more people have been lifted out of poverty in capitalist-type governments (exchange systems) than in any other type of system ever.

It should be pretty easy to see the difference — it's easy to be empathetic to those closest to you. Your husband or your child is sick. You literally feel for them. You want to help them because you hate to see your loved one suffering. If your husband is in bed moaning from the pain of the flu, your first inclination isn't to go in there and tell him, "Okay, fine, I'll fill in and do your chores the next few days. I'll take out the trash (or do your laundry or unload the dishwasher, whatever chores are normally his), but I expect you to do my laundry next week (or load the dishwasher or cook or whatever you normally do)." No, your focus is on helping him.

Same with your children, and even when they're not sick! You care for them, make sure they get the best education, nurture their particular interests and activities. Your primary interest in doing all that isn't to get paid back later. Sure, your child might get a high-paying job thanks to the great preschool you found, or your son might become a world-famous soccer star and buy a house to thank you for the soccer league you put him in, or your daughter can invite you as her plus-one to the Oscars thanks to school plays you attended. Of course, we have hopes and dreams for our children. But as parents we're not looking after our own interests; We do what we think is best for our children.

That's partly built into genes. We have an innate ingroup/outgroup mindset; we tend to favor those in our group (whatever that group may be, alma mater, religion, sports team, fandom). In fact, a group of researchers tried to perform an experiment which required groups that were totally random, but found it impossible to do so, because every time they put people together into a group, those in one randomized group thought their group was better than the other randomized group!

We have this innate us/them mindset that is not learned. It's most likely inherited from tens of thousands of years ago, when humans clung to the safety of our own groups to defend ourselves against marauding groups of outsiders. While we are not born racist or prejudiced, our brains are built to think whatever group we're in is better than other groups. After all, it was the "racist" groups who won over others, when we look back through history, because they banded together to beat out others for food during shortages. In a modern market economy, where wealth is generated through cooperation rather than preserved by exclusion, racism and xenophobia are a huge hindrance. But looking after people you know, who can be counted on to cooperate with you rather than steal from you, still makes sense.

Consider where the United States is now, in the 21st century. We have a very large country with a very large population. Do you have the same level of everyday concern for someone living a thousand miles away from you as you do your own family? Unlikely. Please note, I'm specifically talking about everyday concerns, such as someone having the flu. We are, and have been, the most generous nation on earth, and give to complete strangers in this country and around the globe for catastrophes and emergencies, but how willing are you to, let's say, work an extra 30 minutes per day so that a child a thousand miles away can attend a slightly better school? Your own child, sure. A stranger you'll never meet? Unlikely. Communism breaks down when there are few reciprocal and familial ties.

I saw this in action at my disk-duplicating company, in the days it was winding down. We had a large, rush order to get out, and were short-handed. One of my employees had a friend who was out of work, and said she would ask her to help out. Luckily, the friend showed up the next day, so there were about six of us working at a table, instead of five, which was a big help. Yes, on this day I rolled up my sleeves and was also in the assembly part, rather than my usual office job of running the company, because we needed all the help we could get on such a tight deadline. We had about a week to complete this large order.

At this point, I need to mention that the work was a bit tedious. We were collating 3.5 inch floppy disks, putting them into plastic bags, and sealing the bags. The nice part about the work is that we could all chit-chat, tell jokes, and listen to music, so good conversations could be the focus. Kind of felt like a quilting bee.

The next day I was concerned when the friend didn't show up. My employee told me, *"Oh, she said she absolutely hated the job. She said it was so tedious that she'd rather get unemployment than work at this job."*

I was a bit surprised, as she seemed like a very nice person who would show up for a few days just to help others in a crunch. But, of course, who were we? We weren't family.

And the "unemployment" she spoke about? Basically, getting a check in the mailbox (this was the 1990s!), from a large faceless government. Again, she seemed like a decent person, I just could not imagine her going to her family members and saying, "Hey, I'm out of work, and the only work I can find is this boring job that I don't want to do. Would you please give me money so I don't have to spend my days putting disks into bags?"

I really don't think she would do that. I don't think she would have wanted to be a burden on her family. But it was no problem for her to be a burden on a faceless government, in which money seems to magically appear when we need it. She didn't have to see all the hard work of fellow Americans (some doing very boring jobs themselves!) that paid for the opportunity for her to be paid to stay home, instead of working a job she didn't enjoy.

I read an article in the Wall Street Journal in the early 1980s with a similar bent. A laid-off worker in Michigan (auto industry, which the government helped destroy, but that's another story for another time) moved to the boomtown Houston, flush with 1980s oil money. He hated the heat and the humidity, so moved back to Michigan, stating he'd rather be on welfare in Michigan than working in Houston.

Another example from our business. We had a great team working for us, partly because we offered such flexible hours, and had a starting salary above minimum wage even though the work was minimum-wage level. Most of our employees, as in the story just mentioned, were friends of other employees or heard about us through word of mouth, so we never advertised for help. Our company was in a business park, and my desk was right up against a front window, so I could see people drive up to the parking spots in front of our business. There were several times when I would see someone drive up specifically to our business, come in and ask for my signature on an unemployment form that they had asked for a job, get back in their car, and drive off. In other words, I did not see them park in the distance a bit and go down the line of businesses, asking for work. Our business was singled out. What made things worse is that the business right next to ours (about 20 steps from our door to theirs) had a "Help Wanted" sign in the window, and I didn't see a single person leave our business and go next door to actually ask for a job at a company that wanted to hire someone.

Talk about a messed-up reward system! Public subsidies unfortunately reward some people for not working by paying them to not work. And pays them to stay in areas of the country where their work isn't needed. Wouldn't it be better to have a system that rewards those who go where they're needed?

By now you're probably saying to yourself, "But we need to help those who really need help!" Absolutely. I couldn't agree more. But the way to do it isn't by a large communal system, which is bound to fail, as did the Soviet Union.

If you're going to insist that the government take on the role of charity, then it needs to be done at the local level. In fact, for many years in our country, that's the level that looked after the poor, and it did a pretty good job (as well as can be expected by a government program). Not only could those in charge of the system more easily find out who needed the help and who didn't, but those asking for help realized they were asking their community for help. They were imposing (hopefully for a short time) on the generosity of their friends and family, not the large, faceless bureaucracy of the federal government.

Of course, I'd take it a step further, since private charities have a level of accountability that's not found even in local government. If an organization isn't getting money to those who really need it, then donors stop supporting them, and instead give their money to those who do a better job.

The example I used often in my 1996 VP campaign was that of United Way. It was report-ed at the time that the President and CEO of United Way spent hundreds of thousands on lavish office decor and spent donor funds courting a much-younger woman. When donors discovered that, they were outraged, as they should have been, and donations went down. United Way revamped their policies, making sure more of the money got to those who really needed it, and donations increased again.

We can't do that with the government. If the government is wasteful (and by the sheer size it's going to be) we can't decide to give those charity dollars to organizations who are going to do a better job.

You may have heard of countries that seem to do okay with socialist systems. Denmark is one I've heard of often in the past (although they are having more of their own problems now), but it makes a poor comparison. First of all, there's the size of the country. It's small, so when people take from the system, there's more of a communal feeling of taking from friends and neighbors.

Secondly, until fairly recently, it's been a very homogeneous group. When people were clamoring for us to be more like Denmark, 90% of that country was of Danish origin. Like it or not, we have that innate us/them ingroup/outgroup mindset that we are born with. In Denmark, the majority of the population is 'ingroup,' more like family, which thrives on communal relationships.

A side note about the happiness of Danes. Denmark is frequently found at the top of rankings of countries for "happiness." Sometimes people try to draw a cause-and-effect relationship from socialized medicine, or socialism in general, to their happiness. Upon further inspection, the reason that the Danish are happy is because their expectations are so low! They don't expect things to go according to plan (they assume the bus will be late or the store will be out of the item they need), so when the bus is on time, they're elated. In America, we just assume buses arrive on schedule.

All that being said, though, how Denmark could keep a system going better than most, I need to point out that it was Denmark that my grandmother "escaped" from. The grandmother I mentioned in my stump speech. When I was young, she would tell me how awful it was — that you could work and work and work and it didn't matter, because the government would take away all your money anyway.

Not that she and my grandfather (also from Denmark, but they met here) became wealthy in the United States. She told me those stories as we sat in the trailer that they had retired in (or mobile home as she would always correct me!). Granted, their mobile home park was nicer than most, and it was in nice weather (Florida), but they never made it big. What they were allowed to do, though, was to keep what they earned, reinvest it in their business (cement contracting, north of Chicago), and decide best where the money should go.

Unfortunately, our current government is increasing taxes to the point that we may soon be like Denmark, which won't be sustainable in our large country. To design a system to build a great nation, reward entrepreneurship and job creation, motivate people to organize impressive things and seek their own wellbeing...you almost couldn't do worse than the IRS income tax system.

I absolutely hate doing my taxes, and it isn't just the ADHD brain that is so paperwork averse. (On the campaign, after complaining every day for about two weeks that today was the day I would force myself to put together my corporate information to give to my accountant, someone on the bus quipped, "Now we know why you're running for president - you just hate doing your taxes!" That wasn't why I was running, but taxes are a big part of why I'm a Libertarian).

I really do hate it, not just in practice, but in principle. Taxing income and employment couldn't be more on brand for *Rewarding A, While Hoping for B*. Taxing earnings makes people hesitant to keep increasing the value they bring to society, because they're penalized for earning more. If the goals of your society include innovative ideas, economic growth, and increased employment, income taxes punish exactly the behavior you'd otherwise want to encourage.

Our tax system punishes creation, trade, productivity — and rewards lobbying instead. At each step of exchange, you pay another tax: tax if you sell your land, tax on what you buy with the money, or on the returns if you invest it wisely. Tax in the form of inflation, which eats away at your savings even while they're sitting in the bank. The only ones who don't pay are those who negotiate special exemptions and deductions, which are just another set of incentives aimed at engineering our behavior. It's a system acting on us, without our consent, and it's literally draining us.

Employment taxes make it harder to hire and keep employees. When I was running my disk duplication business, we grew from just two founders and our initial personal investments to 25 employees and more than two million in annual revenue (in 1990s dollars, not our currently highly inflated dollars). Each time we hired someone, we had to account not just for the wages we'd pay them, but also for the huge tax burden associated with each hire. If we hired someone full time, we also had to pay the government for Social Security and Medicare, which is a separate expense we're paying out in order to employ someone, but that the employee never sees. Same goes for Federal Unemployment taxes. Failure to withhold our workers' wages from them would be met with stiff penalties. Our country wants more jobs to grow the economy, but the government punishes companies who hire new employees by requiring endless paperwork (all subject to steep penalties if not done correctly), along with additional costs.

One concept I teach in my Social Psychology class (it's been a few years since I've taught this class) is the tragedy of the commons. Unlike liberal professors, I don't randomly bring up my own personal politics. I realize that students and parents are paying a lot for tuition, and I'm being paid to teach psychology, not my pet political ideas. Fortunately, this topic does fit into the class nicely and is mentioned in three different places in the social psych textbook I used (thank you, Dr. Roy Baumeister!)

The tragedy of the commons occurs when resources are shared, leading to people frivolously wasting them. The typical situation given is fishing waters. Different fishing companies have access to the waters, so, as predicted, the fishers try to catch as many fish as possible, but since no one person or company is responsible for the waters, no one worries about restocking the fish or making sure the waters aren't overfished. I was pleasantly surprised that my textbook authors, in a field composed almost entirely of liberals (many of them extreme liberals), used the Soviet Union as an example. Farms were collectively owned, giving everyone incentive to take the food they needed, but not put much effort into it. After all, it's not their farm, so why put in extra hours only to have a fellow compatriot take, literally, the fruits of their labor? People were starving in the U.S.S.R., because of this tragedy of the commons, so the government very reluctantly introduced capitalism into farming by allowing people to own small lots they could farm themselves. In the end, 30% of the food was produced on these private lots, even though they only accounted for only 3% of all the farmland!

The tragedy of the commons explains why people turn to the government for help when in fact, it's the government causing the problem. That's not limited to the Soviet Union. We hear about some tigers being an endangered species and elephants being slaughtered for their tusks, and the knee-jerk response is to get the government to fix it. It turns out, much of this poaching goes on in quasi-government areas, or areas that are jointly shared (such as the fishing waters), so hunters have the incentive to hunt as many animals as they can, without the responsibility to make sure the different species procreate. On my VP campaign trail, I would point out that you never hear about a farmer coming back into the farmhouse and excitedly telling his family, "I had a great haul today — I just shot 25 cows out back!" when the farmer only had 25 cows to begin with. Notice cows, even with so many people eating burgers, are not an endangered species! That's because cows (many of them, anyway) are privately owned, with the owners having the incentive to replace the herd as time goes on.

Can we fix the tax system? I sure hope so. But it's going to require a level of overhaul that will be fiercely resisted by a lot of people who like our current, broken system because it serves their special interests. The system *is* working for some people, and they won't want you to change it into something that works for you, instead.

Keep in mind, before World War I, America didn't even have an income tax. We paid taxes, generally, on imports and exports, and on consumption: that is, mostly sales taxes. That encouraged saving and investment and allowed people to keep more of what they earned, so they wanted to keep creating. That was certainly a better way of doing things than how we're doing it now. The system we've designed — or fallen into — is almost entirely backwards. We need to start rewarding what we want more of.

Do What Works for You — And Keep Improving It

Most systems you live under aren't anywhere near as difficult to crack as government taxes. Even those that feel rigid, like working 9-5 or commuting to an office, are increasingly able to be adjusted. If traditional college doesn't work for you, choose something that does. If a traditional workplace doesn't work for you, you'll have to work harder in other areas, but you can opt-out of that system. If your household or family routines are doing more harm than good, change them. If a government consistently acts against your interests, challenge it.

When you're focused on your own success, and aware of what you find motivating or demotivating, you can develop systems and habits that encourage you to do your best.

Get Real

Be Authentically You

I'm not sure how I ended up emphatically indifferent to designer labels or fashionable trends, but my small-town Midwestern upbringing and pragmatic parents probably played a role. I favor quality and my own eccentricities over the hottest new look. I did spend quite a bit of money on those 1980s power suits for my job at IBM, in a cookie-cutter style that quickly went out of fashion, and I'm now a bit embarrassed about it. I could have been one of those outdated, shoulder-pad-clad models on the "*Dress for Success*" book jacket. In the years that followed, perhaps emboldened by that experience, I started to develop a style of things I liked, a style, or perhaps a non-style, I consider to be authentically mine.

When people ask me what the hardest part of my campaign was, I think they expect me to say exhaustion, or the grueling travel, or staff drama, or political hostility. But the real answer is — they made me wear *polyester!*

When you run for national office, lots of people have lots of opinions about what you wear. I received complaints that my campaign wardrobe made me look too much like a schoolteacher, but hey, I am one! I was asked to get a lot of new clothes (some we rented) to spiff up my look, but there wasn't enough time to sort through all those nice-looking options in search of natural fabrics, which I prefer. In the 1970s, I would've never believed it'd be so hard to find 100% cotton clothes when I got older. Cotton used to be basic and "plain," and now it's a luxury fabric.

I didn't have a very deep wardrobe of business clothes, since I had been out of the corporate world so long. My teaching clothes consist of long cotton dresses and long cotton skirts with casual tops (cotton, of course!). While I like to think of myself as dressing Bohemian, my family calls my style, "corporate Bohemian," and unfortunately, that's pretty accurate. I occasionally wish it were a more "cool" style – more "Bohemian" than "corporate," but that's where I landed.

The campaign staff made it clear that I couldn't keep wearing the same three or four outfits. I didn't quite see why it mattered — they were clean, after all, and nobody in Pittsburgh on Friday knows or cares what I wore in Dayton on Tuesday, so what's the big deal?, but at the higher levels of politics, this indifference is apparently unacceptable. They hired a stylist for me who took away my turtlenecks and told me to "open up my neck."

I can't wear wool (allergic), and polyester feels terrible on my skin. My daughter has sensory integration issues, which started when she was just becoming a toddler. Sometimes we'd go through three or four outfits in the morning, just for her to find something that didn't hurt her. Once, I remember putting her new shoes on, and she screamed bloody murder. I thought, "Oh, no, maybe there's a needle in there from my sewing (I hand-smocked the dresses I sewed for them)," but no, she was losing her little mind because one of the shoelaces was further down than the other and was touching the floor. But anyone passing by would have thought I was scalding the child with boiling oil. I can't say the polyester felt *that* bad on my skin in 2020, but it would've been nice to scream.

At the time when we were seeking a diagnosis for her, the specialist asked me, "*Do the tags on clothes bother her?*" and I had to say, "*I don't know. They bother me, so I cut them all out of her clothes before I ever put them on her.*" So, perhaps we can begin to guess where some of those strong preferences came from.

And for me, it was professional political consultants who wanted to change my outfit three or four times. This was a whole new world for me. In fact, when I threw my hat in the ring in 2019, I bought mascara for the first time in four years. And the only reason I had bought some four years earlier was to wear it to my daughter's wedding, and then never picked it up again. (Perhaps I should be allowed to drop the "corporate" part of corporate Bohemian because I don't usually wear mascara?)

I didn't find out until after the campaign that I was criticized for not wearing nail polish. It didn't even occur to me; I prefer not to wear it. These are issues — the right earrings, the right makeup, the 'approachable' neckline — that men in professional positions never have to worry about. Americans seem not only to care more when a woman wears the same suit twice in a week than when a man does, but many people seem to care more about what a woman wears than what she thinks or how she will govern. I'm really not sure authenticity can be elected president in this image-obsessed age.

During the campaign, there were pictures of me in the media, and circulating on buses and flyers and such. During one of my online Clemson classes I was teaching, I received a note in the chatbox about my campaign. I said thank you for the kind words, but I don't talk about politics in class. She replied something along the lines of, "*I thought it was a big coincidence that you looked so much like that lady, and then I realized it was you!*" She was more right than she knew. My reply: "*Yes, hair and make-up does a lot.*" Granted, it was an online class, but there was a live video stream of me in the corner of the screen. In those photos, in those clothes, it was me, but it wasn't.

But I did find some pieces that the campaign approved of, that met their specs, and that I could stand to be in. As it became clear that I'd maintain a professional presence at conferences and conventions for years to come, I have patiently (and with careful shopping of sales) built up a non-polyester wardrobe of business-friendly separates that both look good and feel good. More importantly, they don't feel like I'm putting on someone else's clothes just to make a good impression.

One of the biggest things I've had to accept about myself, and learn to live with, are my shortcomings from ADHD. With a lot of work, I have learned to overcome, or at least get better at, certain aspects. One thing that a lot of people don't realize is that some researchers have found that ADHD symptoms in girls are different than those in boys, and I have the classic female ADHD symptom of interrupting people. I was told by my teachers, from grade school to college, that I interrupt too much and ask questions that are completely irrelevant. This is one area where I think I've been able to improve. No, I haven't completely stopped interrupting too much, but I'm so much better at forcing myself to wait than I was when I was younger.

Unfortunately, the one big area I haven't been able to overcome, and may never overcome, is being able to follow instructions. It's maddening to be smart enough to earn multiple graduate degrees, including a Ph.D., and yet not be able to follow simple instructions.

I just had a case of this while writing this chapter. I bought an appliance (which I won't name, to save myself complete embarrassment), that was advertised as being easy to set up and use. My daughter found a YouTube video of a fresh-faced young woman gushing over how quickly and painlessly she set hers up, and if she can do it, then anyone can.

Well, anyone, but me. I literally got stuck on step one of the "Quick Start Guide." Skimming ahead to the section showing the different buttons, I was hopelessly lost.

I called the support line and was on the line with the guy for about 15 minutes. I think the young woman in the video had hers set up in less time than I spent on the phone trying to figure out step one. After getting off the phone, I was absolutely exhausted. Worse than the end of my long teaching day, in which I teach a class online, quickly eat something before the hour commute to school, hold office hours and take care of other tasks before teaching two 2 classes (almost three 3 hours), finishing up at 8 p.m. Oh, then the drive home, which means I never get home before 9 p.m. That long workday doesn't come close to how I felt trying to follow fairly simple instructions.

Did I get it set up? No. Too overwhelmed. I never felt overwhelmed on the campaign trail, even with sixteen-hour days and sometimes getting three hours of sleep. But the instructions kicked my butt. My plan was to set it up a few days later, during business hours, so I could call the support line again if I needed help. But it was still overwhelming. Finally, about two months later, my daughter came over and set it up for me. As she started, she asked me, "*So what went wrong? What happened when you plugged it in?*" I had to admit that I hadn't even plugged it in yet. And, yes, she successfully got it set up without a 15-minute phone call with a support guy. (In my defense, I did get some valuable information from him!) My daughter shared this story with her in-laws, which apparently supplied quite a bit of entertainment. ("*And she didn't even plug it in!*")

Another misstep of mine on the first step of instructions was almost comical. As COVID was starting, I needed a new phone after damaging mine. Because of COVID restrictions on face-to-face customer service, my phone provider wouldn't switch the SIM card for me. I open the box with the new phone, set it next to the old phone, and started reading the instructions. Step 1 was to type in a URL that was provided, so I take out my MacBook and type it in. The very first question is, "Which phone are you reading this message on?" Well, neither! So I picked up one of the phones to enter the URL, but the phones were already communicating, which wasn't supposed to happen until that website was brought up on one of the phones. (I ended up switching phone providers to one who would change my SIM card for me, despite the lockdown.)

I'm very thankful that Clemson has great computer support, because, as you might imagine, I'm a regular. I met with one of the technical support people to learn how to use Adobe Illustrator and InDesign for my new online class. When I introduced myself, she said, "*Yes, I know who you are. I used to work on the Blackboard staff.*" (Blackboard was the online learning management system we were using, although now we've gone to Canvas.) So, yes, everyone who works on that staff knows my name well, and that was before running for president. Although, in my defense, I do use advanced features that many instructors don't use, but I doubt those instructors would need the help I did. (If you're wondering how I became a card-carrying Libertarian without the requisite computer skills - I'm typing this on a Dvorak keyboard, which I've used since 1984.)

I'm terrified of following written instructions. Yes, I could figure out how to tile a kitchen countertop and floor by myself in the 1980s, before HGTV was even a thing, but I can't follow instructions. After switching to a new bank, needing to get my online banking system set up, I actually loaded my desktop computer (a rather large one) into my car to take to my daughter's house so she could figure out how to enter new payees and show me. Me, the one who, as an undergrad student, was tutoring grad students in a statistics class that I was in, learning along with the rest of them. And, yes, I understand it would've been much easier to simply set up online banking on my phone (I take my phone when I visit my daughter already!), but I would never put banking on my phone. I lose it too often. My daughter was pleasantly surprised when she discovered I only needed help setting up the Payees. She assumed she was going to have to set up the entire system, since setting up a Payee is fairly easy. (I'll have to ask her if this story also provided untold hours of entertainment for her in-laws!)

What's ironic is that I had started on the cutting edge of computers, but now I'm at the end. I want from the top 10% to the bottom 10% (perhaps 1%!). I learned FORTRAN IV in the late 1970s, dutifully carrying my punch cards around campus. In the early 1980s, I learned Basic and RPGII. Most people would consider those programming languages more difficult than filling out a form online, but to me, programming a computer was easier than using it. Different kinds of smart.

I rarely cry. I don't really remember crying from being sad. The only time I cry is when I'm frustrated. Not very often, but it has happened. Unfortunately, it's happened every summer for the past few years when trying to fill out my annual performance and goals plan at Clemson. (Luckily, though, this is the only part of the job I hate.) If I understood how to use the software, it wouldn't take me longer than an afternoon to list my accomplishments, teaching goals, and service contributions to the department. But I have to enter it into a convoluted program that we've had for a few years. Of course, because it's so frustrating, I put it off for a little while (as a coach, I would recommend that anyone tackle these kinds of goals first, but I'm human, so I procrastinate). That night I opened my computer with resolve. I took "cheat-sheet" notes the previous year as the administrator walked me through the process (I took her out to lunch as a thank you, since I was so hopeless). So I had high hopes, as I took out my cheat sheet, only to find myself in tears within literally five minutes. I clicked on the first two links that were listed, only to find myself at a dead end with nowhere to go. Yes, smart enough to earn the Ph.D. required to teach a science (yes, it's a real science!), but not smart enough to fill out a form for that job. Yes, different kinds of smart.

And even getting that Ph.D. had challenges. I struggled with a graduate-level class (a very difficult, abstract graduate class taught by a Harvard alum), which I had a hard time following. I finally asked the professor if I could record his class, which he agreed to. I spent hours and hours on this — I recorded class, then would go home and painfully transcribe it, pausing after each and every sentence to write down exactly what he said. Then, after reading a few of the transcribed paragraphs, I would completely understand what he was saying. In fact, the material seemed pretty easy when I could read it. I have no idea how something could be so hard to comprehend when I listened to it, but so easy to comprehend when I read it. This was one way I was diagnosed with ADHD. My IQ was extremely high when I read passages and answered questions (in the top quarter of one 1% of the population), but below average (literally, below the 50th percentile) when I had to pay attention to spoken passages and answer questions. This was part of my frustration as a child — everyone thinking I wasn't very bright, but I knew I was smarter than they gave me credit for. Well, everyone except my parents. They had faith!

I should mention that being so inept with computers has helped me teach online classes and setting up the online grading system. Because I get confused so easily, I set up my classes so even I could follow it. I always tell my students, *"If my online learning system isn't the easiest one you've ever followed, please tell me because I want to fix it so it is!"* I do receive several compliments each semester that the computer portion of my class is the easiest to follow.

My absentmindedness was frustrating on the campaign trail. I'm not sure what I would've done without Jess Mears, the Deputy Campaign Manager, who traveled with me. She arranged for me to get many of the things I left behind, or replacements for what I left behind, on our trips. In addition to that, I'm sure I left hundreds of dollars of items behind in hotel rooms across the country, including one of my favorite turtlenecks (a casual turtleneck, not the turtlenecks they took away from me!). She would also help me in my chaos of getting from one place to another.

I had some interesting mishaps on the 1996 campaign trail, as well. I often stayed at people's houses, instead of hotel rooms, to help the campaign save money. I had fun meeting new people across the country. One time I stayed with an elected Libertarian state rep in New Hampshire. It was nice that I could use his stove to make fresh brown rice, instead of carrying around the cold bag of cooked rice and lentils. At least, it was nice until we got back to his house after a full day and they discovered I had forgotten to turn the stove off before we left. Yes, the stove was on for seven full hours. At least it was on low. I felt horrible, given they were so gracious to allow me to stay in his home.

My one consolation is my profession — perhaps it's okay to be an "absentminded" professor, even if that absentmindedness meant forgetting I left a needle in a friend's couch while I was sewing something, only to have her dad later sit on it!

Just as I became emotional when I was first diagnosed with ADHD, I recently had another emotional experience (the first one since I was diagnosed), while watching a television show. It turns out that apparently John F. Kennedy, Jr. had a similar cluster of symptoms as I have. The diagnosis of ADHD has two lists of symptoms. Some people are diagnosed exclusively from the inattention list, while others can be diagnosed exclusively from the hyperactivity-impulsivity list, so two different people diagnosed with ADHD could easily have two different descriptions. It's impractical to list over 20 characteristics. In summarizing a description of ADHD as applied to JFK, Jr., Dr. Michael Hunter, on the show *Autopsy*, sounded like he was reading a description of my life. The list included a few characteristics not specifically listed, such as risk taking. Dr. Hunter believes that John's ADHD played a role in his airplane crash, including impatience (flying the shorter path across the dark water instead of the longer path over land with lights) and differences in the cerebellum. I could see myself being tempted to take that short route, as well. I saw myself as the story of his life was laid out — crutches a few times (perhaps related to balance problems in the cerebellum), taking risks in starting companies (granted, my companies weren't as prominent as his was, but I have given up a stable income to start three companies over the years), as well as being too impatient. Even little things matched up, like procrastination. All those 4-H ribbons I mentioned earning at the County Fair? Every year, I would finish at least one project on the way to the fairgrounds. My mother would drive me as I would furiously crochet those last few rows on the afghan or do the last bit of hand hemming on an outfit. Sometimes we would get there a bit early, and she'd wait about 15 minutes in the car, as I sat there finishing up. Every year I would say, *"Okay — this time I'm going to get my projects done well in advance,"* and everyone in my family would say, *"No, we think it'll be another year of finishing at the fairgrounds!"* And my kitchen has never been cleaner than when I should have been finishing my dissertation.

I think I hold the world record for impulsive home renovation. While up late reading (as I often do), I decided at around 5 in the morning that it was time to finally put an island in my kitchen. I had been waiting until I could afford top-rate renovation, but realized that would take some time. So why not build my own now? I woke up at 10 the next morning and called my then-husband at his work, telling him I was going to swap cars (he had the SUV) so I could get supplies to build an island. He was shocked to arrive home from work in the early evening greeted by a kitchen full of cabinets, plywood, trim, door handles, etc. strewn about, waiting to be assembled into an island. *"You got all this?"* he asked me. *"Well, yes, I told you I was going to do this."* *"But not all in one day!"* Yes, it was about 9 hours from the time I made the decision to build an island to having all the components piled in my kitchen.

While I don't have dyslexia, I can easily transpose numbers. That would tend to scare passengers when they first flew on my small airplane with me: I would tell them to listen to the air traffic controller for a 4-digit code that goes into the transponder. I would point out the transponder and tell them to please enter the numbers for me, because I often scramble them, and it takes a couple of tries for me to get it right. Of course, the response is a horrified, *"What? Are you sure you know how to fly this plane?"* My reply — *"Yes, I can fly the plane just fine, I just can't put those 4 numbers into the dial!"*

I can't leave my authenticity description without talking about my small-town, blue-collar roots. That's who I am. When I started junior high school (we didn't have "middle school" in the olden days!), my northern Illinois town had a population of about 4700. I was the oldest of three children — I have a younger brother and sister. We never locked the doors at night, while we slept, let alone during the day. I usually got a ride to that school, but when I walked the approximately one-mile trip, I literally cut through a corn field (a short cut). Grayslake wasn't considered a commuter suburb of Chicago at the time, but the population has exploded, with people now commuting to professional jobs (at least, before Covid). When I lived there, though, it was very much blue-collar, out in the middle of corn fields, with only one traffic light in town. I remember picking asparagus with my aunt on the railroad tracks. I went to public school from kindergarten through 12th grade; there wasn't even a private school in my town. I only knew one family in town with a Mercedes (and it was a small town so I knew a lot of people!).

In the 1990s, newly single, I became friends with my two flight instructors, who had been college buddies. I didn't date them — they were dating others, but sometimes I'd hit the town with them. Their favorite spot, where I went a few times with them, was a very preppy-type sports place. Pool tables and guys wearing khaki pants and blue button-down collar shirts (left over from the 80s). I felt very uncomfortable there. Looking around, I'm sure the place was full of accountants and engineers. At the time I had a BS and an MBA (no Ph.D. yet), but somehow, I felt out of place in this crowd.

One of my employees had told me about some event going on with different bands, so my flight instructors decided to go with me to check it out. It was quite the heavy-metal scene — black leather, studs around necks, and long hair on the guys as well as the girls. I said to one of my instructors, "*Okay, now this is the crowd I feel comfortable with!*" His reply, "*And I bet there's not one college graduate in the entire crowd!*" (Outside of the three of us, of course.) That comment really opened my eyes. Yes, I probably did feel more comfortable in a non-college crowd, because that's how I grew up. My parents and grandparents hadn't gone to college. My high school had no AP classes, no calculus or psychology classes, and lots of shop classes (I took Woods, Metals, Plastics, and Mechanical Drawing). There was a class in which students (all guys, of course) rode in a bus to build a house. I was a blue-collar child who strayed and got a Ph.D.

Furthermore, yes, I was a member of Mensa, but not because I wanted to hang out with a lot of college grads. In the mid-1990s, my best friend, my business partner (who was introduced to me by my best friend), and my realtor were all in Mensa. They invited me to a few Mensa Happy Hours, and I had a great time. (They were held every Wednesday at 5 p.m., at different bars and restaurants around the city.) Finally, they told me I couldn't attend the Happy Hours anymore unless I were a member, so I took the test, and was surprised that I scored high enough to get in (this was years before entering the doctoral program). After all, my husband at the time was a plastic surgeon, so "he was the smart one," not me. I was the one who "just" stayed home with the kids and had recently joined a small company now that they were in school.

I brought my kids with me every week, who were well behaved, thanks to the practical applications of behaviorism that my Abnormal Psychology professor taught us (and that I now teach my students). After a year or so of this, another member brought a child who really acted up (I missed it, but I was told the child, after many other antics, ran out the front door of the restaurant and put a stick in the handles of the 2 front doors, preventing anyone from the restaurant getting out!). After that, they instituted a rule of no children at Happy Hour, so I allowed my Mensa membership to lapse. That was over 25 years ago. One of these days I think I'll join back. If I ever get the time!

As it was, I graduated with my Ph.D. at age 45. My doctoral class had three students in it – me, someone about 10 years older, and someone about 10 years younger. All three of us graduated on time, which (at least at the time), didn't happen very often. If you've ever considered going back to school, I encourage it. There's a level of maturity that you don't have when you're younger, that helps to get you through it, but also to appreciate it more. College was a completely different experience in my early 20s. In the PhD. years, I already owned my own business, and I literally knew what it was like to "meet a payroll."

Getting homework done on time or studying for a test is nothing when compared to making sure others get their paychecks and you can pay office rent and file the many tax reports on time, dealing with the IRS. Even university administrators are easier to deal with than the IRS.

If I'm to be truly honest, I must admit I'm somewhat of a rule-follower, especially for being a Libertarian. I carried three different MacBooks with me on the campaign — one was the campaign laptop (for interviews and speechwriting), one was my Clemson laptop (yes, I taught an online class during part of the campaign and answered student emails), and one was my personal MacBook. I'm terrified of the IRS, so I wasn't about to do any work on the wrong computer! The campaign and I were strongly criticized by some factions of the movement for not being willing to get arrested in an attempt to participate in a presidential debate. That's not how I do things — I try to change the system from the inside, rather than by any notion of overthrowing the system. Besides, I'd hate wearing prison jumpsuits, which are likely now made of polyester instead of cotton.

What Research Tell Us about Authenticity

If you don't know which of two paintings is an original, and which is a mass-produced print, the two impact you (cognitively, aesthetically, emotionally) the same way. But scientists can perceive, at the level of brain activity, which pleasure centers are activated when you're told you're looking at an original Rembrandt, instead of a clever forgery.

In an art auction, our perceptions of authenticity might dramatically change how we value things, in ways that are much the same for everyone. But authenticity isn't a universal experience because we value different things. When someone asks, "Is this leather jacket authentic?" they're very likely to be asking whether the jacket is genuine cow hide.

Personally, while I'm happy to wear a vinyl coat that looks vinyl, like a fun raincoat, but a vinyl one made to look like leather wouldn't feel 'authentic' to me. (For the record, while I don't eat red meat, I do buy leather products. "Vegan leather" is often made from plastic, derived from fossil fuels. And more animals are killed for food than for leather, so I'd rather see a cow hide put to good use than end up in a landfill while at the same time manufacturing extra plastic.)

Very often, people, especially young women, are encouraged to "fake it till you make it." There's some validity in that, especially when what you're trying to overcome is nervousness or inexperience that prevents you from seizing opportunities you care about. But "acting the part" has limits. When you're acting in a way that feels inauthentic to you, that distortion seems to creep over into other areas of your behavior and self-perception.

A study conducted among college-aged women attempted to discover whether wearing counterfeit products, and feeling less 'authentic,' would influence people's behavior. Half of participants were led (based on a bogus survey they filled out) to believe they preferred counterfeit products, relative to others in their group, while other participants were told they preferred authentic, designer items. Each was asked to choose a pair of sunglasses from one of two boxes (marked 'authentic' and 'counterfeit') and were given a task to do with those glasses on. For the record, all the sunglasses, in both boxes – and this is crucial, were exactly the same designer brand frames, with an average price of $300.

First, study participants inspected some posters on the wall while they got used to the sunglasses. Then they completed a brief problem-solving task. Each correct answer earned them 50 cents, they were told, up to a total of $10. But there were no names or identifiers on the task paper, and after completing the activity, participants were told to simply report their scores to researchers for payment. People wearing sunglasses they believed to be counterfeit, and being told that they preferred counterfeit goods, were more than twice as likely (71% vs. 30%) to fib about having done better on the test than they really did.

When people believed they were wearing a counterfeit product, they projected what researchers called, "a counterfeit self," which made it easier or more tempting to lie.

Even when the element of preference was removed (in the second study, participants were informed that their assignment to 'counterfeit' or 'authentic' glasses was entirely random) the effect persisted. Among those who thought they were wearing counterfeit glasses, unethical behavior — in this case lying with a side of theft — was notably more common.

Wearing 'fakes' seems to make people behave less ethically and authentically. A follow-up study found that people wearing fakes also believed that other people, people they knew, were more likely to act dishonestly or inauthentically.

If something as simple as wearing knock-off sunglasses can make us feel inauthentic enough to influence our values behavior, what can the reverse, the authenticity effect, teach us?

UK-based psychologist Stephen Joseph did groundbreaking work on authenticity. He found that authentic people understand their own core values and align their actions with those values. They try to know themselves and live up to their own expectations. They tend to care less about what other people think of them, based on values they don't hold. They pursue goals that are personally meaningful, and that are consistent with their strengths and abilities. If they act in ways that feel out of character, or conflict with their values, they experience that negatively.

Because they're experiencing less stress, authentic people have lower incidents of depression, digestive ailments, chronic fatigue, sleep disturbances, and substance abuse. Authenticity even seems to be correlated with a stronger immune system.

In addition to being happier and healthier, authentic people are fun to be around. They aren't threatened by failure, or other people's success, and they can admit their faults without beating themselves up about it. Because they're not trying to win anyone's approval, they're less likely to gossip, and more likely to praise and compliment others. They formulate a position carefully, weighing the evidence against their values, and only then do they explain that opinion to other people. They tend to lead interesting lives, because they're less worried about what other people think, which means they often pursue interesting hobbies or unique avocations. They win their own approval. They're wearing the "authentic" sunglasses.

Babies are perfectly authentic. Toddlers are who they are, and they'll say just about anything without considering other people. But from the time we're small, others begin to shape us. We receive more recognition, praise, and affection for behaving in certain ways. We begin to edit ourselves in the ways that are socially rewarded.

When I was about four years old, I was imitating Elvis, doing "The Twist" in our living room. My parents had friends over, and someone noticed me, and they found it very amusing. Every time I would start dancing again, everyone stopped what they were doing to watch me - "Look - she's doing it again!" It may be the last time I danced unironically (I'm not much of a dancer), but for a year or two I did it pretty often when people came over, because it always resulted in positive attention.

Dance like Elvis, draw a pleasing picture, get good grades, win awards and trophies. Some ways of being "us" are rewarded with love and a sense of belonging. Other behaviors, which aren't necessarily less "us," garner stern looks from our parents, disapproval from teachers, disappointment from coaches. Maybe we are forced to clean our plates and learn to override the internal knowledge that we're done eating. In the teenage years, the urgent search for belonging can cause us to act in ways that contradict our values, in order to get peer approval. In each case, we may learn that we must behave in certain ways to get acceptance from those around us, whether those things feel true to us or not.

All of our teenage years, and much of our adulthoods, are concerned with figuring out who we are and who we want to be in the future. We try on identities, figure out what to keep, and what's "just not our thing." We get messages from all over about what we "should" be, but slowly, we can come to care less. We become aware of our own shortcomings and failures, without getting mired in them. We explore our own strengths and areas of interest. We become ourselves.

We also tend to spend a lot of energy wrestling with that "self," and wanting it to become something else. That gap between what we believe we should be and how we actually behave is important. The difference between our perceived and imagined selves can cause a healthy, restless dissatisfaction, of the kind that makes people quit their good jobs and start a world-changing business. Or give up eating meat. Or go back to school.

Sometimes that gap in authenticity becomes negative. You're hiding part of yourself, or so preoccupied with your shortcomings that you feel like a failure or a fraud.

At some point during my thesis completion process, I didn't think I'd be smart enough to finish it. I went to my thesis chair and told him that I thought I should drop out of the program, and in fact I probably never should have been admitted in the first place. This confidence gap is often called "imposter syndrome," and is particularly pernicious in professional women. It probably keeps us from accomplishing as much as we could if we were able to internalize our successes and confidently pursue our goals. In extreme cases, that disconnect can lead to crippling guilt, addictions, and sociopathic behavior. All too often, seems to lead people into politics.

Inauthenticity can be corrosive both to the inauthentic person and to those around them, but not everyone experiences it that way. John Fund, who wrote for the Wall Street Journal, once told me about his days working on the Clinton campaign bus back in the 1990s. Bill Clinton would speak to supporters, or at a campaign rally, or to a reporter, in whatever town the campaign was passing through. In front of a group of people, he'd answer someone's question and very earnestly give someone information, tell them his views, or make a campaign promise. Then a few minutes later, he'd turn towards someone else on the other side of the crowd and say exactly the opposite to the other person. Clinton's true gift, according to Fund, was he genuinely seemed to believe what he was saying both times, even though they were complete contradictions.

Clinton was renowned for a chameleon-like ability to present himself as whatever a voter or donor most wanted him to be.

In 1993, the Rush Limbaugh TV program, then in its second of four seasons, showed side-by-side photographs of the then-President Clinton which seemed to reveal he was dying his hair based on the issues he was speaking on. Gray to appeal to senior citizens when his presidential schedule called for meetings with them, then back to brown, barely graying at the temples when he spoke to college students. Then back to a full head of gray to be on the Phil Donahue show, to make himself approachable to its graying audience.

A man with so little sense of self, or sense of integrity, that he can leave everything from his views on abortion to his hair color up to the pollsters and image-makers cannot also be depended on to govern with any integrity. The total lack of authenticity is a liability; he's an empty suit for sale to the highest donor.

Authentic people, especially misfits, have long since become accustomed to ignoring others' expectations. We don't mind being ourselves, unapologetically. We're not so good at conforming to expectations, twisting ourselves into the image constructed by journalists and campaign strategists. Either we lose ourselves, or we lose to the Bill Clintons of the world.

I do consider myself to be an authentic person (even though I got bullied into wearing mascara and polyester sometimes) and I think that comes from being kind of an outcast as a child. My gregarious, physical, blue-collar parents didn't quite know what to do with their bookish, reclusive kid who could win every ribbon at 4-H club, but not a spot on the cheerleading squad, like my mom did.

After my nomination as the presidential candidate, my social media team scraped conversations about me to learn what words people were using to describe me. I'm very proud to say that the most-used word was, "genuine." I was thrilled, because I couldn't think of any way I'd rather have people think of me. (The number two word, if you're curious, was "smart." I'm sure other candidates would have preferred to have "smart" as their top word, but that's validation I don't need). Genuine, authentic people not only live interesting lives, but they also free other people to do the same. It was exactly the energy I think the country needs more of.

I have changed my mind in one area of authenticity. I never "played hard to get" in order to get a guy to like me - after all, that doesn't seem very authentic. But research in cognitive dissonance shows that we tend to value what we have to work for more than what we don't. Perhaps it's better to find out early in the relationship how many hoops a guy is willing to jump through for you.

Government Attacks on Authenticity

Authenticity only has meaning in the context of individual choice. Your values have to be your own, if you are to live authentically, according to them. Values can't be imposed on you from the outside, unless you individually choose an influence (anything from a religious commune to an HOA) to control your actions. And even then, you must be free to leave at any time, to change your mind. You're free to join any peaceful community or organization who shares your interests and your values. You can form a group based on shared identity or form a community to celebrate and express shared values. Only when you are free to choose and associate can your authentic self be expressed to others.

My campaign was focused on promoting Libertarian principles, which rely on self-ownership, bodily autonomy, and freedom of association. Freedom from force, including government coercion, is a prerequisite to living authentic lives.

How you want to live, or present yourself to the world, or express yourself, or live in community with others, that's up to you. And as long as you're not harming others in the process, it's no business of the government's. But government gets in the way, all the time.

At least a quarter million US families live off the grid, often in eco-conscious communities experimenting with sustainable living. Even if they're perfectly peaceful, these communities often face strong opposition from state and local governments. It's often illegal to live "off the grid," even on property you own. Camping, growing your own food, collecting rainwater, and not connecting to local utilities are often violations of local codes, and so, criminal acts. Requiring these folks to navigate permits and inspections, or to connect to public utilities that they reject (often because they are provided unsustainably) makes it impossible for them to live both authentically and within the bounds of the law.

The same is true for the increasing percentage of the population who use psychedelic substances like LSD, or psilocybin mushrooms, or MDMA for personal growth. Empirical and anecdotal evidence indicates these substances help people recover from trauma, break out of depression, and achieve spiritual clarity. It's heartbreaking that research on these, begun in the 1950s, was shut down by the government, apparently because they thought it was behind the anti-war movement. (My 1996 pre-nomination stump speech included Randolph Bourne's quote "*War is the health of the state.*") Not only did government stop research on LSD, but they also classified it as a Schedule I drug under the Controlled Substances Act, characterizing it as having "*no currently medical use in treatment in the United States.*" Only now are researchers going back to exploring this possibly life-saving treatment. Think of all the lives that could have been helped or even saved over the decades, if those in power hadn't arbitrarily dismissed these substances, while promoting other drugs that can be much more dangerous (but make huge profits for drug companies), or, worse, as suspected, outlawed it because it got in the way of their deadly wars. Exploring your consciousness and investing in your own sense of self are among the most self-authenticating actions you can undertake. When government restricts access to these substances, or threatens to jail you for peacefully experimenting with your own brain, they outlaw one path to authenticity.

People also engage in civil disobedience, breaking unjust laws that violate their personal principles. From lunch-counter sit-ins during the civil rights movement, to burning draft cards during the Vietnam War, to blocking traffic around a government building, these are legitimate forms of "petitioning the government for redress of grievances," explicitly allowed by the First Amendment to the Constitution. Government may still meet these practices with fines, police violence, and criminal convictions. We are forced to live inauthentically and conform to unjust authority just to keep ourselves out of jail.

How To Become Yourself

So how do you become more authentic? It's too simple to say, "be yourself," because many of us, most of the time, aren't particularly clear on who we are. We have a series of stories we tell ourselves about why we are the way we are, not all of them in accordance with our more deeply-held values.

Being authentic isn't a matter of uncovering a core, deep-down authentic self, and learning to act in accordance with it. How you act *is* who you are. And people change much more than we generally give ourselves credit for. We speak about personality as if it were a very consistent pattern of traits throughout your life (such as being extraverted or optimistic), and most people think of them as being stable. In fact, many people think personality is so stable that they're stuck with how they are. Actually, personality traits are surprisingly unstable and evolve and shift throughout our lives.

You (your self-concept and behavior) are changing anyway, so you might as well put some thought into it and be deliberate about those changes. As we mentioned in the Optimism chapter, yes, you can change how optimistic you tend to be, and you can change other tendencies and behavior, as well. Of course, you still have an internal compass and values that you need to remain true to, but those values often shift over time, too.

Just as we underestimate how much we change, we expect that other people stay the same. They don't. The example I use with my students when discussing this concept is to think about the first time they went back home from college. Did their parents still treat them like they were in high school? I get very emphatic nods from that question!

I had my own experience with this, but a bit more extreme, over a longer time period. I was a goody two-shoes in high school, no getting around that. When I was in high school in the 1970s, it was pretty common for teenagers to drink at parties, but I never did. Not even once. (My well-known appreciation of bourbon came later, and yes, my parents did the trick of giving me alcohol when I was young so I could see how much I hated it and not want any. Actually, to the dismay of my mom, I loved it, and my parents would allow me a sip every now and then, but that was the extent of my drinking in high school.)

Fast forward to my 10-year high school reunion. We all received raffle tickets, with several prizes lined up across the stage. When they got to the bottle of red wine, I thought, "*Ooh — I hope my number is called!*" I love red wine, and with a husband in medical residency after completing medical school, we didn't have a lot of money for such indulgences. I was ecstatic to have my number called next (what are the odds!). I walked up on stage to pick it up, and I was instead handed the jade plant that was the prize after the red wine. As I confusedly walked off stage with my new shrubbery, my former classmate who was in charge whispered to me, "*We know you don't drink, so we gave you that plant instead!*"

I was speechless. At this time I was married (had been for eight years) and had a young child (the one who needed three outfit changes a day). Just because I didn't illegally drink alcohol as a minor didn't mean that I wouldn't enjoy red wine with a nice dinner as a married woman, well over the legal age. But that's how my high school classmates saw me.

This is why social psychologists say the best way to change your self-concept is to change your social environment. It's much easier to reinvent yourself when others don't already have preconceived expectations about who you are.

Be Unapologetically, Authentically Yourself

Here are some more strategies for living more authentically:

<u>Observe your actions</u>

In your interactions with others, ask yourself to what extent you are deceptive to make a better impression. In the activities you choose, are you doing them because you want to, believe you should, or for some extrinsic reason? That is your level of inauthenticity.

<u>Listen to yourself</u>

Awareness has to do with listening to the signals from inside your own body and mind. It takes conscious work to sweep away what you've been told to want and find your own intuition again. When you feel conflicted about how you behaved in a situation, examine that feeling. Listen to your gut.

<u>Look back to your childhood</u>

As mentioned above, children just blurt out their truths. A friend of mine who did color analysis (a very complicated system in which she would hold up 2000 different pieces of fabric, not the oversimplified seasons), told me that children intuitively know what colors look good on them.

My mom had gone shopping with me in preparation for my first girl/boy party in high school. I was drawn toward a red and black outfit (very harsh), but I let her talk me into the pale baby blue and pink outfit. After that advice from my friend, I realized that it was my mom that looked good in the pale colors, not me. I should've gone with the red and black.

<u>Understand your own values</u>

Most of us were raised with a set of strong values: what was important, what to think, who matters most, how the world should look if everyone did what they should. We don't live in that world, and maybe you don't want to. Just because your parents or community or college friends believed something doesn't mean you need to keep carrying it out. Don't be afraid to question things.

Engage a new identity

When you decide to make a change, try to internalize the change as a new identity, getting a different picture of yourself in your mind. You don't just want to occasionally make healthy dinners, you want to be a healthier person: the *kind of person* who makes healthy dinners. Think of yourself as someone who takes healthy actions, and then prove that to yourself through actions. Buy healthier groceries, cook healthier meals, exercise. Before you know it, you're living authentically, because your actions shape you into the kind of person you've committed to being.

Tell others your intentions

If you share the changes you want to make with someone else, you're more likely to follow through on them. You might have trouble holding yourself accountable, but in general we hate to be hypocrites, so it works much better if you let others know. If you tell others you're going to stop smoking or go to the gym twice a week, you're more likely to do it than if you simply make that promise to yourself.

Find places where it's safe to be yourself

Feeling free to be authentically yourself means finding or gathering a supportive community where you can belong. It's very difficult to continue to act authentically in the face of ostracism or constant criticism (more on this in the chapter Choose Your Circle).

Keep a sense of humor

Your faults and flaws are part of the human condition. Even on your worst days, you're probably doing fine. Learning to laugh at yourself and reminding yourself that other people also have problems and foibles, can lend important perspective.

Ask yourself why you want something

People are great at rationalizing. (Yes, even if you're smart - it just means you have more brain power to rationalize with!) You may think that the reason you need new outfits is to look professional at work, but are you fooling yourself? Are you sure it's not because of that cute guy who just transferred to your office?

While I'm still a little annoyed at how I was treated as a candidate — not the least being made to wear polyester! — ultimately the campaign came from a place of authenticity, and so did I. I didn't mind being powder-puffed, and dressed like a doll, because my appearance wasn't what I was trying to sell to voters. If all that is what it took to get us in the door, taken seriously, for people to listen to our ideas, then bring on the hairdresser, I guess.

Also, I am a strong believer that if Libertarians are to get anywhere, we need to dress for the occasion. If we dress in outrageous costumes or too casually, we won't be taken seriously. When the campaign spiffed me up a bit, it was just polishing my look, not a complete makeover. It was my decision from the start to dress professionally, as though I were going to a job interview, because that's what running for office is.

Behind the lectern and in my public statements, I was an authentic voice for the values that so many people, including not-yet-Libertarians, believe in, but can't quite name. The ideas themselves are where my values and commitment lie. Freedom for all, to express themselves and their identities, to embrace unconventional ways of living, to experiment with their own experiences. We should be tolerant of everyone and anything peaceful.

For the record, I don't wear either designer or fake designer sunglasses, on the rare occasions I do wear them. Right now, I'm wearing my mom's sunglasses, one of about four pairs I found cleaning out her car after she died. My mom was frugal and I don't think ever bought a designer brand in her life. Her sunglasses were from a regional not-very-fancy department store. I can't find a name anywhere on the sunglasses — I have no idea who even made them if I wanted to buy another pair! On top of that, the plastic frame broke, so it's being held together with glue. And I've gotten compliments on them. They're just "me."

Life is too short to spend it trying to be someone you're not. Listen to your own intuition, and embrace it, even in the face of adversity, or in defiance of authority. Be authentically you. Accept no substitutes.

Stay Curious

Don't Believe Everything You Think

I don't have a lot of regrets, but I did something dumb at my 10-year high school reunion. The organizers took votes for superlatives in lots of categories, one of which was "who has changed the most."

My high school best friend Bambi (yes, that was really her name) was one of the three people we voted on. Now she had, in some sense, changed a lot since we were students, when we were two socially invisible wallflowers against the world. She'd been the feminist revolutionary who successfully fought for the right for girls be allowed to take metals shop at our high school, and the boys could take cooking classes. She'd joined the Marines after graduation to get out of our small town and even ended up appearing in Playboy. After Playboy ran a spread of something like "Girls of the Southeast College Conference," she wrote to Playboy and suggested they do a "Girls of the Armed Forces" and include her. She didn't merely answer an ad; she created that opportunity! Evidently, she had become more fit from the rigorous Marines bootcamp and had really grown into herself.

But I didn't vote for her. I didn't see the change. I always thought she was beautiful, and she looked the same to me. Instead, I voted for Barry Burgett, because he'd so visibly grown up, had facial hair, and looked very much like an adult. To me, men's appearances change more than women's after high school.

That really hurt Bambi's feelings. I don't remember whether she won or not, but she was pretty upset that I didn't vote for her. Anyone else might have realized that I was supposed to vote for her because she was my friend, but I didn't. I answered the question honestly, because I was asked in a survey, and I wanted to preserve the quality of the research. I forgot that it was just for fun. I should have lied, but it was more important to me that we collect accurate data. Such a geek - just call me Sheldon.

That example stands out to me, but I've always been a bit more analytical than most of my peers. I want the data. The facts. Show me how you figured it out, and then I'll decide if I believe you. Besides, one of the first unjust things I remember happening to me was in a similar situation of students voting a verdict. While participating in a math bee in my second-grade class, a student noticed that I had my hands in the very large pockets of my lime green dress (it was the 1960s). I had them in there because it was comfortable; one of my fellow students, however, accused me of doing it for nefarious reasons — counting on my fingers to get the correct answers, since I was one of the few remaining finalists. The teacher handled it by asking the class to vote on it — was I innocent or guilty? The class voted guilty. The injustice of that accusation — and deciding an empirical question based on student observations that couldn't possibly have answered it — still stings. The irony is, crazy as it sounds, is that I didn't even know how to count on my fingers; it was easier for me to simply memorize the numbers.

It might be obvious, as I'm a college professor (technically "Principal Lecturer," but no one knows what that is), that I'm a believer in the benefits of college education for those who honestly want it. As colleges and universities have moved ever-further to the left, it's become popular for some people to express disdain for the whole institution, and to say things like, "What's that degree even good for?" and "Don't go to college."

Yes, there was an overblown push for a long time to make everyone follow the same path of college. There's no reason to go into debt if you genuinely want to become an auto mechanic or a welder. But a college education has a lot to offer most people, in terms of critical thinking, and a richer cultural life. Even the tropes that turn up on TV or references in movies, if you can recognize that's from Sartre or that's from Shakespeare, offer a deeper appreciation of what's going on (part of what I love about Monty Python is that it's just full to the gills with sophisticated references to Western history and philosophy).

History really does repeat itself and if, as a people, we have some understanding of history and what happened before we were born, how other cultures handle a particular issue, and what mistakes humanity has already made, we can avoid making some of them again. There are certainly plenty of new mistakes we can be making.

Is it possible to gain this perspective and depth of understanding without going to college? Absolutely. It's the kind of thing public high schools should be teaching, were they not at least four decades into a process of deliberate dumbing-down of the curriculum and the population.

In high school I took an English course called something like, "Sports in Literature." It was a "contract learning class" which was an experimental education model from the 1970s. We sat in a classroom with seats on one side facing the seats on the opposite side, and we sat and read the books we'd committed to reading (in a more rigorous time, the reading would have been done at home). The range of book choice was very wide. I was seated looking across the aisle at a guy who was a wrestler and who also played football. I remember seeing the paperback book he was reading, which had a cartoon picture on the cover of a big football, with a woman wearing a skimpy bikini straddling it. That's what he was reading for the class.

I have no objection to anyone reading what they enjoy. I suspect he might have read that sort of thing outside of class, too. That book didn't need to be assigned in high school and read during class time. Might he have been better off reading something that would have given him a richer life, with a greater understanding of the world around him? I think over time he'd have a better sense of what's happening and be able to put it in context. What's the point of requiring people to read for a certain number of hours, if you don't even suggest to them that they might read something that challenges them to fulfill their potential?

Of course, for elites and politicians, a less-skeptical, less-capable, less-informed citizenry is a good thing. Critical thinkers are difficult to rule; skeptical voters are difficult to fool. It's one of the many reasons we shouldn't put government in charge of educating kids: politicians' values are not aligned with the long-term interests of the people. And that's not merely my observation. I recently heard an educator being interviewed, complaining about parents who dared to want a role in deciding what should be taught in schools and which textbooks their children should use. She went on to remind everyone that part of the purpose of public education "is to teach them what society needs them to be taught." No mention of what a child needs to know.

If you don't know how to skeptically consume science, or media, or research, you'll be led around by manipulators and con-men (con-people?) who are feeding you conclusions. That's true even if you stick to peer-reviewed research — bad research gets published all the time. It's true even if you're reading a reporter you really trust; sometimes well-intentioned people get things wrong. One of the key things our educations should include, but usually don't, is an understanding of what makes a "good study."

In the sciences, we have straightforward criteria for what makes a study a good one. It should test one or more things while holding other variables constant. It should have a control group, with random assignment of subjects to the experimental and control groups. Findings should be able to be replicated by other researchers. And the sample size should be large enough, and the variables valid enough, so that the conclusion can be applied to subjects who weren't actually studied.

Years ago, a study came out about some difference between those who are happily married and those who aren't. It would have been interesting, except the experimenter defined a "happy marriage" as couples married longer than 13 years, and an "unhappy marriage" as couples married less than 13 years. I don't know about you, but I've known some very unhappily married people who've been married a heck of a lot longer than 13 years! And some happy couples married less than 13 years. So, the results are completely worthless. Worse than that, the study wasn't just useless, but generated false conclusions for others to read and reporters to spread.

Several years ago, I had a debate with someone about whether you can lose weight by swimming. Yes, I realize exercise is one way to help keep a healthy weight (although using it as the sole way can backfire), but for me, swimming is different. For some reason, I'm always really hungry after swimming. Maybe it's the chilly water, I'm not sure. The person I was debating said it burned a lot of calories, so it'd be a great way to lose weight (anecdotally, Olympic swimmer Michael Phelps was reported to have eaten 9000 calories per day while training, and he looks great). I later ran across research reported in the media that supported my side — people who swam ate more calories, so it didn't help lose weight. I was excited to show the other person results that seemed to back up my view — until I read there were only eight participants in the study. That's not an experiment —

that's eight individual stories! To be generalizable, experiments need large numbers. The classic study on aspirin helping to prevent heart attacks included 10,000 participants. The swimming study was the equivalent of telling eight friends, "Here, take this aspirin every day and let's see if you have a heart attack or not." That's not research. That's dinner party gossip.

Deciding to demand evidence can be an uncomfortable way to live in the social world (not that being weird has ever stopped me from doing *anything*). A couple of people who were close to me around the time that I was getting my Ph.D. said I had changed quite a bit, and they said it in a negative way. Had I become too proud, or hateful, or scornful of my friends? No. But I'd gotten oriented toward asking for data. (You know what they say: "In God we trust. All others must have data.") And for my friend who wanted to tell me about my astrological projections, what I viewed as a question of interest about her data set came off as hostile. If your beliefs are not based on logic, or evidence, or provable claims, then the whole idea that claims can be weighed for their truth value can be quite unwelcome.

It hasn't stopped me from being friends with people who value things differently. I'm very much a scientist, with a Ph.D. in a science, but somehow my friends tend to be sort of new-agey. That caused small conflicts, for example when I suggested that, to protect your health, antibiotics work better than crystals. I even read a book on feng shui, though it was not as convincing as the giver hoped. Because I have been, and expect to be, misunderstood, I guess I'm more open-minded and willing to take the time to tinker with ideas and investigate new claims.

For the things that matter, empirical evidence, data-gathering, and critical inquiry are the best way of seeking knowledge — even if it ruffles a few feathers at a reunion.

What Research Tells Us About Thinking Critically

Critical thinking is an essential skill, but it's frequently undervalued (or ignored) by the education system that's supposed to prepare young people for a complex world. To think critically, you've got to evaluate information effectively, and to the best of your ability, objectively. Only when we can understand not only our own thinking, but the hidden motivations behind our own reasoning, can we make better decisions and form more reasonable views.

One thing we know about critical thinking: it takes work. Our brains are wired to be cognitively lazy (social psychologists refer to this as being "cognitive misers," economists would call it "resource efficiency"), far more than they're wired to be accurate. Jumping to conclusions based on limited evidence kept us alive on the evolutionary savannah. Those skeptical souls who went to investigate whether it really was a lion behind the bush were unlikely to live for long.

We're also pretty resistant to changing our minds, or admitting when we've been fooled. Social psychologists, when talking about cognitive dissonance, like to use the example of doomsday cults, who often require members to turn over all their worldly goods to cult leaders. When the expected day of deliverance or doom arrives, and the world doesn't end (the "end" has been predicted hundreds of times throughout history, and we're still here) people generally don't just leave the cult. It's too difficult to admit we've been fooled, or change our attitudes or behaviors. It's too painful for cult members to believe they've given up their life savings for a lie, so they double down, adjust their calendars, and continue waiting for the end of the world. This is cognitive dissonance.

The crucial skills of critical thinking begin with identifying cognitive biases. Our brains go wrong in predictable, anticipatable ways. Often these biases would serve us well evolutionarily, when survival was paramount, but create problems in the modern world. My graduate school cognitive neuroscience professor used squirrels as an example: the way they dart and sometimes stop and change direction works in the wild, but becomes a liability on a road full of automobiles. When we use mental shortcuts to evaluate claims, we are prone to poor judgment and flawed decision-making. Here are a few examples of these traps we fall into.

<u>Confirmation Bias</u>

If you already believe something, you may find that information coming your way seems to support your already-held conclusion. This is confirmation bias, and there are actually two parts to this one. First, we seek out information that backs up what we already think is true, and second, we ignore or dismiss information that contradicts what we already believe.

In a study in the 1970s, 48 undergrads (our favorite subpopulation to study) were given two papers to read, one seemingly confirming their already-formed beliefs about the death penalty, and the other contradicting them. Across the board, people found the research results that confirmed their beliefs to be more persuasive and convincing. Even though they'd read two different opinions, students emerged more polarized and certain of their own view.

It's crucially important that you seek out alternative viewpoints. That doesn't just mean more than one cable channel, or more than one podcast. You must try to find people who disagree on some fundamental values, and then see how they approach a particular issue. Maybe you'll have your mind changed, but maybe you won't. But you owe it to yourself, and to people who disagree, to genuinely try to understand many sides of an issue.

John Stewart Mill, in his 1859 essay, *"On Liberty"*, explained it in context:

> *"He who knows only his own side of the case knows little of that. His reasons may be good, and no one may have been able to refute them. But if he is equally unable to refute the reasons on the opposite side, if he does not so much as know what they are, he has no ground for preferring either opinion... Nor is it enough that he should hear the opinions of adversaries from his own teachers, presented as they state them, and accompanied by what they offer as refutations. He must be able to hear them from persons who actually believe them...he must know them in their most plausible and persuasive form."*

In other words, don't avoid people who disagree with you. Hear them out and assume their good intentions. Try to figure out what their framework is, why they are so adamant in their opposition.

Sometimes, our investment in our own views is obvious. If you watch true-crime documentaries, you'll often see an interview with the families of both the accused and the victim (either in clips of a televised press conference, or an interview for the program itself) giving completely different accounts of the trial or evidence. They say, "I just don't understand how the jury made that decision. I must have been watching a completely different trial than they did." Well yes, actually, they were. People who went into the trial with their minds already made up paid attention to information that confirmed their beliefs, discarding any evidence, no matter how credible, that challenged what they so desperately wanted to be true. Those with an emotional stake almost literally can't see the other side of the case.

Here I must add a caution against Google and similar search engines, especially as I'm writing during the very first waves of ChatGPT, the first mass-appeal, AI-language model capability. Google is a confirmation bias machine. These search results rely on a business model. It isn't to give you the truth, or the thing you need to see that you hadn't considered; it's to give you what you'll click on, rate highly, accept. What you're already looking for. A few times in the researching of this book, I was looking for the details of a particular study, and I searched Google Scholar for the conclusion of the research: "pets provide social support, psychology." There was very little risk I'd see something other than the conclusion I'd looked for, because I already held it. If I did see a study with a totally contradictory finding, I'd be at great risk of ignoring it, because it wasn't what I was looking for, and I wouldn't take it too seriously. But that isn't how we, as a culture, should be deciding what is true and false.

<u>Confusing Correlation with Causation</u>

We've known for almost 100 years that people with schizophrenia sometimes have enlarged brain ventricles (fluid-filled cavities). Which causes which, though? Does schizophrenia cause the ventricles to become large because nearby parts of the brain degenerated, or were those parts of the brain already small, causing the schizophrenia? Adding to the problem is that not everyone with schizophrenia has the enlarged ventricles, and some people have enlarged ventricles without schizophrenia.

Many classroom examples are less nuanced and a bit more laughable. For quite a while, people suspected that eating ice cream might cause polio. In fact, polio rates just rise sharply in the summertime, right along with ice cream consumption.

A researcher called Tyler Vigen has compiled a lot of these "spurious correlations." The more movies starring Nicholas Cage in a particular year, the more people die by drowning in swimming pools. Those variables move almost in sync from 1999 to 2009. The divorce rate in Maine seems to track identically to the per-capita consumption of margarine. The more it rains in Washington D.C. each year, the higher the sales revenue at Staples office supplies.

Most of the time, the relationships are not so laughable. They may even be intuitive. So we must be wary. Just because variables move together, doesn't mean one causes the other, or even that they share a common cause.

<u>Ignoring the Base Rate</u>

This is one of the first biases, or decision traps, that I learned in my doctoral program. I stole the following example from my professor, and now use it in my Intro class. Included in an article in a respected management magazine (before the internet took over) was advice on how to hire an employee. The writer pointed to research that showed that more than 90% of CEOs had pets as kids, and they probably became CEOs because they learned dependability and responsibility from owning a pet. Walking the dog, feeding the cat, etc.

It doesn't take long for someone in my Intro class to see the problem with this thinking, "Hey - what about non-CEOs?" I then ask students who've had pets to raise their hands, and after jokingly doing a *Rainman*-type calculation, I point out that 95.4% of the class has had pets. ("Congratulations - you're all CEOs!") My class is too large to do an exact count, but it's clear it's an overwhelming majority. But what if more non-CEOs had pets than CEOs. Now do we say, "Hire someone without a pet?" as if that were more meaningful?

This study was described in a respected magazine, with editors looking over the articles. We are at an even greater risk of running across seemingly legitimate advice on the internet.

The decision trap here is ignoring the base rate. You can't look at how many CEOs had pets as kids, and arrive at any conclusion, without looking at how many non-CEOs had pets as kids. Even then, it's correlational, so you can't draw cause-and-effect conclusions. But it's a good exercise to go through when someone gives you that kind of statistic. What are they comparing against?

I used to tell people that my first-ever sentence, as a toddler, was a question. I thought it said something interesting about my inquisitiveness. But I realized recently, I don't know what the base rate is for that, either. Perhaps most kids' first sentences are questions, and I'm not that special at all. (Yes, I could check that out, but I think I'll just continue in my pleasant confirmation bias that believing I had all those questions because I was a budding young scientist!)

One base-rate I did get to the bottom of was a scare tactic that my parents had used on me as a child. When visiting Florida as a young child (so my dad could do his cement work when the ground in Chicago was frozen), I was told to stay away from the canals, because I could drown. The horror story my parents told me was that a family had driven into a canal, and when their bodies were found years later, they could only be identified by their dental records. So, for years I was terrified of canals, since death in a canal was apparently so grisly that you would be rendered unrecognizable. It was only years later that I discovered that dental records are a very common means to identify people who die in all kinds of ways, such as fires or being exposed to the elements for years.

This is one that a lot of people fall into, so if you're listening to a talking head or supposed expert, ask yourself if they're making conclusions based on faulty evidence. For instance, I've heard people in the media making a political point by pointing out that trans individuals who transition from male to female seem to be in the news more often, and are more politically active, than those who transition from female to male. I haven't kept track, but they could be right, but it may not be for the reason they think it is. They are making a hidden assumption about the base rate that equal numbers of people transition from male to female and female to male, but that's incorrect. Actually, three times as many people transition from male to female (referred to as "natal male" or "assigned male at birth") than transition from female to male. So, you can't say it's just because they tend to be louder. There are simply more of them. It could be both, along with other reasons.

Which leads to another point...

<u>Multiple Causes</u>

The average person, when asked about why a particular person acts a certain way, usually gives just one reason. "It's the drugs" or "She came from an abusive household." Scientists understand, however, that very rarely is there only one cause for a behavior.

In my Intro class, I go through a class demonstration. First, we vote on someone whose behavior we can discuss. (I never use a politician as an example! One year I taught two Intro sections, and the class who chose Adolf Hitler was quite annoyed when they found out that the other class had chosen Miley Cyrus — they didn't realize the field was quite so wide open.) Then we go through different perspectives, which include the unconscious (perhaps there's something in the past she has forgotten), behaviorism (people are more likely to do things they are rewarded with money and attention), biological (drugs, hormones), cognitive (how they process information), and evolutionary. One evolutionary study showed that exotic women dancers received more tips from men when they were fertile than when they weren't, but of course men weren't thinking "I'll put $10 in her G-string instead of $5 because she could bear a child for me now!" All our behaviors have layers, because that is who we are. By the time we go through the list, students understand that humans act in response to a wide range of causes.

<u>Availability Bias</u>

Which causes more deaths each year in the U.S. — tornadoes or asthma? Many people pick tornadoes, even though over 40 times as many people die from asthma. (Even if you guessed asthma was the correct answer, did you think it would be over 40 times as many?) In fact, the number of people who die in tornadoes each year is matched by asthma deaths in just a little over a week. So why do we get this so wrong? Because we see images in the media every time there's a tornado, but we don't see many images of people dying from asthma. I'm not a broadcast journalist, but I've seen enough local stories on tornadoes that I can predict the scenes they'll show: an aerial shot over some homes, a child's toy or stuffed animal lying by itself, an interview with survivors talking about how fast it came, and perhaps a video shot through a storm-chaser's windshield.

People also often report a fear of flying, but that's also an example of availability bias. I tell college students, "Imagine a jumbo jetliner crashed right now, during class, and everyone died. And it happened next week, during class. And the following week, for a year. All those hypothetical crashes would still kill far fewer people than car accidents in the same year." This doesn't seem to comfort them, exactly, but it's a useful illustration. Plane crashes are big news specifically because they are so very rare. Car crash deaths rarely appear on the news, because they happen much more often, so we don't see all those deaths from across the country.

Both of these are examples of availability, which is basically, "if it's easy to remember, it must happen often." If we can call an example easily to mind, then it must happen pretty frequently. In another poignant example, we hear more about, and worry more about, homicides than suicides, though suicide is about twice as common.

Over the past few years, and particularly around the death of George Floyd, there were a lot of stories about police officers killing Black men. When asked in a survey to estimate the number of unarmed Black men killed by police in 2019, half of people who called themselves "very liberal" (and likely to be exposed to footage and stories of such deaths) estimated more than 1000 deaths. The actual number? About 10. Each of them a tragedy, but on the scale of things, hardly an epidemic.

<u>Anchoring and Adjustment Biases</u>

If I were CEO and you were my sales manager, and I asked you to give me a forecast of this year's sales, what would be the quick and dirty (and fairly accurate) way of doing it? Take last year's sales and adjust up or down, depending on how things are going this year. There are traps you can fall into, doing it this way.

First, we tend to not adjust enough up or down. This can really cause problems if a recession comes about. On the local news, during the 2007-08 recession, I saw a local construction worker (I think it was a roofer), saying that business was 20% of what it was the year before. I thought I had misheard that — that perhaps business was down by 20%. But, no, after rewinding the show, he clearly said business was 20% of last year's (so it was down by 80%).

The second part is the anchoring part. Maybe you have a valid anchor (last year's sales), but that's not always the case. An interesting study was done in which participants spun a roulette wheel. Unbeknownst to them, it was rigged, so that it stopped on a high number for half the groups and a low number for the other groups. A later task asked the groups to estimate how many countries in Africa belonged to the United Nations. As expected, those who heard the lower (random) number introduced by the wheel guessed fewer countries than those with the higher number.

My dissertation chair was working on his own dissertation around the time this study came out, and he had a hard time believing it, so he tested it in his study. He randomly gave half the participants a lower experiment number that they had to write down, and the other half a higher number (the experiment numbers were completely bogus - it was all one experiment). To his surprise, those randomly assigned to the higher experiment number predicted they would type more words in a short amount of time than those assigned the lower number.

The moral of the story is that if you are making a prediction and don't have a valid anchor (like last year's sales), your brain might go searching for one on its own. It could be the room number of your boss's office, or even a number on a digital clock.

<u>Peak-End Rule</u>

We tend to perceive experiences differently based on their peaks (the highest or most intense part) and whether there's a peak at the end. If you watch a scary movie, you'll remember it as being scariest if the peak, or scariest part, was exceptionally scary, and/or if a scary part appeared right at the end.

To test the peak-end rule, researchers divided colonoscopy patients into two groups. The first group had a regular colonoscopy, where the uncomfortably intruding instrument was removed at the end of the probing. The second group had an identical colonoscopy, but the instrument was left in, after the active scoping was done, for an extra three minutes. Leaving it in certainly isn't pleasant, but the pain was much lower than the colonoscopy itself. Those whose experiences (while otherwise identical) ended with a less painful waiting period rated the whole procedure as less painful. Leaving the probe in longer than you have to may improve people's perception of the experience, which is important if you want people to return regularly for the recommended screenings.

This certainly clears up the time-honored battle that kids have with their moms. Moms have always said to rip the Band-Aid off fast, because it's less painful. Perhaps it's objectively less painful, but we don't experience the world objectively. The kids are right on this one — if you're a human, lifting the Band-Aid off slowly will probably feel a lot less painful.

<u>Framing</u>

A while back, some gas stations started offering discounts if you paid in cash. Perhaps you've taken advantage of the offer, glad to save a few dollars. Maybe, though, you thought it wasn't worth it to mess with cash, and continue to use your credit card, thinking you're not out anything since you're paying the "regular" price. How would your thinking change, though, if the price difference were framed differently? If your local station set the cash price as the "regular" price and then charged you a surcharge to use your credit card, you might be quite upset about the extra fee. But by setting the "regular" price higher, and offering a cash discount, the station used framing to accomplish the same thing without ticking you off.

<u>Gambler's Fallacy</u>

I flip a coin five times. I get heads five times in a row. What will the next likely toss be? Many people will say tails, because it's "tail's turn." If it's a fair coin, the heads/tails chances are 50/50, every single time. Gambler's fallacy occurs when people think that things will even out in the short run, as if the coin or Roulette wheel had a memory. Is it unlikely a coin will come up heads 500 times in a row? Sure. But in the short run, it's not unusual to see long streaks.

If, as a parent, you really want to have a girl, don't assume that you'll have one just because you already had two boys. A family I know apparently wanted a boy after having girls. The first child - a girl. The second child - a girl. The third pregnancy, as though the universe were laughing at them - twin girls! The fifth child - a girl. Finally, the sixth child was a boy. I don't know the family well enough to know if they had so many children because they were trying for a boy, but I do know that the father played a lot of football with that sixth child. Yes, biological factors like chromosomes, sperm strength, and fertilization rates play a role, but the advice of gambler's fallacy still applies. If you and your partner have given birth to three boys, don't assume the next one will be any more likely to be a girl.

<u>Illusory Correlation</u>

Everyone was shocked when John Lennon, at just age 40, was shot near his home in New York City. I remember where I was and what I was doing when I heard the news. His killer was diagnosed with multiple mental disorders. There have been mass shootings making headlines by someone diagnosed as mentally ill. This has led many people to believe that those who are mentally ill are dangerous, but the statistics don't support that. One study is often cited that shows no overall differences between the mentally ill and the general population, although there are a few diagnoses that do have a slightly higher rate.

<u>The Barnum Effect</u>

A classic study was done in 1948. An instructor handed out a personality test to all his students and then collected the results. A week later, he handed back personality descriptions based on the responses and asked the students to rate how accurate they were. The response? Yes, this sounds exactly like me! Students gave it an average rating of 4.3 on a 5-point scale. The punch line here? The personality descriptions were all identical! The personality test was bogus, and was never even scored, and the students received the same write-up, similar to astrological columns in newspapers. The descriptions were very vague and could fit most people. ("You have a tendency to be critical of yourself." and "You have a great deal of unused capacity which you have not turned to your advantage.") The Barnum effect is common to conmen and cold readers, advertisers and astrologists, as we tend to see general descriptions that could apply to anyone as being particularly applicable to us.

Knowing and naming these cognitive biases (and there are dozens more that impact our thinking in different ways) won't make you immune to them. The shortcuts are just too effective in protecting us in the world for us to unlearn them as adults. But if you develop an awareness of the likely ways that you might be misleading yourself, you have a much better chance of evaluating things more honestly and making decisions that contribute to your own happiness.

As always, though, there are systems working against your happiness in this regard.

Government promotes uncritical thinking

Critical thinking skills (which government-run schools are unlikely and ill-prepared to provide) can provide a crucial antidote to political tribalism and polarization.

Have you ever wondered about whether the narrative you're being fed, by cable news or newspapers, or magazines, or the blogosphere, is a fair representation of a complex issue? Very often, what we feel are our personal convictions are fed to us by corporate or governmental interests, who have studied how to make us feel like those conclusions were our own.

Supporters of an increase in local school taxes used framing to make their increase feel very small to taxpayers by requesting "a penny for our children." After all, who wouldn't give a penny to a child? Only someone cruel and heartless. Like those upset about paying extra to use a credit card, taxpayers are not going to be happy when they discover the "penny" they agreed to pay might add up to hundreds or thousands of dollars per taxpayer.

We see framing from the government that really amounts to outright lying. Those elected to "slash" spending will point to their proposals to cut millions from the proposed budget. Notice, they are cutting from the proposed budget, so your next question needs to be, "How much is the budget?" Upon further inspection, you're likely to find that the budget was a huge increase from the current budget, and the "cuts" don't even bring it down to current spending. In other words, it's like saying, "I had planned on gaining 10 pounds, but now I plan to only gain 4 pounds. Look — I just lost 6 pounds!" Small-government crusader Michael Cloud calls this "the Weight Watchers test." "Get on the scale," he admonishes government. "Are you really cutting spending or are you really increasing it, while calling it a cut?"

Unfortunately, many of us fool ourselves by poorly framing our yearly tax "refunds." If we were to cut one huge check to pay our taxes every April, (1) we might not save enough throughout the year to pay the large tax bill, but, more importantly, (2) if we paid it all at once, we would see a huge number of dollars leaving our bank account at one time and protest, saying we're paying too much and not getting enough in return. Government saw these trends clearly and set up automatic withholding, where 92% of workers have their taxes siphoned off paychecks before they arrive in our accounts. All too often people see their tax refund as a Christmas bonus: "Isn't it great that the government gives us this big check every year?" But it's not a Christmas bonus; it's our own money that we worked very hard for and involuntarily loaned to the government without interest. Some organizations have tried to shift this framing by designating a Tax Freedom Day, designating the point at which Americans start working for themselves. In 2023, that date was April 18. Everything we earned from Jan 1 to April 18 went straight to the government.

Confirmation bias was rampant around the COVID-19 fight and the release of the first vaccines. Cameras followed Dr. Anthony Fauci, then Chief Medical Advisor to the President, around during the pandemic, and he is seen advocating for the vaccine, including telling people that it would be extremely rare for a vaccinated person to contract COVID, and that the symptoms in vaccinated patients would be so mild in that case people wouldn't even know they were sick.

That was absolutely wrong. Perhaps he was only looking towards the vaccines he was familiar with in the past, such as measles and polio (the chance of getting those diseases after being vaccinated actually *is* very, very rare) while ignoring all the new research on the COVID vaccine that disconfirmed his view. And, yes, it's a good idea to be skeptical, perhaps even about this explanation. Long before COVID-19, Fauci explained in an interview that natural immunity (from an infection) is very effective against illness, yet ten years later he was insistent that even those who had been infected with COVID should still be vaccinated. Whether he was telling what he believed to be a helpful white lie, or was acting out of some desire for personal gain, or he really tricked himself, we don't know. But confirmation bias carried the day, with serious public health consequences.

Sometimes thinking critically about government programs doesn't take any more effort than, "Did the government cause this problem?" In 2010, when negligence of a major oil company caused millions of gallons to spill into the Gulf of Mexico, many people clamored for more government regulation, hoping to prevent a recurrence. What they didn't realize is that government had capped the amount any oil company would have to pay in the event of an accident like this. Government intervention caused the oil company to take extra risks. Had the oil company been required to go to a private insurer, that company would likely have refused to cover the risk, and the drilling wouldn't have gone ahead. Or if it had, the insurer would have demanded to do very regular and thorough inspections, to protect their own bottom line. If either company had failed in its diligence, both might have gone out of business cleaning up such a disaster. But in this case, taxpayers could be imposed on to cover the cleanup, instead.

Government "protection" made them careless, and made a large-scale spill more likely, not less. This is a clear case of profits benefiting the environment, as they usually do.

Another thing to consider: The U.S. Department of Defense is the largest polluter on the face of the planet. Why would you go to the largest polluter for help in reducing pollution?

Often we hear people on the left rail against the greedy big companies of our "capitalist" system, not understanding that without big government, most of these companies wouldn't be as big as they are. And without campaign donation cronyism and regulatory capture, companies would be held to a much higher standard of behavior.

Even before Rosa Parks refused to give up her place on a Montgomery, Alabama public bus, people have demanded that government eradicate racial discrimination. But of course, Ms. Parks was arrested for breaking the government-enforced color line on a government-owned bus on a government-owned bus line. When the bus boycott began, 70% of bus riders were Black. If a private, profit-driven bus line had discriminated against 70% of its own customers, they'd have been out of business by the end of the week (imagine two-thirds of Uber riders experiencing discrimination), as well they should. But the government, with that unquestioned power and near-unlimited funds, discriminated and forced others to, without any consequences. It's heartbreaking to see people in very genuine distress begging for help from the very people causing their pain — government.

Slavery and the dehumanization of Black Americans was the epitome of racial discrimination, but almost immediately after they were freed, there were new uses of government to keep them down. Black master craftsmen, suddenly entitled to be paid for their work, opened up small businesses and slightly underpriced existing businesses, as start-ups often do. (This is what I did when I started my business.) Did White-owned businesses lower their profits, and improve their quality and service to customers? No. They turned to the bully power of government to oppress the newcomers, in what became the Black Codes and Jim Crow laws.

People who are aware of, and willing to question, their own confirmation biases, may be more likely to seek out the viewpoints of people who disagree, and attempt to figure out why people (who are likely, if counterintuitively, just as sensible as you) might hold such a radical view. Overall, we're not as philosophically different as we suspect.

Turning us against each other is a classic tactic of divide-and-conquer politics. Establishment political media can easily make a broad grassroots movement look like a reactionary fringe group, and the other way around. We are not encouraged to cultivate empathy, nor appreciate alternative perspectives, so "us vs. them," "with us or against us," "friend or enemy," binaries are allowed to stand, leading to greater tribalism and polarization.

Milton Friedman (whom I once had the unbelievable experience of accompanying on a private jet from Oakland to Dallas) wrote, "*One of the great mistakes is to judge policies and programs by their intentions rather than their results.*" This is another way that government prevents us from thinking critically or making good decisions: by distracting us from the most important pursuits of our lives, regardless of the results.

Even government programs designed to help people generally cause more problems than they solve, at least partly by obscuring the evidence we should weigh to make good choices.

When the Department of Agriculture is subsidizing or rebranding certain foods (pork is not a white meat), it becomes difficult for people to make informed decisions about what to eat. When the Federal Reserve bails out banks who've made bad investment decisions, the true costs of those decisions become unknowable, which leads to moral hazard (reduced incentive to make smart choices, because you're protected from the consequences). When government manipulates health insurance and health care, it's very hard for people to decide what kind of care they need or can afford (and moral hazard crops up again, because people aren't as likely to take responsibility for changing unhealthy behaviors). When regulators control who can test and patent new pharmaceuticals, fewer of them end up being made, and only the most profitable (not the most life-saving or promising) drugs get off the drawing board.

When subsidized loans obscure the costs of college, it's harder for families to evaluate whether college will be a good investment, or whether a particular degree program will pay off. When a federal agency claims to be providing the best K-12 education available, many parents don't investigate whether that's accurate, or learn about alternatives that might, in fact, be better for their child's needs.

When Social Security claims to have our retirement well in hand, we save less than we'll need, especially as the program is likely to pay out less than promised. Even if you have all the critical thinking skills a person could hope for, you'll get worse outcomes when government is manipulating your information and choices.

Lots of us in the 1970s were raised with misconceptions that did genuine damage, because they were so divorced from evidence. Plenty of those myths were promoted by well-meaning government bureaucrats. The whole idea of cannabis as a gateway drug was indoctrinated into our society. But it just isn't true. The data reveal tobacco is absolutely the gateway drug to more damaging substances, but that rarely came up in public school teaching, which I suspect is a legacy of lobbyist money from alcohol, tobacco, and pharmaceutical companies. Together they supported Partnership for a Drug-Free America when it formed in 1985, putting out scary, but unsupportable claims about the dangers of cannabis (called by the xenophobia-inducing Mexican name "marijuana"). If you look at most people's "first drug" experience chronologically, Children's Tylenol would likely be their gateway drug. If you look at it casually, experimenting with alcohol comes first in most people's youth. And the data on the dangers of cannabis just doesn't add up to the framing we were sold, by an ad campaign funded by companies who saw cannabis not as a national crisis, but as a potential competitor for American dollars.

Another great myth of my childhood, since disproven by statistical evidence and skepticism, was the "Stranger Danger" scaremongering. Kids of that era, and well into the

1990s, were taught that strangers were a huge threat to children's safety. In fact, I remember making a poster on this in 4th grade, complete with a man holding some kind of black-cape-looking thing in front of his face, demonstrating just how scary a stranger could be. This overlapped with the panic about satanic influences and ritual abuse of kids in the 1980s, which was also not based in fact.

We were taught to be wary of anyone we didn't know, especially those who tried to talk to us, or offered us gifts or rides. While it is certainly possible for a stranger to harm a child, it's statistically very unlikely. Children are, unfortunately, sometimes sexually assaulted or abducted, but someone a child knows is much more likely to commit such an awful crime.

Parents should, and must, teach their kids about danger. But the vivid, fearful cultural myths are actually harmful, because they stop us from discussing evidence-based, realistic risks. Ironically, molesters often groom the parents to get access to the child, so the parents themselves are the ones who need to be on the lookout.

How To Stay Curious, And Think Critically, Even If You're Done With School

There will always be someone, and sometimes whole governments, trying to manipulate your conclusions and convince you of one thing or another. The only way to determine if you're making the best choice (or at least the best available choice for you, right now) is to hone your ability to question what you're told and seek out concrete evidence both for and against your assumptions.

If you've been holding yourself back with thoughts of "I'm just not smart enough," the good news is that "being smart" (IQ) is different from critical thinking, which can be taught. In fact, while IQ has no effect on happiness and well-being, being able to critically think to arrive at better conclusions does improve people's lives. You've probably known some very smart people who make very dumb decisions. That's because yes, there really are "different kinds of smart," and because being smart isn't enough. Critical thinking involves goal-directed thinking that considers biases, such as those listed above, deliberately considering probabilities with a healthy dose of skepticism.

Question everything

If you're given a statement of fact, be prepared to ask how reliable it is. Question your sources, and evaluate the source credibility. You might realize that it's an actor playing a doctor in an ad, but are you unconsciously letting your guard down because someone in a white coat with a stethoscope is trying to convince you of something? Also, we tend to be persuaded more by people we like. Are you sure you're being persuaded by the logic of an argument, and not the attractiveness or accent of the speaker? The question, "How do we know that's true?" can unlock a magical world of new possibilities.

Watch out for biases

Seek out people with expertise in the field, but understand that experts are also just humans, who can be misled by errors in thinking or judgment. One classic study showed that medical doctors recommended surgery based on how the outcomes were framed, even if those outcomes were the same. Only the framing changed: 60% chance of success, or a 40% chance of failure shouldn't change a doctor's calculus. In many cases, you can spot the bias or vested interests that might lead someone to promote or deny a certain fact. It's no shock that tobacco companies pretended their products didn't cause cancer for so long. It's no more surprising that people invested in public schooling might not be very forthcoming about the weaknesses of that system.

Also be aware that some of our confirmation bias is being fed to us by algorithms in social media. These companies direct information towards us based on what we already view, so information isn't presented to us to help us try to disconfirm our beliefs. If your social media never causes you to question whether your beliefs are completely correct, it's time to go outside social media to look for it.

Evaluate the evidence

Use your knowledge of what factors go into high-quality research, and see what can, has, or should be tested for veracity. Even if a measurable effect or relationship between variables does exist, be careful of drawing too quick a conclusion. Consider other possible explanations for what we observe: would some other framework better explain the evidence?

Update your worldview

If you aren't at least a little embarrassed by something you used to believe, it probably means you're not growing as much as you should be. Always be ready to change your mind based on new information, or better explanations. We all get emotionally invested in what we believe, and that can make us resistant to changing our minds. But the most significant value in learning new things is to update your worldview, so that your mental model is at least a tiny bit closer to reality.

<u>Seek alternatives</u>

If you find yourself going down the path too quickly to arrive at a conclusion, ask yourself if there are other alternatives you haven't considered. An expert on a news show said that we know genetics are the main cause of obesity, because if the parents are overweight, then the children are more likely to be overweight. Well, one obvious alternative explanation is that the children are overweight because they're eating the same types of food that are making the parents overweight! One type of scientific study, known as an adoption study, compares children to both biological and adoptive parents, to assess whether children are more similar to their biological parents (which would point to genetic causes) or their adoptive parents (which would point to how they were raised, or environmental causes).

You'll never be done learning and growing, and I hope you find that exciting. Stay curious, think critically, and when you go to bed at the end of each day, be a little bit smarter (or at least a little less wrong) than you were when you woke up.

Stand Out on Purpose, Instead

I love to go barefoot. I really do have a granola-hippy element inside of me and always have. I prefer to drive barefoot. When I got my pilot's license, I asked, and the instructor told me it wasn't illegal to fly barefoot. So, I took my pilot's test barefoot, because I do everything barefoot that you're legally allowed to do.

Going barefoot does have its risks, though - I once realized on my drive to Clemson that I hadn't even brought shoes with me. I often leave the house and just toss my shoes onto the passenger floorboard, so it was bound to happen eventually. Campus is a 45-minute drive from my house, and there was no time to turn back. I stopped and bought a pair of cheap sandals on the way to school. Apparently, I'm not willing to stand out so much as to teach barefoot. I ask my students to put up with a lot, but that seemed excessive.

If I can get away with going someplace barefoot, I will. Once, I took my car to the mechanic. This was back in the mid-90s, before cell phones were popular, and I needed to make a phone call. So, I asked them *"mind, if I use your phone?"* (which used to be the kind of thing you could ask strangers, when phones were attached to locations, and not extensions of ourselves). They agreed.

I walked behind the desk to use their phone, and there were little scraps of paper everywhere, with the mechanics leaving messages for each other.

And I saw a note that said, *"Shoeless Joe will be here Thursday at 2"* — and then I realized *my* appointment was Thursday at 2! I had no idea, but for years, apparently, behind my back, that's how they referred to me. (The namesake there, Shoeless Joe Jackson, was born in Greenville, SC — his museum is within walking distance of my house).

I walked all over Chicago barefoot, with my friend Bill, who took a class on urban sociology at Northwestern and wanted to show me all the cool stuff he learned in that class about different parts of the city. We walked from about 4 to 6 in the morning, which is supposed to be the safest time. I actually walked down Skid Row barefoot, over all the glass and stuff, because my feet are that tough.

The more you go barefoot the easier it is to do. And to be known for it, apparently.

It wasn't the plan, but I ended up barefoot in Minneapolis, in June of 2020, when I was a Presidential candidate. The campaign sent me to view the place where George Floyd had been killed by a police officer — who knelt on his neck for more than eight minutes — three weeks earlier. I'd taken strong stands on ending the drug war, qualified immunity, no-knock warrants (the kind of policies which create conditions for these violations of rights) and my campaign felt it was where I should be.

I was scheduled to be out in the sun all day, visiting different sites. While we were walking through areas of very recent riots, in the June sun, my shoe broke. The strap separated from the shoe within the first 30 minutes. The campaign staff started brainstorming, and I said, it's not a problem, I'll just go barefoot.

So, for the next three hours, I walked barefoot on the streets of Minneapolis, on the side of the road where the buildings are tattered. Broken glass, and shards of steel on the ground, barefoot. One of the Minneapolis hosts started laughing, and told me, "*Uh, your campaign had actually called us a couple of days ago and asked us to get a wide-brim hat for you so you wouldn't get sunburned, and here you are, walking on broken glass!*" I was a bit horrified that, while well-intentioned, someone would ask a host to get me a hat. I didn't want to be seen as a diva. I must also add that I'm glad the state party, as they explained to the campaign when they called, were too busy with other things to worry about a hat. I would definitely categorize hats in my column of responsibility.

I've gotten really mixed feedback about that visit to Minneapolis. I think it was the right place to be, the place of the moment to talk about these issues of power and corruption. We were there on Juneteenth, the 155th anniversary of the last U.S. slave being made technically free. And we got good publicity out of the appearance, because only the

Libertarian Party candidate showed up. Neither Biden nor Trump went to Minneapolis — it was too politically loaded.

(Then again, someone from Fox News was there doing a national telecast from the makeshift memorial. Somebody from my team went over to say *"Hey, Jo Jorgensen is here, you know, Libertarian presidential candidate,"* and he made it very clear he couldn't care less and wouldn't interview me. For third parties, national media attention is always pretty relative.)

I did feel as if I had to put in a lot of extra work as a candidate to be heard and taken seriously, not just in the broader media conversation, but within my own campaign. A man in my position would not have had to do this, but I did.

We spent a lot of money on a reputable firm to create an official campaign logo and branding for us. It would appear on the banners behind us when we spoke, and on our printed materials, and t-shirts, and all over the web. So it was pretty important for setting the tone. We hired professionals who know how to do this branding, for politics specifically.

The hired firm showed us a brief history of what was in use at the time. The classic is the 2008 Obama-Biden, often considered the gold standard, which won a whole bunch of awards. It's the blue circle that looks like a sun rising over red stripes, that makes an O. And beneath that, Obama's name is large, prominent, and dark. Then Biden's, smaller, beneath, and slightly grayed out. The paid experts were very clear about the fact that the presidential candidate's name needed to stand out from the vice-presidential candidate's name, for a few reasons.

The new designer wholeheartedly agreed with the original designers that the presidential candidate's name needs to stand out in either size or color. The mockups the firm did for us followed this conventional format, with Jorgensen large and white, and Cohen (my running-mate – Jeremy "Spike" Cohen) smaller and grayer, very similar to Obama/Biden. We chose his logo for the campaign.

To save on costs, the campaign manager decided to use the campaign graphic designer to create signs, banners, and the like for the campaign, instead of hiring the guy who designed the logo. I confirmed and reinforced these rules to the campaign graphic designer who agreed to follow them.

But then I arrived at an outdoor event, and the backdrop used new branding. Cohen's name was as large as mine, and the same color, so there was no differentiation at all. Since his name is shorter than mine, his name was just as prominent as mine, if not more so. The campaign graphic designer had ignored my request (and ignored award-winning, professional advice) and I was told later that it turned out the graphic designer the campaign manager hired wasn't my biggest fan.

I went back to the original guy who had designed the logo and asked him to create a new backdrop for me, and they gave Cohen the other one. I had to wonder if male candidates had to personally call graphics designers to have their names prominently displayed. Or work with campaign staff who were less than supportive of their nomination.

Years later the designer who created my logo mentioned to me that this new designer created a branding deck, out of his logos, altering his logos to make Cohen "equally relevant" to my name (whether it was the size, color, or other prominence of his name). He was frustrated, after all his hard work, to see his designs bungled, no longer following well-established design practices. He protested, explaining to them that I was the presidential candidate, and my name needed to be more noticeable.

Another campaign manager who has hired many graphic designers for both candidates and his business pursuits explained to me that many of the items with the VP's name prominently displayed with mine shouldn't have even had the VP's name on the item anyway. After thinking about it, I realized that yes, many of the Democrat and Republican presidential material over the years has had just the presidential candidate's name on it. (Yes, Biden/Harris was a noticeable exception, but that was a strategic decision in 2020, given Biden's problems.) So, I'm fighting to keep my name noticeable on material that should have only my name on it.

It would be sad enough if this only happened in the campaign. It had also happened in the national convention signage, with the decision being made by someone who was part of the convention (and later fairly high up in the campaign). The graphics designer (the one who actually listened to me!) created many different options of how our names were displayed. Most of them had Cohen in smaller letters. One sign had Cohen's name in the same-sized letters, but his name was shaded, so my name would stand out. For the lectern where I gave my acceptance speech, this person did an end-run around the official logo, putting Cohen's name in the same color as mine. Since the sizes were the same, again, no differentiation. I did complain to the person who had the sign printed, and he told me he wanted to save money by having three-color printing instead of four-color. Libertarian campaign's strategies to "save money" have been known to be a bit short-sighted. He also told me that the appearance "wasn't televised — it was just the internal national convention." Actually, my speech was streamed across the country, carried live on C-SPAN, and will be in the LP history books for many years to come.

Our campaign spent a lot of money to get advice from a well-known firm who understood the design rules to make us look as professional as the Democrats and Republicans, and person after person ignored that, erring on the side of making my name less prominent. I worried that pushing back on this, even now, might make me seem whiny and entitled — even though all I was asking was that Libertarians follow professional and creative norms for a serious campaign.

I tell this story to demonstrate the work that was required, the diplomacy and deliberate following up, that was required to make my own voice heard on my own campaign. It's not that I'm a narcissist and I just irrationally demand that my name be bigger. But I believe we need to follow certain conventions to be noticed, and to be accepted by people outside the third-party movement as a viable political choice.

The same applies to campaign colors. There were also a number of disagreements about using purple and gold signs, or gray signs. People in our country are primed for political signs to be blue and/or red. There are some established conventions that we should follow; a well-established practice of what people expect from political parties. Red and blue signs are political signs. Passersby know it isn't a roofer, a real estate company, or a patio-renovation place, or other miscellaneous advertising. Political signs are red, white, and/or blue. You have to give people some of what they expect, to break through that barrier and get noticed. Libertarian campaigns are trying to attract attention and acceptance. We have to appear at the starting gate with a certain decorum, to show that we're contenders. To show that we understand how things are done. We don't have to love the confines, and we can challenge them, but to some extent we've got to live within the set norms, or risk becoming noise. Or another roofer advertising.

Some of the early branding, before we decided on the gold torch, included two red triangles. That seemed to be what the campaign wanted. (I wasn't thrilled with it, but I didn't hate it, so I went along with it.) At the time, President Trump was under fire in the press for using inverted red triangles in some campaign ads, which many people interpreted as a Nazi symbol, because inverted red triangles were used to mark political prisoners.

Someone at LP Headquarters told me they weren't going to use our red, white, and blue color design because of the Trump controversy, which had happened very recently. Being on the campaign trail, I hadn't heard about that controversy and was appreciative that they brought it to my attention. I called my campaign manager to tell him that we had a problem — we couldn't use the logo that was chosen because of the red triangles. My campaign manager, ever the scientist (he had taught chemistry) and ever the logical Libertarian, said, *"Oh, don't worry it's not a problem because theirs are equilateral triangles and ours are isosceles."* While I was very amused at his Ayn-Rand-like rationality, I knew we had to change it. I didn't put my foot down very often, but this was one of those times I did. The red triangle branding didn't make any sense — why would we be asking for controversy for symbols that weren't even very relevant? A little long-term thinking can go a long way. What other people perceive matters, even if we believe those people are wrong.

It was such a clarifying moment, in a way. I love Libertarians. They're so analytical, and someone that analytical would see two different triangles. But the average person, the voter, would just see triangles. The incident seemed to highlight what I feel is a strength of mine as a Libertarian candidate — the ability to see people where they are, with perspectives different than mine, and try to meet them where they are, not where we are.

Part of what upset me is that we paid money for this advice, and then the campaign just ignored it without consulting me. And I shouldn't have to oversee the little details. I should be practicing my speech, or checking my email, or talking with donors, but no,

I had to spend my time running interference with a graphic designer to make sure that our material meets a certain standard.

You can bet if I were a man this would not have been a problem. If a man had made the same request, it would have been taken seriously. This would not have happened to a male presidential candidate with a female vice-presidential candidate. I know that because I ran with Harry Browne in 1996, and you never saw my name as prominent as his, and often didn't see it at all (the accepted way the Democrats and Republicans do it). I was treated like an errand boy, which is what I expected. I wanted to be a team player, and was happy to be a support person, to help make the presidential candidate look good and support his platform. After all, that's the job of the vice-presidential candidate — to support the presidential candidate. I went to the places he didn't want to go, and I gave the message my candidate had decided on, and I backed him up.

Once I gave an interview on a Texas radio station about immigration, and Browne didn't like my answer. That night I had a three-hour conversation with someone from our campaign about how I was supposed to answer the question. We practiced exactly how Harry wanted me to respond to such questions. The next time I was asked, I gave the answer that reflected the presidential candidate's views. Harry was clearly in charge, and if I'd continued to say things he didn't like, someone probably would have been fired.

I requested that two people be fired from my campaign, and they weren't.

Harry lucked out. Would I have given answers I wasn't thrilled about, if those were the answers that Harry wanted me to give? Yes. Again, that's the job of the vice-presidential candidate. But luckily, I didn't have to. I was more than glad to receive the three-hour tutorial on how to answer the immigration question, because Harry and I were philosophically the same, and we were pragmatic about campaigning. We both supported the Libertarian Party Platform and were in the movement because we wanted *"a world set free in our lifetime."* We were there for freedom's sake.

Neither Harry nor I believed that an abstract message of freedom and liberty was the way to go. We figured that most of the people who wanted freedom for freedom's sake had already joined the movement. Now we just needed to show the average voter how liberty and freedom was a practical solution to their everyday problems. How people could more easily pay their bills, go on a vacation, and find educational options that worked for their families. How education could be higher quality, meet the needs of the parents, and yet still cost less than the status-quo. We wanted to spread the word of how people could make their own choices, such as whom they wanted to marry (this was still 17 years before Obama and Hillary Clinton publicly said they were against gay marriage). How we could drastically reduce health care costs while increasing quality and increase the standard of living for retirees.

We both wanted to present a positive, practical message to voters on how freedom can improve their lives, so I welcomed the advice of one of Harry's assistants on how to answer the immigration question.

Unfortunately, as a presidential candidate, I did not receive a vice-presidential candidate who agreed with that idea of a VP candidate's role. I definitely did not receive the level of support I gave, as a supportive VP candidate. Often, Cohen was out there preaching a message that actively went against mine.

I'm a very positive person, and throughout a pretty rough year (2020 was complicated for all kinds of reasons) I worked hard to maintain a positive demeanor with everyone I spoke with. Masked-up conventions, socially distanced photo shoots, contentious protests, and lots of hot tempers...people were frightened, and angry, and trapped (often literally). It's easy for me to be optimistic and I felt a responsibility to share that energy whenever I could. Voters would often say that I had good policy solutions, but also that I was genuine, and really cared about people and solving their problems. And that I could explain complex issues in a way that made them understandable (I am a teacher!). People needed calm, and hope. I wanted all of our messaging to be very positive.

Then-President Trump had won his first election by asserting that he was a successful businessman who understood how to run an organization. He promised he would reduce the deficit and the debt to run the government profitably, so to speak, but he did nothing of the sort.

Trump increased spending in the government every year he was in office, and increased both the debt and the deficit more than President Obama had, even though that's what he campaigned against. On a personal level, he became known for assigning derogatory labels to his opponents, such as "crooked." He was also accused of not so flattering behavior with women, with one cringeworthy conversation of degrading comments towards women being recorded.

My other opponent, later-President Joe Biden, is a dismissive, arrogant, angry, mean guy. He's got a famously short fuse and a foul mouth (insiders say he uses the F-word more than anyone else in the White House), is callous with his staff, and cruel to anyone who questions him. That's become more visible to the public during his administration, but it was clear to me even then, and not just because of his thirty-year policy history that ruined millions of lives.

I wanted to differentiate myself as someone positive (because I am!) and sincerely wanting to fix the problems of our country. Being the granddaughter of immigrants, I wanted to be the candidate that reminded people what's good about our country, and how much we have to look forward to. After all, research shows that candidates with positive messages tend to do better than candidates with negative ones, with Ronald Reagan's "Morning in America" campaign message breaking records.

While I fully understand the righteous anger that police violence creates in people, the messaging from the VP's team quickly went off the rails. His team put out an ad with images of cars on fire, and the words, "killer cops." It was right down in the weeds, name-calling and bashing like Biden and Trump. In my view, it was clearly hurting the brand and undermining my presidential campaign team's strategy. Even worse, the overall message (of the federal government playing a role in local policing) was the opposite message I was pushing, and, more importantly, a direct contradiction to the Libertarian Party Platform and libertarian philosophy. I saw one of my tasks as showing voters what a Libertarian government would look like, and it certainly wouldn't have bureaucrats in Washington micromanaging small towns across the country about how they should run their local schools and police departments.

It was an important way I wanted to stand out, and I felt like I was shouting into the void in 2020, just trying to remind people to be decent to each other.

These days, with my shoelessness and my candidacy, it may sound like I embrace my distinctiveness, that I'm excited to stand out, or at least indifferent to other people's judgment. It's a luxury of adulthood, and entrepreneurship, maybe. It certainly hasn't always been true. As a kid I was very concerned about what people thought of me.

My childhood wasn't fraught with trauma or dramatic mishaps. My parents were good people who cared about me and tried so hard to understand me. My stay-at-home mom ferried us around to activities and came to see me do a highland fling at Scottish day in high school, or compete in basketball games and track meets, attended my band concerts, and drove me to the county fair to submit my work, later viewing it on display and taking photos of my ribbons. In that regard my childhood was very easy and not painful. But it always felt painful for me, because I never felt like I fit in anywhere. Especially in a small town, and even within my own family, I was always very aware of the ways I couldn't seem to fit in.

I remember that we were instructed to wear white shoes for junior high school graduation. They didn't sell women's size 10 dress shoes in white, at any store, within 30 miles of my high school at that time. I know because my mom and I drove to and checked every single one. And there was no online shopping or mail order like we enjoy now. So even when I wanted to conform, and to do what everyone else was doing, I couldn't. I did the best I could and got white sandals (too small, but at least my toes could hang over the edge whereas they wouldn't fit inside too-small shoes). And I was chewed out by a teacher for not following instructions I literally couldn't follow, which felt at the time both deeply unfair and depressingly symbolic. Back then, very few stores offered a woman's size 10 in any style. (Yes, pretty much every shoe store now carries women's size 10, but unfortunately I've graduated to a size 12 many years later.)

There were many ways I was happy to stand out, too. I won ribbons at the county and state fairs in 4-H for my sewing and other crafts (finished in the car on the way). I placed in competition while on the gymnastics and track teams. I was generally a very good student, getting high grades and honors. But kids can be cruel, and I often felt like my best efforts, and even my little victories, only won me more scrutiny and sometimes ridicule.

College was a chance to start over, and like most young people I saw it as a time to reinvent myself. My best friend Bambi was very much like me, although not as nerdy, but we were generally wallflowers who didn't drink or go to parties at that age. And she told me, *"You're going so far away to college. Nobody there will know you, or what you're like. You could completely change, you can pretend to be popular, you can be anyone you want to be – and no one would even know!"* But I've only ever really been any good at being me.

From the moment I arrived at Baylor, from orientation on, I was aware that I didn't have much in common with these very formal and proper kids. Women spent literally hours getting ready for class in their fancy clothes. Moving from the Chicago area to a Southern Baptist college did put me in a different place on the identity scale. I was now among students who never drank alcohol. In my new group, I was considered a bit of a wild child because of my love of Monty Python, with its fairly subversive-for-the-time satire, and my stereo playing Led Zeppelin "on 11" (whom I had seen in concert not long before going to college).

By the time I was a college senior, I was married and working part-time as a bartender. Whether on campus or off, I seemed always to be the outsider, caught between worlds. Most days I'd leave this zero-alcohol, buttoned-up campus to go work as a bartender, in a country bar called the Continental Club. It was a rough sort of place — there was even a knife fight once while I was working. Disco was all the rage, but filtered through a Texas sensibility: boots and big hats, with all that late-1970s glitter. And as far as that felt from a Southern Baptist college education, there'd be me, behind the bar with Greek vocabulary words on Fortran cards (the punch cards required for computer programming back then), trying to memorize enough that I could fulfill the professor's final; a former Baptist preacher, he had us translate the first four chapters of the Gospel of Matthew from Greek. I'd glance at the cards between serving up drinks to the cowboy types, and there'd be little flecks of beer foam or droplets of liquor on my flashcards for ὁράω (see) and ἐσθίω (eat). Being nerdy at the bar while a bit "wild" in class, wherever I went, I was always aware that I didn't belong, or fit into a crowd or environment the way other people seemed to.

While I certainly did reinvent myself in college, I didn't magically find a way to be more like other people.

I'm sometimes credited as being the "first woman" to do something, and that's always bothered me. Yes, I was the first woman to appear on the ballot in all fifty states, twice. But being introduced as the "first woman" to do something always seems to undermine the accomplishment. Being a woman doesn't necessarily mean I had to overcome more than the 37th man to accomplish that thing, except if you believe that being a woman makes me innately less competent somehow. And if I don't agree with that premise, that I'm at a disadvantage in the world, then why should I think it's special? I'm fully aware that some things in my life were harder, and some easier, because I'm a woman. I just don't really find that core to my identity.

I do recall an early feminist (if you can call it that) fervor while I was in high school, at a public swimming pool in Florida. The posted rules said that women had to wear swimming caps. In those days I had super-short hair (we all wanted the Mia Farrow pixie cut, I guess), but I was traveling and didn't bring a swimming cap with me. The lifeguard insisted I get out, because I didn't have a cap. And while my hair was very short, the style in the 1970s was for men to have much longer hair. I pointed to a young man swimming nearby, with hair down to his shoulders, and asked why I needed a cap, but he didn't. "Because you're a woman," seemed to be the only reason. As soon as the lifeguard lost interest I jumped in again. I do tend to be a rule-follower, but that one was just so outrageously unfair that I decided they could kick me out, or live with it. If I had a moment of feminist rebellion, it was a modest one.

My accomplishments, and my shortcomings, have to be my own, and not with qualifiers or disclaimers about my gender. If I 'don't fit in' with men, I 'don't fit in' with the majority of feminists, either.

As an aside, I have an attraction to counterculture, but even then, I'm too much of a rule follower to get totally immersed. Although I did almost single-handedly stop a Pink Floyd concert. The "almost" refers to the single-handedly part, not the stopping the concert part. That part I did pretty completely.

I hadn't yet gotten my pilot's license yet (actually, it's called a "certificate," as my flight instructor would continually correct me on), but was getting quite close. I heard about an outdoor Pink Floyd concert that would be going on at Clemson (years before I became a student or taught there), so I thought it might be fun to fly out there and take a look, especially since lasers would be involved. My flight instructor and I double dated (no, I wasn't paired up with him – he brought a woman he was dating and I brought a guy I had briefly been dating), and the four of us flew out there.

We found the outdoor venue, and flew around waiting to see the lasers, which seemed to be taking a really long time to start. Then we received a message from the local tower to please vacate the area, because they couldn't start the laser show with us up there. Evidently, one of the lasers hitting our plane could have brought it down! We quickly left the area.

We did feel bad that we held up the show for tens of thousands of fans. Also for the trouble they had to go through. After all, they couldn't simply use a megaphone to shout up to us – they had to figure out how to contact us through the FAA. It's hard to think of a more incongruous pairing — the countercultural concert crowd using federal regulators to get a message into my clueless brain high overhead.

If I've made peace with standing out as an adult, it's mostly because I had no other choice.

What The Research Tells Us about Standing Out and Fitting In

Psychologists refer to "optimal distinctiveness," which describes our struggle to fit in, and also to stand out. We exist in constant, precarious balance. If we feel like we're getting overlooked among people around us, whether it's the clothing we wear, music we listen to, or even our racial group, we look for ways to be different. If we feel too different from or visible to others, then we try to find ways to be similar and blend in. One study found that Black Americans identified most strongly with their racial group when living in areas in which 40-70% of the population were also Black, making them feel similar enough to their neighbors, but just different enough to be unique. I do have concerns about the trend for people to segregate themselves into groups. Sure, they have the right to do that, and I'm not about to stop anyone from interacting with whomever they want to. But these rooms in buildings in which only members in certain groups are allowed in might be detrimental in helping us feel that right amount of "special."

Imitation is a key part of likability. Nobody wants to be an exact clone of someone else, but we commonly copy behaviors, patterns of speech, styles of dress, and interests from people around us. From high school cliques to world cultures, a certain level of conformity gives us identity and a sense of belonging.

In one study, participants were paired up with a confederate, someone who goes "undercover" in an experiment and is employed by the researchers, but the real subjects think they're another subject, who had been instructed to vary their behavior in specific ways. When the person they were talking to touched their face more, or waggled their feet, or smiled, the participants did more of each of those behaviors, too. Even without realizing it, and even though this person was a complete stranger, they unconsciously behaved at least a little bit more like the people they were interacting with. In a separate experiment, participants had a conversation with the confederate about some trivial topic, while the confederate deliberately (but subtly) mimicked the participant's body language. After the interaction, people whose behaviors had been mimicked rated the confederate as more likable, and the interaction as more smooth and enjoyable. We instinctively like people we perceive to be like us. Mimicry runs parallel to the idea of reciprocity, which we already discussed. Mimicry happens in many other realms, as well, such as eating. In groups, whether it's family or friends, if someone eats something, those around are more likely to eat the same thing, or something at all. This is why we tend to eat more when we're with others, even though we're not aware that we are.

Mimicry is often taught as a tactic in sales situations, sometimes called mirroring in the business world. Even speaking faster or slower to match the prospect's speech can make a difference. For a humorous take on this, Phyllis demonstrates this to Karen on a joint sales call in the show *The Office*. I've wondered if the faster pace of my Northern speech hurt me when I went into sales in Texas, which was my first professional job, since I had only been there since college.

My mom did tell me that she noticed I started talking a lot slower after moving down here. I never purposely did this, because it seemed a bit underhanded, but I would use terminology that clients use in order to aid communication. In the disk business, we usually labeled the 3.5 inch floppy disks. One client kept calling the labels "stickers," so I went along and started calling them stickers as well, just to make the conversation easier for him. I'm happy to speak the language of others. I strongly believe that speaking the language of others helped me as a candidate, with more votes than any other first-time Libertarian presidential candidate.

In college, I took an outside class in sign language, just "for fun." I thought it'd be interesting, and it certainly wouldn't hurt having a new skill. I ended up volunteering as a Campfire Girls leader for a group of deaf girls – the Bluebirds group (the youngest group, at the time). I wasn't sure what they were saying half the time, but it was fun, and their mothers were all very grateful that a hearing person cared to help out.

Never in a million years would I think I would need these skills. Enter my first daughter, who had a learning disability. By the time she was 18 months old, she only said a handful of words (which oddly included "credit card," which she was fascinated with because she recognized the decals in store windows as being the same as in the phone book). The speech therapist suggested we teach her sign language, which she took to right away. My husband would come find me in another room to ask me, "*What does this mean?*" asking me about some sign she was using that he'd forgotten. She used it in at least some form until she was around six years old, when she finally verbally spoke everything. (Of course, like all parents, while I was thrilled she was talking, it was nice to have quiet spaces between the talking as well!)

So many times you hear people say, "I always thought this (whatever this is) happened to other people, but not me." That was my experience with sign language. I was thrilled to help others' children in the Campfire Girls tribe, but how nice I was rewarded by having that quirky skill ready when my own daughter needed it.

On top of everything else, I chose the most misunderstood science to receive my Ph.D. in, one that doesn't get much respect. So many people think that psychology is all about feelings, and point to Freud and his pseudoscientific ideas, at best. (Many of his ideas I would label as pure storytelling.) The fact is, not only is Freud not the father of psychology, as he's often thought of, he wasn't even a psychologist - he was a medical doctor! One prominent psychologist (a real one) strongly advocated that the field of psychology was set back 50 years thanks to Freud. I'm not as critical; I do give him credit for the advances he did bring.

It certainly gives many people the impression, though, that psychology is all "touchy-feely" and there are no right or wrong answers. Tell that to my dissertation chair, who was first author on the article, "*Interdependent Infrastructures as a Multiteam System: Enhancing Resilience.*" Tell that to my former department chair, who was the lead author in the peer-reviewed paper "*Emotional Dampening in Persons with Elevated Blood Pressure: Affect Dysregulation and Risk for Hypertension.*" Or to the Sensation and Perception professor down the hall from me, who tests students on the lateral geniculate nucleus of the thalamus and the physics of frequency and amplitude on hearing. Heck, I test my Intro students on the role that the suprachiasmatic nucleus of the hypothalamus plays in the physiological pathway of the biological clock. (The answer is "B" on the test!)

No, my field of Industrial/Organizational Psychology isn't as biology-oriented as some other subfields, but at points during my thesis and dissertation, I thought I was going to have to drop out of the program because the rigorous process seemed so far over my head. In fact, I showed up at my Thesis Chair's office and announced that I would be leaving the program. Despite excelling in math in junior high and high school (my 8th grade teacher gave me an A++ on my report card and told my mother he didn't know what to do with me because I was so far above everyone else in the class), and despite doing very well in statistics as an undergrad, I felt as though all the studies I needed to read and quote and all the stats contained within them were all written in a foreign language. Literally. The numbers included. And while I was fairly good in math throughout my schooling, I didn't do well in English, so it took me about three times as long as anyone else to simply read the articles to understand what all those long words meant. Running for president was nothing compared to completing my thesis and dissertation, which were the two most difficult things I've done in my life.

I have an MBA and an MSW, even graduating with a 4.0 in my MSW (with a graduate certificate in Drug and Addiction Studies, also 4.0). Neither one of those are research degrees, however. Both were like extensions of undergrad, so the rigor didn't compare to the Master's level work in psychology. No, I did not receive a 4.0 in psychology studies.

Yet, armed with my Ph.D. in a science that was fairly difficult to get, I'm not looked at as being a "real" scientist with a real doctorate. I explain to my Intro students: My field doesn't (with apologies to Rodney Dangerfield) get any respect. No one says, "I saw an apple fall from the tree - I'm a physicist!" or "I just put a Band-Aid on someone - I'm a medical doctor!", but so many people say, "I can tell the kind of person someone is by shaking their hand!" Everyone's an armchair psychologist. (And, by the way, studies have been done and no, handshakes are not a good way to tell anything about people, especially when interviewing for a job position.)

If you have concerns about some personal trait that causes you to stand out in a negative way, or gets in the way of connecting with people, a shift in context can be very useful. The Campfire Girls were in a group of other deaf girls for a reason, and they were excited to see me for a very similar reason. It isn't only about finding your "tribe," but in finding places where your full self is welcome and appreciated.

My Master's thesis ("*Can Context Change the Interpretation of Body-Weight Cues?*") sought answers about how context changes our relationship to negative cues about other people. All sorts of research shows that fat people are treated negatively in the workplace and elsewhere. The term fat, though it seems pejorative, is the preferred term some overweight people use for themselves. The argument made by the National Association to Advance Fat Acceptance is that normalizing these words (like "We're here We're queer,") takes the sting out, reclaiming them from negativity. They also stated that "overweight" points out a gap between a body and some other weight or body shape it "should" be; fat simply describes a body that is.

My research goal was to find positive terms used about fat people, and identify a job or career in which fat people would be preferred over skinny people. "Normal weight" people generally have an easier time getting hired than heavier people. Economics research links women's size with income, with each added dress size reducing her annual income. Men suffer from this discrimination, but considerably less — overweight men are actually overrepresented among CEOs.

I did manage to find a job for which being fat increased people's favorable opinion: it was day care workers, but only the younger ones. Whatever your particular presentation in the world, there's someone who finds that valuable. If you love it about yourself, find others who'll love you for it, too.

A Third-Party Voice In A Two-Party System

In many ways, I found my tribe with the Libertarian movement. The movement is full of, defined by, people who don't fit into the traditional two-party mold of American politics, but who are invested enough in change that they can't just tune out. The most powerful political opinion in the nation seems to be apathy: while the 2020 election was the first time in decades that more than half of eligible voters turned out, "Did not vote" continues to beat both Republicans and Democrats in every election.

Libertarians are animated by dissatisfaction with the two mainstream parties, but mostly frustrated with the political system as a whole. We see the "old" parties as broken, corrupt, too entrenched in their views, and bought off by special interests and high-dollar donors. We accept the paradigm of voting for candidates that share your views, and want to work within that system to challenge the status quo. We want to be heard not only by voters, but by other parties, as a way of incrementally influencing the policy direction of the country, even if we don't win a given office. We want to broaden the national conversation, contributing our part to a robust representative republic.

The Libertarian stance on adult use of cannabis, and our acceptance of LGBTQ+ rights and personhood, were considered radical, fringe views when they first appeared in the Party's platform in the early 1970s. But now those views have become mainstream, and the political movements behind them have seen revolutionary successes.

Third parties (and fourth and fifth!) can offer a different vision for the future. We lobby for equal access for smaller parties to appear on ballots, without jumping through needless hoops like collecting thousands of signatures (while larger parties do not have to do). We reject the insular, exclusionary practices of two-party debates run by the parties themselves, who have a vested interest in limiting competition. The Let Her Speak campaign, which lobbied for my inclusion as an equal party in the 2020 presidential debate, should not be as edgy and revolutionary as it in fact was.

I wish I didn't have to write about this. 'Mises Caucus' is just a blip on the radar and will eventually be forgotten by most people reading this book. But it wasn't a blip to me.

The Party has many caucuses, some very serious and policy focused, such as the Radical Caucus, and some purely for fun, mostly on Facebook, like the Middle Earth, Star Trek, or the Waffle House caucuses. So, when I first heard about the Mises Caucus, I didn't think too much of it, I just figured it was one of the many.

I hadn't yet realized that it was an authoritarian group that was determined to undermine the Party. I got a sense of it in the 2020 primary for the presidential nomination.

When you're on stage and at a microphone every night for months, you can tell if you've had a good night or a bad night. There were times I knew I wasn't at my best. And there were nights I could tell the other candidates, whom I debated, in varying combinations, at dozens of state Libertarian Party conventions, had off nights. But gradually, the vote totals diverged from the quality of the performances. Loyalties were emerging.

One night (I won't say which state) someone came up to me after the debate, and he said, *"I'm in the Mises Caucus, and I was told to vote for X, but I actually voted for you. Please don't tell anyone, though!"* And he said it to me in an undertone, like he was trying to sell me an illegal substance. Solemnly and in a whisper, in this big auditorium.

Now what he said wasn't totally unusual. Sometimes after a vote people will say, "Yeah, because I'm with this group, and we're supporting this, I put my vote behind this person; but you were my second choice," but it's usually jovial, back-slapping. Or someone will say, "I support this guy, but he was really not on his game tonight, so I threw my vote to you this time, but my guy will have to work harder."

But something about this time was rather odd — the way he said it. Not something a Libertarian would normally say — that they were told whom to vote for — and that he told me like he was telling state secrets from China. He was dead serious about not wanting to be found out as disagreeing with his group. Typically, I'd want to dig into the psychology of odd behavior, and why people do what they do, but that time it just didn't sit well. I should have thought, "Hmm, wait a minute. Okay, these people are different.", but I just didn't realize.

Eight months later, after the nomination, somebody in the audience at the Florida State Convention asked me if I regretted marching with Black Lives Matter. And I was taken aback a little. I wracked my brain, trying to think of a snappy comeback, or make it seem like it was such an outrageous question that it didn't dignify a response. Of course I didn't march with Black Lives Matter! The last thing I wanted to do was to appear defensive, but I was so thrown by such a ridiculous accusation that the only thing I came up with was, "*I never marched with Black Lives Matter.*" Usually I think pretty quickly on my feet, and you have to if you're going to debate week after week, but in this case, I had nothing.

I saw the writing on the wall in a forum at the Minneapolis State Convention in 2022. A couple of times I clearly answered a question better than the Mises Caucus candidate had, which caused him to raise his hand and say, "*I'd like to add something,*" with that "something" being changing his answer to be closer to mine. I was pleased with my performance, and after being the candidate, had high expectations. I was surprised by the responses in the crowd, though. Many attendees came up to me afterward, and in hushed tones similar to the person who voted for me but "wasn't supposed to," was told wistfully, "*as always, your answers were by far the best and right on. . .* " And then they trailed off as if to say, "*. . . but it won't do any good because the Mises Caucus now has control.*"

I finally found my "peeps" in Party, committed years of my life to it, felt like I finally found a place to belong, and then all of a sudden I'm an outcast there, too. I finally found the group that says, "we accept all modes of life," and then suddenly, they don't. It doesn't seem to matter which direction I go. Even the outcasts have decided I don't belong!, but I'm fiercely proud of the message I carried in 2020 — I would be ashamed to carry the message that the national party leadership promoted in 2024. The ruling caucus wouldn't be likely to accept me as a candidate, and not necessarily because there's someone better out there for the broader Libertarian message. But because they view me as an outsider. And there are some groups you shouldn't want to fit in with.

How to Stand Out (in a Good Way)

There's no quick fix to fitting in, even if you are willing to drastically alter your environment or social set. But there are ways you can help yourself to be more accepting and feel more accepted.

Focus on self-acceptance

Everyone has something to offer. Instead of allowing "different from others" to always be a negative, recognize the ways you're exceptional in a positive sense. Make time for activities that make you feel good. Spend time with people who value you, in all your uniqueness. Challenge negative self-talk and talk to yourself like you'd talk to a friend. Treat yourself with compassion.

<u>Decide what is worth standing (out) for</u>

"Fitting in" usually requires adopting, or at least abiding by, the values and social norms of a group you hope will accept you. But only you know whether pursuing or sacrificing those things is worth it to you. There's no value in gaining the acceptance of others if you lose your self-respect to get it.

<u>Find Common Ground</u>

Even if you feel very different from other people, you can build positive relationships with them.

Try really understanding their perspective, and the values that ground their opinions and actions. Even if we express ourselves through very different actions and choices, our underlying values may not be as different as we believe. If nothing else, we can gain a better appreciation for the diversity of human experiences.

Political campaigns, like high school or college, provide a strange simplification of the fitting in/standing out balancing act. You have to stand out from your opposition enough to be noticed, but not so much that you alienate people. You have to fit in enough that people find you approachable and relatable, but not so much that you're beholden or forgettable. Everywhere you go, and everyone you meet, will be trying to convince you to be more like them. But the only approval you should be willing to change your actions for — is your own.

Improve Your Relationship with Food

When I told my deputy campaign manager that I intended to write this book, the first thing she said was, "*Well, you have to talk about your food!*"

"My food" has been something of an entertaining novelty for those around me. My meals mostly consist of unprocessed foods, what we used to call 'whole foods' before corporate branding took over that term. I haven't eaten red meat (yes, that includes pork! - more on that later) since 1996. I never cared for fatty beef, like steak, nor did I have any taste for any type of pork products. I don't call myself a vegetarian, and I generally hate those kinds of labels, but vegetarians would label me a "pescatarian." Most accurately, I don't eat animals that nurse their young. After nursing my two daughters, I just can't face it. But that's not a choice anyone can make for you.

These preferences are certainly not inherited. My dad was a hunter and taught me how to shoot a gun when I was about four years old. I was taught early that it's Canada geese, not Canadian geese. He was friends with a guy who owned a farm that had cherry trees on it, and they would shoot at the blackbirds to protect the fruit. He was an avid duck hunter during my entire childhood, until years after I moved out of the house. For a while he also went deer hunting every year. He and my mom had matching jackets made from the skin of deer he'd shot. I can recall cleaning out freshly killed ducks in the basement utility sink, like you'd clean out a Thanksgiving turkey, reaching in to pull out the gizzards, which weren't carefully wrapped in plastic or paper like you get from the grocery store. These innards were authentic. They'd turn up on the dinner table not long after, and I didn't much like the taste anyway. Too rich, like steak.

My dad found my food choices to be atrocious, often telling me that with my way of eating, "*you don't actually live longer, it just feels longer.*" It was hard for me to get him to understand my version of "healthy eating." He told me, "*now they say that ginkgo doesn't help your health at all.*" I tried to explain I've never even tried that, and the basis of my eating was simply unprocessed vegetables, beans, and fruit, and avoiding processed foods and animal products.

He was definitely "meat and potatoes," and I was required to eat meat when I was younger. He told me, "*When I was young we couldn't afford steak. I can afford it so you're going to eat it.*"

While many young adults, when going off to college or leaving the home, rebel by drinking alcohol and taking drugs, or being thrilled they no longer have a curfew and partying all night, my adolescent freedom was not eating meat! Maybe that's why I never used drugs — my newfound freedom was not eating meat, which apparently was enough of a rebellion for me.

My daughters also questioned my food choices at various times. My mother took my young daughters to the zoo, and while standing in line, asked them, "*Would you like a hot dog?*" My younger daughter, around age 4, replied, "*Mama J, what's a hot dog?*" After receiving strange looks from the person in line behind them, my mom was concerned she might get turned in for child neglect or something. After all, how many children in the early 1990s had never heard of a hot dog? My daughter's verdict after biting into it was, "*This isn't very hot!*" I guess she was expecting spicy. My daughters both grew up very healthy, though, with my older daughter towering in at almost 6 feet (I'm so jealous!). They thrived on a reduced-meat diet.

My mom used to reward me with McDonald's milkshakes after I endured each weekly trip to the allergists' office. I was allergic to a lot of things when I was little. Strawberries and bananas, goat hair and elm trees. I remember reading the list, quite long, typed out on an old-fashioned typewriter. I can only remember a smattering of them. So, I was getting allergy shots pretty often, four at a time. In my small town of Grayslake there weren't any allergists, so we'd have to drive twenty minutes to Waukegan, which seemed like forever as a little kid dreading shots. And it was something else that made me feel fundamentally different from other kids. I didn't know anybody else who got allergy shots, or anyone who had to get four shots of any kind that often. It was something else that made me feel like an outsider, like I didn't quite fit even within my own skin, where I had to receive shots just to keep my body from attacking itself over strawberries, bananas, pollen, or hog's hair and goat's hair, if I ever came in contact with those. (Although that may seem a bit far-fetched, I did encounter that every summer at the county fair when entering my 4-H projects.)

But the nearby larger city had not only the nearest allergist, but a McDonald's as well (Grayslake has since grown a lot, and they've certainly got a McDonald's and more than one stoplight these days). My mom would reward me with a McDonald's milkshake if I didn't cry while getting the shots, but after a while, I was too old (and too used to it!) to cry much and milkshakes just became a nice thing we did together.

Our candy drawer was infamous among kids in my neighborhood when I was growing up. Everyone knew about the candy drawer, stocked with all different kinds of candy. My choice always had chocolate in it, and I had a weakness for Mallo Cups (still do!). I had become pretty indifferent about it — it was there all the time, which made it less appealing because having it around all the time made it less of a forbidden fruit. When my friends and other neighbor kids came over, though, it was a source of a lot of fascination, our first stop between the back door and whatever game we were going to play. I can tell you without a doubt, the kids whose parents did not allow them to have sugar at home were obsessed with that drawer. They would gorge themselves, because it was forbidden and suddenly no one was policing them.

Asked to name rewards for children's good behavior, many people (including my students) will say cookies or candy. And from a classical conditioning perspective, that definitely works very well, but reinforcement using food is correlated with eating disorders. Reward kids with a lollipop for a successful swim lesson or pizza for good grades, and before you know it, you've got a 42-year-old businesswoman who earns a great promotion, but can't really enjoy the accomplishment until she rewards herself with a hot fudge sundae.

We're very culturally steeped in food as a form of positive attention and bonding. Look at any tiny celebration or major milestone in people's lives and there's generally a food associated with that moment. And it isn't grapes or broccoli. It's ultra-processed and hyper-palatable, with some combination of sugar, fat, and carbohydrates. There's wedding cake, birthday cake and retirement cake. Ice cream after the big game, Cracker Jack at the ballpark, buttered popcorn and Snow Caps at the movies. Sodas and sugary lemonades at summer picnics and fairs. Chocolates on Valentine's Day. Pumpkin pie at Thanksgiving dinner. Cookies at Christmas. We associate these foods with enjoyment, intertwining hyperpalatable foods with the events and social relationships that make us feel good.

While I'm not always in total control of my snack habits, I've done a better job managing my exposure to medication, which is another manufactured method of changing our bodies' natural response. I don't have an objection to it and am happy to take what my doctor prescribes for serious ailments.

Occasionally, a visitor to my house will say they have a headache or muscle ache and ask if I have any aspirin. And I'll say, "I'm sorry, I don't have any." And the next response is always, "Oh - Tylenol is fine," but I don't have that either. Once or twice someone has gotten pretty upset, sure that I was lying and just didn't want to give them any, as if I were accusing them of trying to scam me out of some over-the-counter pain relievers. But that isn't it at all. I wouldn't say I live completely holistically, exactly, but I'm not a big fan of running to drugs. Just as it has sometimes made me an ungracious host, it sometimes makes me a less-than-sympathetic friend. Once in high school, I was explaining to a neighbor who had terrible menstrual cramps that she ought to drink more water, which I can tell you now, with certainty, was not what she wanted to hear. I guess she thought that free advice was worth every penny.

So how did I arrive at a way of eating so novel that my deputy campaign manager thought absolutely needed to be mentioned? The short answer: I was afraid of getting a hole in my heart, and I didn't know what to make for dinner by the time Thursday rolled around.

In high school, my biology teacher told us a story about a young woman in the 1960s who severely restricted her diet, trying to lose weight to emulate the women of the Twiggy era. According to him, she didn't eat enough protein, and her body started breaking down her heart muscle, in search of protein to sustain her body. That story really impacted me - I've been concerned about getting enough protein ever since - perhaps more concerned than I should be.

It may seem silly now to worry about eating meat every day, but it was a different world back in the 1970s and 80s. Especially in the south, where I first began finding my food ways as an adult. This is the place where macaroni and cheese is still considered "a vegetable" on Southern cooking restaurant menus, and meat is served at just about every meal, sometimes secreted away in vegetable dishes. I did not know a single vegetarian as a young adult, and first heard that it's even possible to not eat meat (I had no idea, given my background) by watching the 1981 film *The Four Seasons*, directed by Alan Alda. In the movie, one of the characters explains how if you carefully time your eating of beans and rice (they must be eaten at the same time), then you don't need to eat meat. He very specifically emphasized the timing had to be correct.

No one would explain that in a movie today.

Then, about seven years after the movie came out, I had a conversation with a doctor (an acquaintance, not "my" doctor), and mentioned I was trying to reduce the amount of meat, but I was concerned about being safe with it. (In other words, I didn't want to get a hole in my heart!) I told her about the food mentioned in *The Four Seasons*, explaining the importance of combining the beans and rice. She told me that new research showed that it's okay if the two aren't eaten at the same time — just so they're eaten in the same day or eaten regularly. Interesting how some civilizations had been eating vegan diets, or close-to-vegan diets, for tens of thousands of years, and yet we're just "discovering" it in the U.S. in the 20th century.

Of course I didn't have the internet to fact-check anything, and doctors actually know very little about nutrition. At the time, people were just discovering that doctors were graduating from medical school without a single class in nutrition. So, I carried on a small amount of ground beef in hamburgers and lasagna, earnestly thinking "I don't want my body to eat my heart!"

The problem with eating only cheap ground beef as a daily meat source, with some chicken and seafood on a few days, is my meals were getting very monotonous. I would have a chicken dish one night, seafood the next, then back to chicken, and then back to seafood. On rare occasions, perhaps some kind of cheap ground beef in spaghetti. Without nights devoted to pork chops, burgers, ham, roast beef, and an occasional steak, dinners were getting pretty boring in my household. After two nights of chicken and two nights of seafood, I found myself on Thursday not wanting to rotate back to either of them.

Trying to figure out how to safely eat stayed in the back of my mind for the next five years, since I had two small children, moved to a different state, and ran for U.S. Congress. Then a solution fell into my lap when a friend of mine told me that a macrobiotic group had started in town. I vaguely remembered hearing that singer John Denver had eaten macro, for at least a little while, so it seemed worth checking out. My true goal was finding new recipes that I'd actually enjoy, that wouldn't cause me to digest my own organs. And that's how I ended up at a table full of people eating a macrobiotic diet, and a new era of my eating began. The nice part about it was that it was all wrapped up into a nice little system, with macrobiotic counselors who checked some kind of additional pulse in your wrist that doctors don't, get your medical history and ask about lifestyle, give you an eating plan. Macrobiotic eating involves no meat, no dairy, and eating a plant-based diet that's relatively local and seasonal, consisting mostly of vegetables, whole grains, and beans or bean products (such as tofu and tempeh). This was a whole new world I was thrilled to walk into. This world did come with all kinds of interesting provisions, including not using a microwave or dishwasher (you're supposed to wash all your dishes between cooking and eating) and not putting ice in your drinking water. While I now use a dishwasher, I rarely use ice, except when packing an ice chest.

When my original macrobiotic counselors tried to instill in me the concept of yin and yang diet and exercise, it was a real challenge. The counselors chastised my eating pineapple, and told me "of course!" I was resorting to an inappropriate tropical fruit, which is too yin, because I was still eating some meat, which was too yang, so I was eating pineapple in an unconscious attempt to counteract the meat. I also gave another counselor a run for his money when I was playing ice hockey every week at the time (so dedicated that I played on Wednesday evenings at 10 p.m., because that was the "over 40" pickup game time, where, yes, I was the only woman), which the counselor told me was "way too yang" and should definitely not be played at 10 p.m. He finally gave up on trying to convince me to take up yoga instead (which I did take up about 20 years later), and gave me a list of yin activities and acceptable food to counteract the extreme yang I had invited into my life. (By this time I had not eaten meat for several years, so hockey was my main source of yang.)

I really enjoyed the people in the local macro community. We would have potluck dinners and counselors and speakers visit our small group (there were no counselors within 60 miles of Greenville). As has been the story of my life, though, I found myself not quite fitting in with the group, as congenial and gracious as they might have been. First, our group was a bit of a misfit group being in the deep south, the land of lots of meat. As expected, these vegetarians were on the liberal side, with conversations about how great a $20/hour minimum wage would be (and that's $20 in the early 1990s). Not wanting to cause too much friction in the group (being a Libertarian, I love to debate to a point that others might call it an argument, but I call it fun), I didn't get into long explanations about how minimum wage laws tend to hurt those they try to help — those at the bottom rung of the economic scale. And while I shared their anti-war stance, they pushed for strict gun control. As usual, I wasn't fitting in, but this seemed extreme. I'm even an outcast in the outcast eating group? Of course my fellow gun-toters are big meat eaters. Meat is as political as guns, and I don't fit into either community.

I white-knuckled giving up dairy and was successful for some stretches of time. My body really seemed to prefer that. People often assume that means I'm lactose intolerant or have digestive trouble, but I've never had those problems. Strangely enough, I found that eating dairy made me more prone to infection, especially in the piercings of my ear cartilage.

Much more recently, my daughter told me that emulating my food habits made her feel like a panda, constantly grazing on roughage, trying to accumulate enough calories to keep going. That's much more like the environment our bodies were designed for. (This worked well for me on the campaign trail — at the time, we had to wear masks except when eating and/or drinking. It would take me an hour and a half to eat one of my large salads, meaning I could be maskless for most of the flight!)

After making the switch to a mostly macrobiotic diet (I continued to eat fruit and other items usually avoided to not become vitamin deficient), I noticed many small changes. A long-broken thumbnail that doctors told me would never heal, finally repaired itself, leading to an improved quality of life since I didn't have to repair it every week. My sleep improved dramatically, to the point that I carried around cooked brown rice and lentils in a plastic bag on the campaign trail for dinner, just so I'd be able to sleep. This was before the days of little fridges in every room, so I'd fill the sink with ice and put my bag of rice and lentils in there. In a few extreme cases, I carried the same bag of cooked brown rice and lentils for four days, eating some every day as I traveled from state to state. Far too much pizza and fast food on campaigns, and my body was craving something healthier.

It was much easier than I thought to give up beef, even the kind I absolutely loved. I still remember the last serving of beef I ever ate – Single with cheese, everything, no mayonnaise, at a local Wendy's with my flight instructor. I still struggle to completely give up dairy. From a moral standpoint, it doesn't involve an animal dying. If I'm to believe the stories of animal advocacy groups, though, mother cows are in distress for at least a little while when their calves are taken away so the milk can be redirected for human consumption. Currently I eat a fraction of the dairy I once did and continue to work on it. (Please don't send the National Dairy Council after me for saying that, like how the cattle ranchers went after Oprah! That case did give us Dr. Phil, though.)

More recently, I encountered the dietary advice of Dr. Joel Fuhrman. His model of nutrient density (eat more things that pack maximum micronutrients per calories) diversifies the American diet in the healthiest way we know of. Dr. Fuhrman's calling card is the acronym G-BOMBs: he recommends eating Greens, Beans, Onions, Mushrooms, Berries and Seeds every day. Research shows this mixture of foods not only gives you more energy with fewer calories, but also improves your overall health, boosts immunity, and may reduce your risk of certain cancers. Dr. Fuhrman's diet strongly recommends eliminating all processed foods, meats, dairy, and sugar. The major changes from my earlier macro diet to this included many more fruits (pineapple is back on the menu!), fewer grains, and less oil. While most Americans may find his way of eating to be extreme, coming from a macrobiotic diet, I found myself going in the opposite direction and becoming more mainstream!

I'm also a fan of Dr. Mark Hyman, who also advocates eliminating all processed foods and sugar and replacing them with whole foods. Dr. Hyman, however, also advocates eating meat, which is now coming back on the "healthy menu" in our country. My not eating meat doesn't have anything to do with health, but, rather, I feel bad eating cows, especially after seeing them in the fields with their big brown eyes. I have started to take Dr. Hyman's advice of eating eggs [no large brown eyes] – another reason I don't call myself a vegetarian, even though those around me do.

Of course, being a "professor," I must have a professor/researcher on my list. Tim Spector, in addition to being a British medical doctor, is a professor performing the thankless behind-the-scenes research. Dr. Spector wants to tease apart nature vs. nurture on the physiological side – a man after my own heart since much of psychology has worked on the role of nature vs. nurture in behavior. His research, a lot of it on the gut microbiome, has shown that we have a lot more control over diseases than we think we do, and control is a good thing to have. Food plays a larger role in health than most people realize.

You'd think, after decades of eating kale, I'd have been excited when it came into the cultural mainstream a few years ago. But I was actually pretty annoyed about it, like a hipster who claims he liked a certain music group "before it was cool." I started eating kale in salads when the biggest buyer of kale was still Pizza Hut, who didn't even use it as food, but bought it in bulk to decorate their salad bars. Then when people started eating kale, they bypassed the salad part and went for kale smoothies and kale chips. Why would you choose to get less fresh flavor? Why would you choose to eat a food without chewing it, when chewing food is one of the things humans like most? While I gave in to smoothies now and then because of my traveling (but only homemade smoothies that I personally made), I feel pretty strongly that if I'm going to eat calories, then I want to chew and enjoy them!

How and what we eat has big implications for who we are as people, well beyond the micronutrient level. I was fascinated to learn from a television documentary that we name our meats according to the class system who eats them. Have you ever noticed that we eat beef and pork, not cow and pig? At the same time, we do eat chicken and fish. The names for those aren't different on the menu than they are in a children's book about animals. But you won't see pictures of a "beef" animal or "pork" in that same book. That's because even a century ago, there was some hesitation over eating Bessie, your cow. So they put some separation between the animals in the field and food on the plates of the noble lords and ladies. Bessie certainly wasn't "Bessie," but she wasn't even "cow" anymore – she became "beef."

Peasants, on the other hand, couldn't afford to eat cows and pigs. They ate chickens and fish. No need to rename those – who cares how uncomfortable peasants are (and the peasants probably didn't have too many fish as pets).

Most Americans completely separate themselves from the animals they eat. One of my guilty pleasures is watching *90-Day Fiancé* with my daughter. (Don't worry – I'm not ruining the mind of a child – she has her own family – husband and two kids. Besides, she's the one who introduced *me* to the show!) One episode (which was actually the series "*The Other Way*") showed an American living in Ecuador with his native fiancé. When it was time to buy the chicken for his birthday dinner, the program showed them going to pick out the chicken, and he was a bit uneasy when he saw they were going to put the chicken upside down into a contraption to cut its head off. That's quite a bit different from our country, in which we go to the brightly lit grocery store and pick out chicken parts, disembodied cutlets on Styrofoam trays in shiny plastic wrapping. No one gives any thought that these were living at one time.

In fact, we don't give much thought at all to where any of our food comes from. But we probably should. And we should certainly be honest with ourselves about what we put into our bodies.

What Research Tells Us About Food

No shock here: Most Americans consume more added sugar, salt, and saturated fats than dietary experts say we should. Even if you make an effort to eat sensibly, you're probably doing some damage to your body with the foods you eat.

Some highly processed foods with these excesses are called *hyperpalatable*, and they're manufactured to appeal to our evolutionary appetites. Food scientists combine fats, simple sugars, salt, and carbohydrates into combinations we can't get enough of — literally. They test recipes with focus groups and track how many grams of chocolate covered pretzels, for example, the average person will eat. Those clusters of flavors (fat and salt, sugar and fat, salt and sugar) are cued directly to our evolutionary brains.

True sweetness is very rare in the natural world, and fruit you find today could spoil tomorrow, or be eaten by someone else, so it makes sense to consume a lot of it when it's available. Our taste for sweetness also encourages us to wait until fruit is ripe, at its maximum nutritional value, to eat it. We'll eat long after we're physically full, because our brains never developed an "off" switch to say "you're done eating that." We never needed one. The limitation was always the scarcity in the food environment. We're built for famine, and when we feast, at some point, the supply runs out. Our genes haven't changed much since our feast-or-famine days; It takes a very long time for genes to evolve in new environments, and our modern abundance of food is a recent environment, indeed.

I point out to my students that in nature, you never see fat squirrels. You also don't see fat deer or ducks or rabbits. That's because they don't have Cool Ranch-flavored Dorito chips. When we're in our natural environment, such high-fat sources are limited.

Skittles and Snickers bars are another perfect example of that evolutionary mindset at work. If, as a primate living on the savannah, you find something that gives you this set of sensory feedback: sweet, chewy, dense, that's an unsurpassable nutritional windfall. You can consume all you want of it — abundant energy! — and you will want a lot of it. With any luck you'll get a little fat, which will protect you in the lean times that are inevitably coming. Once you don't live in that survival space, though, your body doesn't know what to do.

So not only do we have these hyper-palatable foods that don't exist anywhere in nature, but we have a historically unprecedented access to food we do not have to work for, and we do not have to wait for. Not only do you not have to hunt or gather your food, you don't even have to get out of your car. You can access more calories than you need in a week, and have it passed to you in a paper bag through the window of your car.

In some sense, it's a remarkable human achievement that in America, for the first time in the history of our species, you're more likely to be fat if you're poor. More people are in health crises from obesity than from starvation.

When we're under stress, or otherwise unhappy with our lives, we sometimes turn to food to comfort ourselves. Notice in a chick flick, when the character just had a breakup or a letdown, she's often pictured standing in front of the ice cream case choosing a flavor, or standing in her kitchen eating out of the carton with an oversized spoon. She never comes home with an armful of cabbage and carrots, because when we stress eat, we're drawn to high-fat, high-carb, high-sugar foods. Ice cream and chips, not broccoli and beets.

When I was frequenting macrobiotic meet-ups, I remember people talking often about how they all expected that they'd have real trouble giving up chocolate, which you're not supposed to eat with a macrobiotic diet. But everybody said the same thing: chocolate wasn't that hard, but they really struggled to give up cheese. And there's a logic to that. Nature *really* wants babies to drink milk, for survival, so there are calming chemicals in milk. Dairy protein has morphine-like compounds built into its chemical structure. They attach to the same brain receptors as heroin, causing the brain to release dopamine. It's difficult to give up cheese because it's mildly addictive. Engineered, hyperpalatable foods have similar, if very temporary, mood-boosting properties. Like a toddler on a post-party sugar high, eventually, we crash. Then we crave more.

It was (and continues to be!) a struggle for me to give up these addictive components outside of meals. I actually do quite well for my meals, which contain virtually no sugar or fats in oil form. (You might think your meal doesn't contain sugar either, but have you read your spaghetti sauce or salad dressing labels?), but snacking has different psychological cues.

Food is a common way to 'treat' ourselves, and it's one of the most affordable methods around. That was true for my mom, bringing a tear-streaked child home from the allergist, and it's true now, especially for people on lower incomes. If you can't take a ski trip to Aspen or book a 60-minute massage to unwind, maybe you'll have some cheese puffs or a chocolate bar. Drive-through meals are accessible luxuries for low-income families, and are literally branded "Happy Meals" for children. Marketers are constantly researching strategies to make us crave certain foods, and to eat more of them.

But consumers are buying more than cheap, calorie-rich foods. We're buying time with our kids, which would otherwise be spent preparing and cooking foods at home. We're buying the feeling of treating our kids to something special. The high-fat, high-sugar, high-salt combination feels, to the evolutionary brain, like a reward in itself. But our emotional relationship to the food is what keeps us coming back.

You've probably heard of studies that conclude "a glass of wine each evening may be helpful to heart health," but let's throw in some critical thinking here. Whom are they doing that research on? It turns out, it's primarily on people eating a typical American diet of high fat and high sugar. Perhaps, yes, a glass of wine in the evening will suppress some of that activation. But does that really make it a healthy choice, for someone eating a truly healthy diet? No, not at all.

Where you get your information about what's healthy matters a lot. And unfortunately the most prolific issuer of nutrition guidelines, the federal government, seems to get the science almost entirely backwards — because they're not motivated by science, at all.

How Government Food Policy Makes Us Fat, Sick, and Unhappy

The United States Department of Agriculture (USDA) has been issuing dietary recommendations for over a century. At the time, most vitamins and micronutrients we know today hadn't even been identified yet, and plenty of Americans suffered health problems from malnutrition, like scurvy (not enough Vitamin C), pellagra (not enough vitamin B3), and rickets (not enough Vitamin D). Some of these discoveries led to helpful health interventions, like the addition of Vitamin A to milk (to replace what's lost during pasteurization), and infusing table salt with iodine (which helps you make thyroid hormones and reduces goiters).

In my lifetime, Americans haven't generally suffered disease from *lack* of food, but its abundance. In recent decades we've seen a shift toward overconsumption, especially of saturated fats, sugar, and sodium, leading to chronic health concerns.

Government guidance on diet, including the food groups, food pyramid, and its successor MyPlate, have attempted to influence how Americans eat. Overwhelmingly, Americans' health has gotten worse.

The rampant conflicts of interest in nutrition science (and the healthcare system that profits handsomely from diet-related diseases) have compromised the integrity of all such recommendations.

The first *Food Guide Pyramid*, published in 1992, was evidence of the Department of Agriculture's complicated, self-contradictory mandate. As part of its mission statement, the department tries to provide *"healthful diet and nutrition education in a way that supports American agriculture."* It's not at all clear that supporting American agriculture is generally good for public health.

Food lobbying groups, who want the USDA to recommend eating more of their products, have huge influence over national nutritional guidelines. The 1992 food pyramid recommended 8-11 servings per day of grain, which suits the US grain lobbyists just fine, but may be downright detrimental to the individuals who eat that way. Since the issuing of that first pyramid, Americans' rates of severe obesity and Type 2 diabetes (the kind you get from incautious eating) have doubled. I've had to update my lecture notes on obesity in America from roughly 33% to now 42% of Americans being obese. And that's just looking at obesity, not those who are overweight. Adding those two categories means that a significant majority of Americans are either overweight or obese.

The grain farmers' lobby is powerful in Washington DC — just consider the Iowa (corn growers') Caucus, which happens so early in the presidential primary cycle that federal candidates are pragmatically required to choose their priorities accordingly.

The USDA's longstanding recommendation for the consumption of protein, including red meat and dairy, reflects the interests of the beef and dairy lobbyists, while at the same time that recommendation was being linked by multiple studies to an increased risk of heart disease and cancer. Manipulating "scientific" dietary guidelines became just another form of marketing, alongside "Got Milk?" campaigns.

(Important point to note: Despite the marketing campaign the governmental agency National Pork Board paid for with our tax dollars, pork is not "the other white meat." It's classified by another governmental agency, the USDA, as red meat. So, we pay tax dollars to one agency to label it as red meat, and then another agency to market it as *not* red meat. It's infuriating.)

Americans were, as a whole, getting fatter and less healthy already in the 1960s. A small group of Harvard nutrition scientists, who'd been researching the role of butter and red meat in a rising tide of middle-aged heart attacks, developed a thesis that dietary fat and cholesterol were the primary drivers of poor health. Once they'd published that conclusion in peer-reviewed journals, they were approached by the industry-backed Sugar Research Foundation offering some extra funding for research that encouraged Americans to shift to low-fat diets, quietly removing excess sugar from the health equation. Critics of corporate influence often frame this support as the sugar industry paying researchers to point attention at fat and away from itself, but there isn't much evidence that the extra funding shifted the scientists' findings, so much as amplified their incomplete analysis.

What is undoubtedly true is that Americans shifting to low-fat commercial products (with "lower fat" versions of everything from yogurt to candy to salad dressing) caused their sugar intake to increase. When you remove the fat from a fatty product, you remove much of the flavor. To make it palatable again, manufacturers replace fat with sugar and salt. Sugar was added to many foods where it hadn't been present before, creating a slow drip of reinforcement of the American sweet tooth. Pasta sauce, granola bars, breakfast cereal, coleslaw, ketchup. Even when we don't eat sweets like cakes and cookies, we're consuming much more added sugar than our bodies were built to process. A single 20-ounce Coke contains more than the daily recommendation. Even containers of salt have been known to include sugar!

Thanks to a tightly controlled tariff system, pure cane sugar is actually relatively expensive to put into all these products. Over time, alternative sugars grew in popularity, and further confused product labeling by making it hard to spot added sugar, which now went by names like brown rice syrup, malt syrup, barley malt, cane juice, galactose, glucose, and that all-time champion of sneaky sugars, high-fructose corn syrup (HFCS).

Consumption of HFCS has increased tenfold since 1974. I'm not going to get into the debate about whether high fructose corn syrup is worse for the human body than sugar, but it's very clear that it made sugar (in whatever form) a heck of a lot cheaper. Sugar used to be expensive, so it was reserved for those food items that absolutely needed it, like cakes and cookies. Now HCFS is the cheapest way to add flavor to pretty much anything. And that isn't an accident.

The federal government's agriculture subsidies encourage farmers to grow as much corn as they possibly can. None of the tens of millions of dollars in farm subsidies are paid to fruit or vegetable farmers. Subsidies have the effect of making the least-healthy options the cheapest ones: Calories from vegetables are 100 times more expensive than those from HFCS. We subsidize obesity, particularly in children, and then spend many more millions to offset the added health costs.

Nowhere does government have more control over individuals' diets than in schools and prisons. As usual, the vulnerable are hit hardest by government meddling. Federal rec-ommendations control what's served in school cafeterias, where Reagan-era restructuring caused ketchup to be classified as a serving of vegetables. Schools facing budget pressure take these shortcuts to fulfill minimum guidelines cheaply. But in a study of elementary schoolers, boosting a school student's vitamin intake to recommended levels "improves brain function and subsequently lowers institutional violence and antisocial behavior by almost half." Kids given a multivitamin did better in school and got in trouble less than kids given a placebo tablet. Poor nutrition may be a key driver of the school-to-prison pipeline.

Similarly, programs to increase nutrition, both through multivitamins and improving the fresh foods included in meals, have been shown to reduce violence and antisocial behavior in prison populations, with as much as a two-thirds reduction in violence. Supplemental vitamins, minerals, and essential fatty acids lead to better chances of rehabilitation and reintegration, too, as do the psychological impacts of cooking and eating healthier foods. Incarceration is a risk factor for obesity — most people gain weight behind bars, which isn't surprising given the poor food and forced sedentary lifestyle. We also know that boredom, perhaps the prevailing experience of incarceration, is associated with sugar-seeking. The diets fed to prisoners, which are almost entirely controlled by government, make people sick and unhappy, and contribute to violence and reincarceration. The results of these data should trouble us. The more food-insecure the family, the more they rely on programs dictated by skewed federal nutrition guidance. Notice we had a huge government cheese program, handing out free cheese to families in need (with the expressed purpose of trying to prop up dairy prices for the dairy industry), but we've never had a government broccoli program. Our tax dollars fund a system that encourages poorer families to eat unhealthy food, and suffer physically, socially, educationally, and emotionally, because we're artificially making unhealthy food more accessible.

It isn't that I want government prescribing multivitamins to the general population. Nor do I want more restrictive control over the diet and food choices Americans can make. I'm arguing that government already exerts a high degree of influence, if not outright control, over the American diet. The choices it has made with that power are predictably terrible, driven by special interests and positively harmful to individual health. A healthier food system doesn't require more subsidy and lobbying, but less.

How to Have a Healthier Relationship with Food

Humans are different from other animals because we can deliberately shift what we eat, both over time (culturally) and as individuals. Our bodies are designed to handle at least some amount of meat, but can thrive without it. Cooking food with fire increases calorie availability, which means we don't have to forage all day like other apes, and have more energy to grow and run our big brains.

We shouldn't underestimate the impact of evolution on our taste buds, but both empirical and anecdotal evidence indicate that if you start eating a certain way with regularity, your taste preferences change. I remember a husband-and-wife macrobiotic counseling team who had gone on a long trip, and because small towns didn't have health food stores, and macro shuns some veggies like lettuce and spinach, they hadn't had a chance to eat many greens. They were accustomed to eating macro-compliant greens, like collard greens and kale, and after a few weeks were positively craving them. This was during the time that most people hadn't heard of kale, and it was difficult to find in grocery stores (the Pizza Hut kale days). In desperation, they bought a whole cauliflower from some market, and ate the outside leaves of the cauliflower. When you have a craving for kale salad the first time, it becomes clearer. You really can teach yourself not just to eat better, but to *want* to eat better.

I'm surprised how quickly my own taste buds changed because yes, within a couple of years after hearing that story, I found myself craving greens. And not craving meat. Not even burgers. What's interesting is that today, scientists and food companies are trying to come up with new ways to hang on to the old tastes in attempts to "improve" our diet and/or the planet, such as non-meat burgers. So many people have excitedly told me, upon hearing that I don't eat meat, "*Oh, you should taste [fill-in-the-blank] burgers! There's no meat in them, but they taste like real burgers!*" Well, I don't want something that tastes like a real burger. Give me a black bean burger that tastes like black beans any day!

I trained myself to go to the grocery store — never when I'm hungry — and pick up responsible choices I'd be pleased about making later. I only had to have that strong willpower for a little while, and then during the week, the bad choices weren't in my cabinets so I didn't have to resist them. I kept my fridge and my cupboards stocked with good choices. (As a friend of mine discovered in my macro days. She was hungry and went to my fridge, and said, "*I don't recognize anything in here except the cauliflower, and I hate cauliflower!*")

At various points in my life, I've lived with people who were making very different food choices. That makes self-control more complicated. Once the food is in your house, you have to exercise that self-control all the time. Many people now have food delivered to them, groceries and restaurant meals and any snack food you want at any time of day or night — they're asking a lot of themselves, in terms of constant vigilance over those food choices. Deny yourself those foods completely, and you trigger intense cravings, at least for a short time. Franken-foods are engineered to go after the evolutionary cravings, and at some point you break down.

While food is not considered addictive (the only non-substance addiction, according to U.S. psychiatrists, is gambling), junk food can mess with the reward systems in the brain. Rats given junk food have shown withdrawal symptoms in the brain similar to those that occur from other addictive substances.

And unlike with alcohol, or other addictive substances, you can't just decide to abstain from food. You can't give up eating like people give up drinking. You have to indulge this evolutionary hindbrain, to some extent, every 12 hours or so. Changing that pattern requires conscious energy and resolve, which is often in short supply in our busy lives.

Cutting down on quantity might seem difficult, but part of that might be learned by eating food without high nutrition. There are different kinds of stomach cells sending messages to our brains about whether we are full. One type sends messages about how stretched the stomach is — the quantity of food that you've put in your stomach. Have you ever noticed, though, that sometimes you can eat a whole lot of junk food and still feel hungry? That's because another type of stomach cell sends messages to the brain about how nutritious the food is. You can eat a heck of a lot of junk food without meeting minimum nutrition. Eating lots of nutritious foods sends both signals to the brain — that there's plenty of food, and the food is nutritious. I find that I'm not as hungry when I fill up on huge salads that include other vegetables (red peppers, red cabbage, and cucumbers) along with other types of food (walnuts, avocado, and raisins). It's this salad that draws so many compliments from airline passengers sitting next to me.

Food isn't just about physical health. Significant research verifies a link between your food and your mood. Depression is skyrocketing, and diet is a huge contributor. Poor diets make us sluggish and overweight, and they make us sad. But you can leverage that brain-body connection to your advantage. Eating one additional fruit or vegetable per day increases happiness, all the way up to eight servings a day. An increase of eight units of fruits and vegetables is equal to the happiness boost you get going from being unemployed to being employed.

Leafy greens also seem to play a role in keeping us cognitively sharp. Elderly people who eat two servings of green leafy vegetables daily perform similarly on cognitive tests to people eleven years younger. (Sorry, Dad, you were wrong about that one: life doesn't just seem longer — eating healthy can not only help you live longer, but increase your enjoyment of the years you've got.)

Looking for ways to re-engineer your relationship with food? Here's where to start:

Record what you eat

Because so much of our eating is not mindful, forcing yourself to pay attention may shift your eating habits in the direction you prefer. Nutritionists recommend keeping a food journal. (See the Behavior Modification discussion in the goals chapter for specific instructions.)

Some people take phone photos of their food before they eat — not just meals, but anything and everything. Jerry O'Connell, the CBS talk-show host, reports that just writing down what he ate before he ate it allowed him to lose a lot of weight. Sometimes he felt embarrassment about his choices, and sometimes pride. (Think about it – how good would you feel writing down "entire carton of ice cream" in your food log!) The pause allows us to reflect and evaluate the choice against our goals, which shifts the emotional experience of eating toward the things we've chosen, instead of what the evolutionary brain or marketers choose for us. You might choose any number of ways to insert this pause, but recording your food choices is a great one.

Be honest in your choices

Many years ago, my sister and her then-roommate decided they were going to turn over a new leaf and start eating healthier, and perhaps lose a few pounds in the process. My sister got home from work one day to discover her roommate eating candied yams topped with marshmallow fluff. When my sister questioned the food choice, her roommate explained that this was counting as one of her vegetables for the day! Sure, that junk food you're reaching for may be "all natural," but so is arsenic. Food marketeers are using every trick in the book to help consumers feel better about making unhealthy choices. I remember years ago when a food company described their tortilla chips as simply a different way to eat corn! And for the record, "natural" simply means nothing artificial has been added. It makes no claims about how healthy the food is.

Increase the variety of healthy foods

If you've been to a big buffet lately, you probably ate a lot more than you would have otherwise. A wide variety of flavors, textures, and colors subverts your sensory-specific satiety: you don't get tired of a food, and you eat more. Strangely, variety seems to increase our food intake even when the flavors and textures are identical: people will eat more M&M chocolate candies from a bowl that contains lots of colors, than from a bowl that contains just one color. This works against you when it comes to junk food, but for healthy food, can be a bonus. Try a salad mix that contains several kinds of leafy greens, instead of just iceberg lettuce. Buy half as many strawberries, and mix in some blueberries. You can increase your intake and enjoyment of healthy foods by keeping your taste buds on their toes.

Grab a smaller plate

The containers in which we serve food seem to make an outsized difference in our psychological experience of the food we eat. Certainly, you'd be wise to put a small amount of food on a plate or in a bowl rather than eating from the original container, like the movie heroine with her tub of ice cream. But the characteristics of the plate you choose matter, too. We feel more full and satisfied when we eat off a smaller plate, compared to exactly the same amount of food arranged on a larger one. Curiously, researchers have found that when you're very hungry, you're less susceptible to this illusion: your brain compensates for the illusion in an attempt to get you to consume calories you need for survival.

Eat more fruits and vegetables

According to the Centers for Disease Control, only one in ten Americans eat enough fruits and vegetables, so there's a good chance that that may be you. Sometimes it's hard to make changes for our health when we're already relatively healthy (especially when we're young). That one ice cream sundae today most likely isn't going to kill you. And you're not going to gain 10 pounds overnight from it. The damage is long-term and cumulative, just as eating healthy is. Eating your vegetables could prevent cancer, but you're possibly not going to see those results for decades. The good news, though, is the increase in happiness is almost immediate. Even if you hate vegetables, just give it a try for a month or so and see if you begin smiling more.

I've heard complaints that fresh vegetables are too expensive. Two thoughts on this. First, being unhealthy is also expensive: You're no worse off giving those dollars to your current greengrocer instead of your future oncologist. Second, my way of eating (lots of fresh fruits and vegetables, often organic) probably still costs less than the standard American diet that includes a lot of meat, and research has supported that plant-based eating is cheaper. Even chicken is a lot more expensive than beans and tofu. Just cutting out half of the meat frees up a lot of extra dollars. And keep in mind, you don't need to eat organic to gain benefits. You know those studies they do showing that people who eat more fruits and vegetables are healthier than those who don't? They use conventional, not organic, fruits and vegetables. No need to wait until you can "afford organic" to start eating better.

<u>Don't bring a friend</u>

I say this half in jest, because social relationships are crucial for our happiness. But being around other people can also impact how much we eat. You're likely to eat more when you're around people, and the more people there are, the more you'll eat. So you'll eat more with one friend than you would alone, and you'll eat more around six people than you would around two. So if you do bring a friend, be sure it's when you try out that new salad place. There's an interesting exception to this rule, in practice. Women tend to eat less in the presence of a potential partner they find attractive, and the more attractive they find the guy, the less they tend to eat. Women on a date order and consume fewer calories when they're with someone they view as desirable and available. Whether this is due to social pressure (it's more 'ladylike' to eat less), the desire to make a good impression does seem to increase our restraint around food choices. If you find this is true for you, use it to your advantage by allowing a natural desire for social acceptance to guide you as you make up a plate at a party.

I read about a woman struggling with disordered eating, who said she would go to the bakery and order a whole cake to eat by herself. But she would ask for the cake to say, "Happy Birthday, Barbara" (or some other name chosen at random) to avoid the social judgment of bakery employees. When she began to break those patterns, social accountability could play a significant role in keeping her on track.

A larger quantity of food, more variety in food, and eating around other people combine to what I call the Thanksgiving trifecta. I jokingly tell my students they're doomed at Thanksgiving dinner because it has all the main environmental elements that encourage overeating. This explains why most people overeat at big holidays and parties. Psychologically, your restraint is on the rocks.

<u>Be skeptical</u>

Not-so-credible health information is everywhere. You're inundated with "this one weird trick to melt belly fat!" and marketing schemes for pills and potions. We'll talk more about how to critique the plausibility of scientific claims in another chapter, but overall, you're far more likely to be seeing a sales pitch than genuine health advice.

And be sure to not beat yourself up too much when you stray from ideal healthy living, especially when it's something you don't have control over, or have very little control over. On the campaign trail, I reactivated an ice-skating injury from a few years back, which put me on crutches for a few days (thank you, Indianapolis, for being so understanding!). A while after the campaign, I was in physical therapy for about a year, during which time I was told to not run, and for part of that time to not lift weights. Then a year later two more injuries and no exercise. While eating has a greater effect on weight than exercise, I put on some extra pounds during that time. It wasn't fun, but I didn't dwell on it. I knew this wasn't the end of the world.

It's beyond cliche to say "you are what you eat," but what we eat does have a significant amount of influence over how (and how long) we live. If you're looking for changes to improve your day-to-day and long-term happiness, taking a long look at your relationship with food in comparison to science may be a great place to start. It may feel like the whole world is stacked against you trying to make healthy choices, and it pretty much is, but you have the ability to reorder the deck in your favor. Choosing your friends well, the topic of the next chapter, is another underrated way we set the conditions for success and joy.

Cultivate Your Circle

The first (and only) time I played spin the bottle, I was sent into the other room with a boy, and he didn't want to do anything at all. We talked a little and that was it. In retrospect, that doesn't seem like a big deal, but at the time, it was the purest kind of rejection.

Maybe that kid was just being a good wingman, though, because he was the close friend of THE guy I actually liked. THE guy apparently liked me too, though not enough. We were just starting to go out in the evening sometimes in his car, which wasn't exactly a date, but in the 70s counted as half a date. I was helping him with his homework, helping him to type papers and things like that. I was hoping beyond hope that he was going to ask me out on a "real" date any day.

Then one evening I went to see *American Graffiti* with my parents and my brother and sister. (My parents insisted on sitting in a different section of the theater than us kids so we wouldn't see the jokes that they were laughing at.) And it just so happened that THE guy was there with another girl.

I was surprised and hurt, and my dad was angry. But not at the boy. He was mad at me, "*What was that?*" he asked, "*Do you not have enough self-respect? Are you just Homework Girl, helping him get his homework done so he can go out on a date with some other girl?*"

The boy apologized —, but only sort of. When I saw him again he said something like, "*I didn't mean for you to see me with her. I really was going to ask you out but...*" followed by some lame excuse. But I did become good friends with his sister later.

A couple of years later, his sister told me that his dad had been mad at him over me, just like my dad was mad at me over him. He'd said, "*You should have never let Joanne go!*"

(they always called me Joanne, even though I hated that, and yes, my legal name is Jo - long story) *"She's the only girl you ever brought home that your mother's ever liked."* That would be something of a pattern in my life — with one exception, I always got along with a guy's mother, and the mothers always liked me, but the guys not as much. I don't know what that says about me.

Something I've clung to since my IBM days — a young man that I became friends with during my training at IBM said to me, *"I bet you didn't go on a lot of dates when you were in high school."* He could tell by my jaw dropping that he was correct. I asked how he knew that, and he said, *"You probably scared the heck out of them."* (He used the stronger word, though!) Perhaps he was just trying to flatter me, but he wasn't trying to get anything from me. For the record, I did have a steady boyfriend for a year and a half in high school. My expectations were just different from reality — I had expected the 1960s dating scene, but the 1970s were the beginning of groups hanging out more than the stereotypical Frankie Avalon date, although I did have a couple of those as well.

Around that time I would go on a few dates with a guy who was an even bigger nerd than I was. On our first date, he showed me how to build a white noise generator, and I guess I didn't even think that was too weird.

He also introduced me to Monty Python. We started with *Flying Circus*, and later he took me to the premier of *Monty Python and the Holy Grail* at some fancy/historic theater in Chicago. And there was something magical about it. I'd never seen anything like it. The level of insight and intelligence baked into the comedy — it was the mid-1970s and it seemed like everything else was either high drama or low-brow jokes. And then there were these guys, the Pythons, with their stream-of-consciousness comedy and irreverent humor that wasn't afraid to poke fun at things people held sacred. They were doing subversive parodies of the dominant culture, with a real element of the outsider perspective I already felt affinity for, and I was fascinated.

The Pythons were officially formed at a tandoori restaurant in Hampstead, England, in May of 1969 (or so John Cleese claims in his autobiography). John Cleese and Graham Chapman had each already had some success writing for comedy television, but Graham Chapman was also a Cambridge-educated medical doctor who finished his studies between seasons of sketch shows. When they filmed the *Life of Brian*, out in the middle of the desert, he acted as the doctor on set.

I think about that story a lot, the way one man's life, seemingly straightforward and on a predetermined path, was completely transformed when a colleague introduced him to a very small circle of like-minded people. These six young men would become the most revolutionary writing team in comedy, with careers that spanned three decades. They changed what both Britain and America found funny — and Chapman will forever be remembered for his larger-than-life contributions to comedy, instead of ending up as a village doctor somewhere in rural England.

My circles of friends have been less globally transformative, perhaps, than the Pythons', but for someone who's always felt a bit like an outcast, finding people I could connect with has been challenging and meaningful. If someone likes Monty Python, that's a pretty good predictor of whether we'll get along. If you're scandalized or offended by that humor, there's a good chance I will offend you at some point. Within my first month at Baylor, I highly recommended a Monty Python movie to two women from my dorm. I just couldn't see how anyone wouldn't love Monty Python. Well, they didn't. They actually covered their faces for part of the movie. So, for those who aren't fans, sooner or later, I'm sure I would say something that wouldn't sit well.

Even within the macrobiotic friend group, where we agreed on an unpopular idea and were bound together by it, I never fit in. They were all pretty liberal, many of them vegan, and though I stopped eating red meat, I advocate gun ownership. People don't expect those two to go together. If you expect anything from me, I guess, it would be that you shouldn't know exactly what to expect.

While some of my views put me at odds with the macrobiotic crowd, the macrobiotic crowd sometimes made it difficult to connect with others. When my daughter was on the volleyball team in high school, parents each took a turn bringing lunch for all the players for their team meetings. When I told her what I planned to bring, she said, "*Oh my gosh, please Mom, just bring normal food or my friends aren't going to like it.*" She ended up warning them, "*My mom's gonna bring cabbage and tofu,*" which was perhaps the worst possible way to describe that dish. When you're a teenager, being liked by your friends is much more important than eating healthy or preserving your mom's feelings. At some point, we hope we grow out of that. (For the record, the official name of that recipe was "Fried Rice." Much better, right?)

Just because you might feel like an outcast, or not have a lot of close friends, doesn't necessarily mean you're lonely. Laypeople might use those ideas interchangeably, but social researchers don't. You could feel lonely while you're at a busy party, packed with people (I know I sometimes have). And you can live alone in your private paradise for weeks at a time without getting lonely. Loneliness is more of an emotional experience; It's the gap between the amount of social contact you'd like, versus what you're actually getting. What matters is if you have the level of social support that's well-suited to your preferences, and whether you feel like you're getting enough.

Social support might include comforting conversation, a sense of being known and belonging, and also helpful behaviors, like bringing someone a casserole if they're ill or they've suffered a loss. When we feel loved, cared for, and valued by others, we put together a loose network of mutual support. Together, that's your social support network. Your circle.

During the 2020 COVID lockdowns, many of us felt for the first time how much our social networks had been grounding us, once we were suddenly unmoored from routine. The country tried to fill the gap with video chats, virtual happy hours, and drive-by graduations, which in themselves speak to our need for social connection, however intangible. The drumbeat of doom and gloom at that challenging time was made more intense, for many people, because they didn't have access to their support system in the usual ways.

While I think people should do everything they can to be close to family members, sometimes those relationships can be toxic and need to be broken, which can be very hard to do. Ending friendships is also difficult, because we are such social animals. You may have even found it difficult to end non-friend relationships that have come to a logical conclusion. For instance, a physical therapist. You've finished the six months of prescribed physical therapy, and as you walk out the door for the last time, it's almost impossible (unless you really didn't get along with the therapist), to simply say, "Thanks – bye!" No, instead people start coming up with ways they might see each other. "Oh – I'm sure I'll run into you again at some point! Maybe I'll even need physical therapy for another part of my body in a year, so I'll see ya then!", but knowing how to let go of relationships that have reached their natural end is an underrated social skill.

What Research Tells Us about Social Relationships

Social relationships are the number one cause of happiness, according to positive psychologists. People who are married, and people with close bonds with their friends or networks are, on average, happier than those who don't have that support.

Social relationships are so important that extraverts tend to be happier than introverts. In fact, earlier research showed such an overlap between happiness and extraversion that many researchers thought the surveys were actually measuring the same thing, that being happy basically meant you were an extravert. You may be surprised to find out that even introverts are generally happier when they're with other people rather than being alone, provided they get sufficient time to recharge from socializing. (An interesting exception: a highly intelligent introvert is probably going to be happier being alone than with others, but that's a very small percent of the population.)

Social support is a great way to deflect stress, and stress is detrimental to your health. If you lack social support, you have the same increased risk of death as people who smoke fifteen cigarettes a day (I always point out to my students that just because they have a lot of friends doesn't mean it's okay to smoke! Best to have friends and not smoke.) According to the National Institute on Aging, social isolation is twice as harmful to your health as obesity, and nearly as deadly as alcoholism. People without close contacts are more likely to be admitted to hospital, and end up in nursing homes at earlier ages. Social isolation is also correlated with not getting out of the house very often, which contributes to the risk of stroke, heart disease, mental illness, and premature death. People who lack connection and community are more prone to illness, including chronic disease.

How do we measure social engagement? In one study, researchers brought pairs of friends into lab settings, and hooked them up to a variety of sensors and equipment that measure physiological response. When people are talking to a good friend, their cardiovascular function improves and their blood pressure falls. There's a measurable neuroendocrine response in saliva and blood samples, as brain chemicals associated with social bonding are released.

Close, supportive friendships show an increased response for both participants, and there's a lesser-but-still-measurable response for less-close (what researchers called "ambivalent") friendships.

In another study, married couples had the skin on their forearms pricked, so they had a series of little sores. Some of the couples were instructed to fight and disagree, while others got along.

When they showed up some days later to the lab, those who fought had more sores that hadn't healed, while those who got along had nicely-healed arms.

Healthy relationships contribute to physical health, but are also vital to mental health. Veterans who have strong social support report fewer PTSD symptoms, lower rates of depression and anxiety, and increased overall quality of life. Especially in hard times, friends really do make life better.

Long-term friendships and familial relationships benefit us, but so does adding new people to your circle. If you're going through an exceptionally tough time — for example: wrestling with a diagnosis, parenting small children, coping with the loss of a parent or partner — connecting with people who are going through something similar can create levels of empathy and social bonding that take much longer to achieve under "normal" life conditions.

We might think that joining a support group or intentional community around these tough issues helps by providing us with positive influences, help, and understanding. While that's certainly true, some research indicates that you may actually benefit more from offering support than receiving it. *Being* a listening ear and a shoulder to cry on may hold more emotional value for you than receiving that from someone else.

Families, both chosen families and families of origin, are important sources of social support.

Married people are generally happier than single people, have more sex, and are psychologically healthier (although people who are psychologically healthier also find it easier to find a partner and marry). Statistically speaking, the happiest time in an American woman's life is from the time they get married until they have their first child. The same is true for men, but it's not as pronounced.

Does having children in your home make you happier? Well, reports differ. If what made you happy in the pre-child years was going out with friends, partying, or traveling, then having kids might make you less happy, because you get to do fewer of those things, or do them less often.

Parenthood introduces a lot of joys — and a ton of frustrations.

To answer the question of happiness in child-rearing vs. child-free households, researchers handed out beepers to married people and had them rate how happy they were, on a numerical scale, whenever the beeper went off. Non-parents, particularly women, seemed to be happier than their peers with kids. Parents reported lower scores on the beepers, but higher subjective perceptions of their own happiness, overall. Changing diapers, washing dozens of onesies, driving carpool, and scrubbing crayon off the walls weren't my very favorite activities, for sure.

But even if the day-to-day experiences of parenting don't make us happier, the overall experience of parenting seems to make people more meaningfully happy than the minute-by-minute hedonic happiness reports reflect. Certainly my daughters are among the greatest sources of joy in my life — particularly now that they do their own laundry.

We also feel, as parents, an obligation to invest in the meaningful future happiness of our children. The parent-child bond is a life-changing experiment. My parenting philosophy is simple: 1. Understand behaviorism (the psychology of rewards and punishments) and 2. Love your kids to death.

Total strangers used to come up to me and compliment me on how well-behaved my kids were, and my friends would marvel at how they didn't do the usual stalling techniques before bedtime (water, another story, etc.). My kids knew it wouldn't do any good, since bedtime was bedtime, and No means No. When I said No, I meant No.

That might sound a bit harsh, and perhaps that makes me seem like a mean mom. Actually, the opposite is true. The secret to making it easy for No to mean No? Don't say it any more often than you have to. I never told my kids, "*You have to wear your coat (sweater, whatever) because it's cold outside.*" I believed in logical consequences – if they went outside and it was cold, they'd get a coat. (Unless you turn it into a power struggle, which I never did. It was very simple. If you're cold, add clothes.)

After a torrential downpour, my older daughter (around age 5) wanted to play in the backyard, which was basically a mud pit. My then-husband beat me to an answer and replied, reciting what he heard his mother say a million times, "*No, you'll get muddy.*" I had to first intervene and make it seem like he didn't really mean to say that (not a good idea for parents to have a divided front), and I told her to go out and have fun. I then pointed out to my husband that she was already getting a bath that evening. Who cares how much mud pours down the drain – either way she'll be clean after the bath. Besides, doesn't dirt contain organisms that help our immune systems? I tried to make No unusual, and meaningful. And then we didn't have to fight about it.

That's the difference between what they call "authoritarian" (do as I say) parenting, and "authoritative" parenting. Authoritative is being firm about limits, but explaining rules and why things need to be done the way you're requesting, and giving kids as much freedom as possible to make decisions within the boundaries. That means playing in the mud, because bathtime's right around the corner.

It also meant I never made my kids do their homework before watching TV. What do I care what they do first? As long as it gets done. (Now, if their homework stopped getting done on time, then I'd need to start having rules like homework first, with them earning back getting to watch TV first. That never happened, though.) Also, there were never any battles, and they learned at a young age how to manage their time. My older daughter (the one with the learning disability), still takes classes on top of working full-time, and she submits her homework days early!

My younger daughter, however, "blames" me for not making her do her homework first – she thinks she procrastinates because I didn't make her do that. But she procrastinates a heck of a lot less than I do, so she's fine. Even when your primary goal is to generate happiness, you can't make everybody happy.

Parents of *adult* children have higher overall emotional well-being and life satisfaction than their childless peers, which supports the idea that the demands of childcare (and the pressures of balancing family with work) may be making us unhappy when kids are young. Provided your kids move out at some point, you're likely to be happier than those who never had kids in the first place. The results are consistent for biological kids, step kids, and foster kids. The results on grandchildren are mixed, but multigenerational households face other pressures, and people living with their grandchildren are likely to have a strong family support network, predictive of greater overall happiness.

Just as social relationships are a major cause of happiness, social rejection can be a source of pain, literally. You've probably felt the psychological effects of rejection, such as feeling worthless and sad, but you might be surprised at the physical effects. It occurred to one social psychologist that social pain had many similarities to physical pain, so it should be possible to treat social pain with a painkiller, as many do with physical injuries. In his study, students who were randomly chosen to take Tylenol every day had fewer "hurt feelings" than the students who took a placebo. Tylenol only impacted social pain, and not pain from, for example, lower grades. Later brain scans confirmed these results.

Pets offer us many of the same benefits as human friends. My basset hound, Gertrude, and my two cats keep me company around the house, and create warm feelings of appreciation and affection. If a researcher came to my house while I'm petting one of my cats and measured my levels of cortisol, a stress hormone, they'd find lower levels than if I didn't have a little buddy around the house. My blood pressure would be reduced, and my mood improved. Scratching her behind the ears is almost as good for me as it is for her, which is why some colleges are importing dogs during final exam week for students to pet. Some studies have shown that people with dogs live longer, happier lives.

A quarter of American households include cats, and a third include dogs. While many dogs "work," as service animals or guard dogs or herders, our primary reason for having pets is that we like having them around. They're part of our social support network. While we may think of the elderly "cat lady" as lonely, she's actually immersed in a little mutually supportive society. Pets may also make it easier to make human friends, as anyone who's spent time in a cat-cafe or dog park will attest. Having a photo of your pet on your desk at work might make it easier to strike up a conversation with a potential people-friend — especially one who also loves animals.

Dogs' love may be unconditional, but human love isn't. And not all social bonds are created equal. Part of maintaining a healthy social circle is allowing yourself to get distance from people who put you down, or don't appreciate your worth. Like optimism, negativity is contagious. Spending time with people who constantly see the worst in situations, or who complain a lot, but don't work to make things better, can make you unhappy, even more so than a lack of connections. A strong social circle makes you want to be better, and brings out the best in you. The opposite is also true.

Inside the Bubble: The Cultural Cliques of Government Work

The people you spend time with have an impact not just on your mood in the moment, but on your personal characteristics and effectiveness over the long-term.

When I was getting my MBA, I did an internship at a government agency that did job training. The workday started at 8 a.m., and I'd try to get there a little bit early. It was a bullpen setup with about fifteen desks arranged in rows. The guy in the far left corner, when I got there, would always be reading his newspaper. Two women in the back, who as I recall were the girlfriends or wives of Dallas Cowboys football players, would be back there filing their nails — and enjoying good conversation with each other. Others had their routines, as well. And then at 8 exactly, the guy would methodically close and put away his newspapers, the ladies would put away their nail files, and others would stop their routines, as well. Then we'd all start work.

Then I got my job at IBM. I lived in Dallas, but worked in Fort Worth, so I'd always leave early just in case, and generally arrived early. On my first day, conditioned by my experience at the government agency, I brought a book so I would have something to do while I waited for the clock to strike the start of the business day. But when I arrived, a full half hour before work was scheduled to start, the office was already in full swing. People rushing around, people on the phone, sorting paperwork — they were all working. It was such a slap-in-the-face realization for the difference between a government-run agency and a privately run company. And many people, those who came right out of school and went into one of those government programs, wouldn't even know there's another world out there that gets more stuff done in a day. They don't realize that sometimes dedicated professionals come to work early and stay late and sometimes both. You become part of the culture, and you adopt their view of work, like my bringing a book with me. So at age 23, in 1980, I saw close up the differences in work ethic and efficiency between government and private industry. I started showing up early, working hard, and keeping costs down, because that's what you've got to do to compete. But in government, they just take their time, and get to it when they get to it, and if there's a huge, expensive screw-up, no one will get fired; we'll just raise taxes to cover the costs. The results are about what you'd expect.

The culture of the people around you, whether they assume responsibility, take initiative, and hold each other accountable, makes a huge impression on who you are and how you function, what you view as normal.

When I criticize government agencies, many people think I must be claiming that every-one who works in government is evil, or malicious, or just lazy, but it's simpler than that. The culture of government work — getting paid regardless of whether anything gets accomplished, and a program that doesn't meet goals getting more funding, not less — exerts downward pressure on all kinds of otherwise decent and hardworking people. They get neutralized. Demoralized. Discouraged. Their efforts are squandered, and their good intentions stymied. I'm sure the guy with his newspaper and the women with their nail files would start work early if they were in such an environment.

The more social and economic "problems" we turn over to government for solutions, the less likely those problems ever get solved. At the very least, government "circles" capture talent and waste resources that could be put toward workable, voluntary, pri-vate-sector strategies. More often, those inside these "circles" — all the establishment, inside-the-beltway types — solve nothing and create brand new problems.

As I often repeated on the campaign trail, "Government is too big, too bossy, too nosy, and it often hurts the very people it's supposed to help." Generations of politicians have failed the ideals of our country. They've given us over $36 Trillion in debt. (When I was running for President, the stat was $23 Trillion. COVID-response spending and Biden's budget have blown the top off even that. And it was "only" $5 Trillion when I ran for VP in 1996.) They've sent our young people to die in nonstop foreign wars, not declared by Congress as the Constitution requires, transferring billions from peaceful people into the pockets of defense contractors. They've promised us a planned retirement, for the price of 6-13% of our paychecks, then spent so recklessly that many of those promised benefits will never be paid. They've justified the highest rate of incarceration in the world — 1 in 20 Americans will serve a prison term during their lifetime — disproportionately targeting the poor and racial minorities. They've gutted Fourth Amendment protections by promoting civil asset forfeiture, police militarization, and qualified immunity. The incentives of Washington insiders are not aligned with the interests of the American people.

The entrenched, bipartisan political establishment is a circle that serves only itself, and turns everything it touches toxic. Declaring a "war on" something (drugs, poverty, terrorism) seems only to create more of it. The more voters see how this circle treats each other — the squabbling, lying, fear-mongering, power-grubbing — the better we understand how that circle sees *us*. These political types see Americans as tools, meant to serve their interests, instead of the other way around.

While both Democrats and Republicans agree on Washington D.C.'s culture of corruption, they are generally only able to appreciate the "other team's" contributions to the problem. President Trump promised to "drain the swamp," but kept on many of the bureaucrats that were there before him. President Obama promised Hope and Change, but weaponized government agencies against his political critics. Ronald Reagan, portrayed as a small-government politician, increased spending every one of the eight years he was in office.

Corruption has no party affiliation: it is a result of the damaging incentives of seeking power and prestige in a system that disregards the people it claims to serve. Well-intentioned people either give in to bribes, flattery, greed, or other toxic incentives, or they lose their positions to people who do. Personal integrity is punished by missing out on the cushy lobbyist-paid vacations and illegal campaign donations. There is no accountability. No transparency. No fear that the media will call out wrongdoing to voters (although the steady drip of scandals from both ends of Pennsylvania Avenue should show us that not everything remains a secret!). Beltway journalists, whom we should be able to rely on to be the People's eyes and the politicians' conscience, sell out those ideals for coveted pressroom access and an invitation to the Gridiron Dinner.

Corruption in Washington isn't limited to private misdeeds. The guiding principles of public service are tossed out the Capitol windows and locked out of caucus rooms, as short-term political gain is prioritized over actual leadership. Attempts to hold politicians accountable to their oaths of office are treated as attacks.

There's almost no more closed, corrupt, corrupting circle in politics than the insiders who host the presidential debates every four years. While the name Commission on Presidential Debates might sound like an independent, or at least official, government body (and that's what you're supposed to think), it's actually a joint project of the two largest political parties. By charter, it includes only *leading candidates for President and Vice President of the United States.* Who qualifies as a leading candidate is determined by *"nonpartisan candidate selection criteria...to identify the individuals whose public support has made them leading candidates."* This is nonsense.

The "nonpartisan selection criteria" applied in the 2020 race, when I was excluded from the debates, required 15% in several hand-selected polls (ABC-Washington Post; CBS-New York Times; CNN-Opinion Research Center; Fox News; and NBC-Wall Street Journal). Four of those five polls, however, (CBS/NYT excluded) offered only the Democrat and Republican as potential responses, even though I, as the Libertarian option, appeared on the ballot in all 50 states. How can I get 15% in the polls when my name doesn't even appear in the polls? Many thought that the reason I wasn't included in the polls is that when Gary Johnson, 2016 Libertarian Presidential Candidate, was in the polls, he was getting "dangerously" close to the 15% threshold. So how do they keep that from happening again? Simply remove the Libertarian candidate from the polls! Debates, and polls, organized by prominent Democrats and Republicans and excluding all others, cannot possibly capture or represent the will of the People.

After Ross Perot, included in the presidential debates, managed 15% in the 1992 election, the Commission on Presidential Debates revised the requirements for candidates to appear in the debates. This inner circle wasn't going to let just anybody play their corrupt game.

I had hoped that I would get to debate Trump and Biden. Most people don't realize how far we had gotten down that path. A new committee wanted voters to get a taste of all their options. A group of political reformists with enough money to make things happen formed a new debate committee, the Committee for American Debate. They were in talks with ABC news personalities about a moderator. Key members within the Libertarian Party reached out to both the Biden and Trump campaigns. Trump's team was willing to talk with us about doing a debate and requested some statistics to show how we could help push Biden out in the swing states.

Someone on our campaign worked on this data for weeks before presenting it to them, however, when those statistics were provided, they discontinued the conversation. The talks ended up going nowhere since Trump's and Biden's teams refused to consider being in the debate (shocker). I did have hope, though, until the "third" Trump/Biden debate (was to be their third, but the first debate was such a disaster that the second one was canceled). I figured if either one of them completely bungled the third debate, they'd want some kind of rematch, and perhaps it would be with me. The third debate, however, went swimmingly.

At some point I found out that Cohen, my running mate, wanted to be in a separate, third-party debate. And I said, "Absolutely not." My campaign manager, Steve Dasbach, virtually never told Cohen 'no' about anything. But I said, "This is not negotiable." I was happy to finally win one.

I tried to be pretty agreeable as a candidate, not too authoritative, let the professionals do their jobs, but this was a no-go. I told Dasbach, *"Do what you have to do. He is not to go on that debate."* I knew Dasbach was on my side, because he thought it would be a mistake for Harry Browne to be in the designated third-party debate decades earlier, and the reasoning was even more valid today than back then. Most of the national campaign leadership also didn't want to participate in the third-party debates. If we accepted that invitation, with the Constitution Party and the Green Party, it was like agreeing to second-class status, as if we approved of our own exclusion from the main stage with the Democrats and Republicans. We'd be accepting a role in a circle that didn't reflect who we were, or what we were capable of contributing. We don't want to be lumped in with these lesser parties (earnest as they may be, and we wish them luck!) who aren't even on the ballot in a majority of states. We want to be counted in the circle where we have earned our place. It was the in-crowd, or nothing at all. Harry's campaign team tried in vain to talk him out of participating in the 1996 third-party debates, but he was insistent.

When Harry Brown was running, I really wanted him to do the third party debate, because if he did one, I got to do one. I'm a Libertarian — I love to argue for our cause. Put me in any debate and I'm there, because I believe that if people hear our ideas, explained in everyday language, they will see that we have the superior platform. And we did debate, and I am still proud of that performance. Still, it really would have been better for the party not to participate. I don't know if Harry ever came to that same conclusion.

One of the core goals of participating in a televised debate, and running for office in general, is to spread the ideas of Libertarianism. Especially back in the 1990s, when there was no internet, many fewer Libertarians running for and winning offices, and not many had ever heard of us, that was key. So before the 1996 VP debate started, I smuggled a copy of Harry's book onstage to the lectern. I had practiced with the campaign staff, reviewing possible debate questions, and I worked on how to reference Harry's book. I wanted at least one answer to be, *"as Harry Browne says in his book Why Government Doesn't Work,"* and then to read a passage to answer the question. The moderator said something like, *"We're not really here to sell books,"* but I did it again. And Harry hadn't told me to. Even when the moderator told me not to show the book, I did it again. I thought that was my job to support the candidate and his message. I also thought the book was good, and people could get a lot out of it. Perhaps my being a woman earned me slightly easier treatment by that moderator; people would tell me later he had something of a crush on me. Maybe that's true. But from elementary school to adulthood, I could never tell.

I'm not sure Harry was wild about having me as his running mate (and with the Libertarian nomination process, the delegates, not the candidates, choose the ticket), but he definitely warmed up after my performance in the first debate. I finally won him over. Perhaps it was a bump in book royalties that smoothed the way.

I think I'd have done well in a presidential debate with my opponents, Trump and Biden. The media outlets who hosted and staffed the debates do not share the same interests as the voters. They kept us off the stage, and by doing so, were allowed to ignore the major questions I would have raised to Trump and Biden. What about the endless undeclared wars? What about insolvent Social Security and the ballooning national debt? By excluding a third voice, the major parties kept their candidates from being confronted by any real questions or opposition. Americans got weighed down in "us vs. them" rhetoric, and many didn't even know they had a chance to break the binary.

Our 2020 strategy of not being in the third-party debate worked. Reporters are always looking for something new to report. Unfortunately for them, the Libertarian Party platform has remained virtually unchanged for 50 years, so there's not a lot of new stuff there. Had I been in the third-party debate, for the following several weeks I would've gotten questions about the debate. "In the debate, your method for helping the environment is quite a bit different than the Green Party's - care to elaborate on that?" I would've gotten questions comparing me to the very much smaller parties, who were not on the ballot in all 50 states, so people would've heard comparisons between us and "the other third parties." As it turned out, during the entire campaign I only got one or two questions about the other third parties, and that's because that was the focus of the article. From start to finish, reporters kept asking me to compare my position with the Democrats and the Republicans, which is where the focus should be.

The *#LetHerSpeak* campaign was an organic movement aimed at getting me into the presidential debate. Thousands of activists across the country started making their voices heard, on social media, among their own friends, and by calling up the news outlets who'd excluded me from debates. In being excluded from someone else's private sandbox, I somehow attracted a circle of people who were personally invested in my success. In some ways, the vocal support of those highly invested women meant more to me, personally, than the 1.9 million votes I'd eventually get in the 2020 election.

The kind of people who are attracted to you, when you're living an authentic life, are those who will help you to do and be better. It's a little odd — when I get student evaluations in my role as professor, they often say something like, "I like how she acts like a mom to us" and other references to my maternal nature (perhaps because I once rescued a spider from the classroom — I really do have a soft spot for living things). Some professional women would be bothered by that, I think, but I'm not. I care about my students and I want them to do well. If they experience that as mothering, that's okay with me. It might be the same kind of energy that had people during the campaign calling me "*Mama Jo*," for reasons I've never fully understood. But if being myself encourages people to see me as a safe, caring figure, that seems like a cycle of good feelings for all.

Cultivate Your Circle Carefully

A circle of truly supportive people makes a huge difference in your happiness, health, and overall life satisfaction. While it's notoriously difficult to make new friends as an adult, adding new people to your circle, and building truly supportive relationships with people you already love, are excellent ways to improve your outlook.

Make friends and see them

The research is crystal clear. We are social animals, and social relationships are the number one cause of happiness. Researchers have determined that having about 4-6 friends is ideal. And by "see them," I mean in person. Social media is not a good substitute, and has been shown to actually decrease happiness.

Find a job you love

There is a huge interplay in happiness between social relationships and work. If one is going fine, then you're probably okay if the other one isn't. If things are rough at home (fighting with husband/boyfriend, roommate, etc.) then you can find refuge at work if work is going well. If things are bad at work (your boss doesn't seem to like you or you think you might be fired), then you can still be on solid ground if you have a supportive homelife you can take shelter in. If both are bad, then there's no place to run. People who have friends at work are happier and more productive at their jobs and overall.

<u>Get a pet</u>

Furry friends (and even the not-furry ones like birds or lizards) offer similar benefits to human support networks. Consider adopting!, but only if you are up for being a responsible pet owner. My heart broke when I heard about all the pets without homes after the Covid shutdown was over - people who worked temporarily from home (or not at all) who discovered they couldn't keep a pet when it was time to go back to work.

<u>Join a support group</u>

If you're going through a tough time, look into community support groups and other in-person meetings. You'll get some of the support you need, and you'll have opportunities to practice being a supportive friend to others.

<u>Accept help</u>

I'm one who finds it hard to ask for help. But the best relationships have a reciprocal balance, with both people able to give and accept the support the other offers. If it's still uncomfortable, remind yourself that letting people be useful and supportive helps them out, too.

<u>Choose wisely</u>

We tend to mimic and adapt to the habits of people around us, so surround yourself with people who inspire and motivate you. If you don't have those people close to you, reach out and build a network. Join online or in-person communities of people who are doing the kind of career, or hobbies, or parenting, that you want to be doing.

<u>Withhold judgment</u>

The most supportive friendships allow people to say what's really on their minds, without fearing rejection. "We listen and we don't judge." Practice good listening skills, so your friend feels heard and understood. Ask your friend what they need (perhaps, someone just to listen sympathetically) before diagnosing the 'problem' or offering advice. Women do a better job of listening, while men often have a habit of wanting to jump in with advice to fix the problem rather than simply listening. Sometimes we just want someone to listen, and not solve

<u>Let go</u>

Not all friendships are built to last. If someone in your circle routinely makes you feel anxious, drained, or insecure, it may be time to let them leave. While ending a friendship can be difficult and messy, your social circle will be stronger and healthier (and you'll have more time for people you really do like) if you figure out how to say goodbye kindly and firmly.

Surround yourself with friends and family and colleagues who support you, and are eager to celebrate your successes with you, but who are also there on the days you don't do as well as you'd like. Find people who are unafraid to be their authentic selves around you, who are willing to let you see their flaws, if only to reassure yourself that you're not the only one who has a few.

Hold your circle to a high standard, because it's the standard you'll adapt to, and be judged by. If you're unsure, demand better. You deserve better! Decide who you want to be and pull like-minded people into your orbit, and build them up or lean on them (whichever you're capable of that day). But by all means, take care in cultivating your circle, and take care of them once you've got them. Some days your social support is all that stands between you and despair.

Stress Less

In 1995, I'd had my pilot's license for less than a year. I was flying (literally flying, with me piloting my own plane) to the Kentucky state Libertarian convention, the first of two conventions that weekend. My plan was to attend the Kentucky State convention early Saturday, then hop on the plane and fly to Virginia for their convention, later the same day. Because of the commercial airline schedules, even the presidential candidates, including Harry Browne, had determined they wouldn't be able to attend both. But I flew my own plane, so I was the only candidate who could attend both.

The flight path from Greenville crossed over a section of the Appalachian Mountains in North Carolina. I had trouble getting up over the mountains. The plane just didn't seem to want to gain altitude. I was pulling back on the stick, angling the wings to produce more lift, but the plane simply wouldn't go up. I was getting closer to the mountains, until they filled my whole view, and I thought, *Oh my god, I'm going to crash into the mountains!*

I decided I needed to land. I only had a couple hundred hours of flying time by then, and a bad case of the jitters that just wouldn't pass. I was too freaked out to continue safely, so I got on the radio and said, *"I need to land. Can you tell me where the nearest airport is?"* They gave me the closest airport, and with my head still buzzing, I headed for it. I needed a breather, badly. After heading west a bit, I spotted the airport. The runway was literally on the side of a mountain. Like, if you land too far to the left, you crash into the mountain. If you land too far to the right, it's straight down into the valley. The ends of the runways also went down to the valley. And my heart was hammering out of my chest. My brain was screaming, *"I'm crashing, I'm crashing, I'm going to die."* Just writing it out, almost twenty years later here at my quiet desk, my hands are literally shaking.

There was no way I was trying to land on the side of a mountain, when I was only taking a break because I didn't feel safe to keep the plane in the air. So I thought, *"I'm just going to have to take my deep breaths here in the plane,"* but my mind kept volunteering really unhelpful worst-case scenarios, like I'd considered bringing my daughters with me on this trip, and what would I have done with the kids if I crashed into the mountain? I could have killed my kids. None of this was likely to calm me down. My fingers were tingly, every motion felt stumbly. I was lightheaded and sweaty all over. In fact, the reaction was actively making me less safe.

I decided that, unless I were to head back home, I needed to try to get over that mountain again. After taking those deep breaths, though, the six emergency procedures that my flight instructor had drilled into my head came easily to me. The blood was roaring in my ears, my heart racing and the mountains looming. I finally identified the problem as ice on the wings and cleared it, so at least I didn't crash into the side of a mountain, but I couldn't get my body to calm down. Even though the life-and-death situation had passed (for the moment), the reaction hadn't.

While most of the situations in our lives aren't life-or-death (and in retrospect, flying that afternoon probably wasn't either) our bodies often react like they are. And those stress reactions, whether they're acute and short-lived, or general and long-term, can cause us just as much trouble as the circumstance that created them.

What Research Tells Us About Stress

In my classes, I'll sometimes ask kind of a sad question, from a book by a prominent researcher. If you go home for Thanksgiving, which would you be more surprised to find out had a sudden heart attack – a beloved family member like your grandfather, or your dog? To most of them, the idea of a dog having a heart attack seems absurd. But why should that be? Dogs don't have vastly different circulatory systems, they have four-chambered hearts and veins just like we do. It's not like they've got a sixteen-chambered heart and yellow blood. Their anatomy is so similar to humans that medical students sometimes dissect dogs as practice before dissecting a human cadaver. Sorry.

So why, with such similar structural systems, is it so much more likely for a human to have a heart attack? Why do humans experience "stress" and why does long-term exposure to stress create health concerns? Do dogs have it figured out?

Actually, our bodies and dogs' bodies handle stress the same. Our bodies were set up for the types of stress we had 50,000 years ago, which was short-term physical danger, with wild animals chasing us. We needed our hearts to pump blood to our arms and legs for our "fight or flight" reaction, so we could either fight off the attacker with our arms or run away. All that extra energy needed to keep the body moving has to come from somewhere. One place it comes from is digestion, which stops, because there's no sense in trying to digest food when you're about to become food.

The problem today is that very few of us need to handle short-term physical stressors, such as overcoming wild animals. I've only known one person who needed this: my sister when she passed between a mama moose and her calf while hiking out west. Most people don't realize how mean a moose can be. The moose went after her, and my sister had to outrun the moose until she could quickly climb a tree.

For that type of life-or-death situations, these stress responses are *adaptive*. When you need to outrun something, these stress hormones and bodily changes help protect you, just as they helped your ancestors survive. But when's the last time you needed to outrun a moose or a lion?

In our modern life, the "threats" we face don't last minutes, like a moose attack, but days or weeks or years, such as preparing for a better job or figuring out how we'll pay for our children's college. Our threats are no longer physical, in outrunning an animal, but psychological, such as paying our bills and getting to work on time. Blood pumping away from our digestion and toward our arms and legs do not help us as we sit down to pay our bills. Literally sitting. Our evolutionary alarm systems are being triggered far too frequently, by fear of criticism from our boss, or worry about undone tasks. We have lion-fighting, moose-outrunning energy while we're standing at a podium, stressing out over a big speech. Our bodies have us ready to run, to climb, when all we need to do is fill in the bubbles for a high-stakes exam.

I tell my students that if the stress of final exams were limited to the hour they were taking the exam, that would be consistent with what our bodies are designed to do. But anticipating and studying for the exam for weeks in advance — that's long-term stress. Actually, even at the time, if you're sitting in an exam, writing an essay, it is not useful to you to divert blood resources to your limbs just to sit in a chair and move your wrist.

Even when "the worst that could happen" isn't so bad — our bodies don't know that. We're being flooded with stress hormones all the time. There's no real "end" to the stressful situation, so our bodies don't know when it's safe to reduce those hormone levels. Those high levels of hormones and activation are present all the time, or at least far too often for good health.

I've certainly been under stress in my professional life, like when I co-owned (and later owned) a disk-duplicating business. We were often under pressure to get things shipped on tight deadlines, sometimes with a lot of factors I couldn't control. But the real, long-term stress of that job came with the rise of the internet, when I realized that this business (which I'd poured savings into and had become my sole income while raising my two daughters in a separate household from their dad) was doomed to die. Disks would fade from utility. Our lives changing dramatically due to circumstances we can't control can cause long-term stress that no deadline-crunch could rival. But was I more effective at managing that business when I wasn't sleeping, my blood pressure spiking over the stress? Not at all.

The stress response that is adaptive to survival in the wild is downright detrimental to our wellbeing in a sheltered, sedentary lifestyle.

Many "modern" medical complaints stem from this long-term exposure to stress. Heart disease, heart attack, high blood pressure, stroke. Autoimmune disorders. Cancer. Digestive problems, migraines, weight gain, insomnia. Difficulty concentrating, depression, anxiety, dementia. Years ago the term "psychosomatic disease" was used to describe a disease that had psychological roots, such as stress. It's now an outdated term that's rarely used because we've discovered that just about every disease has at least some psychological input, and not just the few that were initially labeled that, such as ulcers.

We experience stress on a conscious level, too, and we all choose to manage our stress in different ways. No one can exist without stress, or without stress-relievers, but we do have some degree of influence over how we manage it. Some people meditate. Some people journal. Some people practice deliberate relaxation techniques, do yoga, talk to a friend or counselor. Many more people, statistically, calm those feelings of hyperactivation with alcohol or other intoxicants. Some people counteract stress by overeating. Some try to regain a sense of control through gambling or self-harm. Not only is the stress bad for us; most of our chosen de-stressors aren't good for us either.

Some threats to your well-being genuinely require an all-out stress response. But moose attacks and home invasions are the rare exceptions. Most of the time, triggering that stress response is doing more harm than good. Even if you really do get fired in that mysterious meeting with your boss, defaulting to, "and I'll be living in a homeless shelter by next weekend" with your heart rate racing doesn't make the meeting go better.

Don't overstress about stress, though! Some people take this too far, thinking that no stress would be optimal. It's not. One of the first graphs I learned in my doctoral program was the Yerkes-Dodson curve. To get maximum performance, it's best to have medium stress. Too little stress and you'll never get around to getting anything done (imagine your work had no deadlines!). Too much stress and you focus inward, not able to look around for better solutions (have you ever had someone ask you a question while you're concentrating and you simply can't handle it?). So there's an optimal level of stress to shoot for: challenging yourself, but not exhausting yourself.

Sleep

Something that can help counteract the effects of stress is sleep. If you are a good sleeper, I'm totally jealous! This is one area of my life that I don't have as much control over, because my body is very sensitive to any substance that could act as a stimulant. (An additional reason I've never had a cup of coffee in my life.) I didn't get to sleep until after 10 o'clock this morning. Yup, I was literally up all night. I've been trying to figure out for about three weeks what is keeping me up at night. At first I thought it might be either the port my daughter gave me for my birthday (some dark alcohols can keep people up) or a new flavored carbonated water (not caffeinated) I had gotten. The only listed ingredients — carbonated water and natural flavor. (It sounds crazy that a non-caffeinated drink would keep me up, but that's what happened a few years ago - a tea with "No Caffeine" written in large letters on the container kept me up because it had other additives.) First, I gave up the port, then I gave up the flavored water. It didn't seem to help, but then I remembered I had started taking a new vitamin. Just a plain ol' multi-vitamin that probably wouldn't keep anyone else up, but that apparently was enough to keep me up. I slept better after giving up the vitamins, but still not quite there. My final verdict - it was both the water and the vitamins keeping me up. I just hate that parts of my life have to be one big experiment. (And while there was something physiological going on, I wouldn't be surprised if there was a psychological component, as well. My book deadline from my publisher could be a factor!)

My life sometimes seems to revolve around trying to get sleep. Pre-nomination I was a guest on a well-known talk show at 9 a.m. By around 5 a.m., I gave up trying to get to sleep and figured I'd just stay up all night and sleep after the interview, which I did. The interviewer, who was well-known, later told my campaign manager that he thought I was the best presidential candidate since Harry Browne, which I took as a huge compliment.

I don't suggest anyone stay up all night by choice. The consequences can be devastating to the body, and I think are the major cause of when I get sick. I would always choose sleep over staying up, but if I eat any type of processed food, I risk being kept up all night from some additive. Several years ago, by the third day of a round of antibiotics, I couldn't get to sleep until around 7 a.m. I called the pharmacist who had never heard of insomnia as a side effect, but after looking it up discovered that the very last side effect listed was "in extremely rare cases, may cause insomnia."

Here are some sleep tips that I pass along to my class, which yes, I try to follow.

<u>Sleep in an environment that a bat would enjoy - complete darkness and cool (like a cave)</u>

Blackout curtains (the real blackout) work great. I sew all my curtains, and get the heavy-duty blackout stuff. If you travel or have no control over your curtains, try a sleep mask. (Or you can do what one of the members of the band Kiss did while on the road sometimes — he was considered to be a diva by at least one bandmate when he requested that the hotel windows be covered in tin foil. The scientist/psychologist side of me has to respect that, at least if he was doing it for sleep!)

<u>Open the curtains immediately in the morning, or go outside</u>

In order to get to sleep by a decent time at night, you need to signal to your body early in the day to start the biological clock. If you stay in bed or on the couch for a few hours in the morning on your phone or computer, on social media or watching movies, your body doesn't know that the day has started, so it doesn't know to end it on time. Sunlight is good for the mood regardless of the time of day, but is especially important in the morning.

<u>Go to bed and get up at a consistent time</u>

Try to go to bed at about the same time every night and wake up at the same time. Every morning every day of the week, including weekends! Or, at least within an hour (so if you wake up at 6 a.m. during the week, you should get up by 7 a.m. on the weekends). Yes, I know that's hard, and this is the one I struggle with most. It's scientifically more important to wake up at the same time every day than to go to bed at the same time every night, so at least try to do that.

<u>Don't stay in bed for a long time if you can't get to sleep</u>

You don't want to train your body to lay awake for hours. I was taught as an undergrad, and have still seen the advice, that if you're not asleep after 20 minutes it's a good idea to get up and do something else, and try again later.

<u>Move to the equator</u>

One of the many things I love about my job is I'm always learning something new. My Clemson students keep me on my feet with questions. During a lecture on sleep, a student asked me if people in Alaska sleep worse than the rest of the U.S., because of the seasonally long days and nights. I figured that was the case, but having a Ph.D. I'm more hesitant to generalize. So I asked the sleep researcher (whose office was only two doors down from mine), who told me that yes, people in Alaska do sleep worse than we do, but you don't have to go as far as Alaska to see a difference. Even those living in New York don't sleep as well as we do in South Carolina, because we're closer to the equator. Thank goodness I don't live any further north than I already do! (Yes, during the campaign I did say Alaska was so beautiful I'd love to move there — perhaps the scenery is worth the foregone sleep.)

<u>Get a full night of sleep</u>

Getting enough sleep doesn't just help us physically, it helps us psychologically. There are different stages of sleep in which different functions are performed. REM sleep is thought to help with learning and memory, and a greater percentage of this psychological sleep occurs towards the end of the night, shortly before you wake up. Your body thinks it is important enough that it will try to make up time in this stage over the next few nights if you don't get enough of it. You may decide, because of something going on, to get, say, 6 hours of sleep when you normally get 8 hours, looking at it like you're only missing out on 25% of your sleep.

Actually, you will likely miss out on more than 25% of the REM sleep so it's best to always get a full night's sleep if you can. And a full night is different for different people. For many, 7 hours is fine, so it's not necessarily the 8 hours we've heard.

Taking care of your sleep health is important for reducing your stress, improving your health, and generally making you happier. Yes, there's more streaming content out there than ever, but don't skimp!

A Batty Incident

I include this story in the book because I must, because it was how a rather shocking number of people first learned I was running for president. I was scratched — not bitten, mind you! — by a bat.

When I heard we were going around the country on a bus, I had visions of catching the bus at Greenville bus station, within walking distance of my house. Nope. I had to fly to Pennsylvania to catch it there. And to get a full day in, I had to catch a very early flight.

Before dawn one morning in early August, I went out my back door to hopefully say goodbye to one of my cats (the other one had spent the night inside) before heading to the airport. She wasn't there. As I turned to go back in the house, out of nowhere something flew into my face. I ran inside and slammed the door, hoping it was a very large moth, but knowing it was something a little more serious. I cracked open the wooden door to see what was going on, and sure enough, there was a bat hanging on the screen door.

I had seen a segment on a news magazine TV show, after a bat had flown around inside a sports arena (maybe it was in NY?), that you don't have to actually be bitten by a bat to get rabies. Simply touching a bat is enough. The bat had definitely touched me, and I later discovered a scratch on my chin. (Contrary to many stories out there, I was scratched, not bitten.)

I also knew that you need to get the first rabies shot within 24 hours of contact. I did get on the plane to Pennsylvania on time, but when I arrived, I said I wanted to go straight to the emergency room of a local hospital. The scheduler had planned for us to go to the ER later that Saturday night, around 10 p.m., after our last event. This was another rare time I put my foot down. I've seen what ERs look like at 10 p.m. on a Saturday night! And, it would be close to only 12 hours left to get the vaccine. What if the bus broke down on the way there, in the middle of nowhere, with no nearby hospitals? What if we get to the hospital and they don't have the rabies vaccine (not all do), and the nearest one is hours away, getting me too close for comfort to the deadline? After all, this is a nearly 100% fatal disease.

So I landed at the airport and caught an Uber to the nearest hospital, just catching a glimpse of the back of our bus. I took a picture of the back of the bus just to send to my mom so she could see it, and her response was, "*Take another picture. I want to see what the side looks like!*" I explained I needed to seek medical attention to possibly save my life, and would take a picture when I caught up with it.

Even though it was the middle of the day, we were at the hospital for three hours. (So glad I didn't wait until the last minute!)

I did experience my first glimpse of people wanting to meet me since becoming the nominee. When it came time to actually get the shot, two people came into the room

— a nurse and some kind of "assistant." I had heard that rabies shots were large and very painful (yes — I did get bruises from them!), but I couldn't imagine that it would take two people to give me the shots.

Later on, someone else in the hospital had explained that the assistant (a very nice young man) had recognized my name when it was written on the patient white board, and that he had been "fan boying" the entire time, wanting to meet me. So the nurse had allowed him in.

After I found out, I asked the employee if she would ask that assistant if he wanted a picture with me (I knew that hospital rules would most likely not allow him to ask me, so I offered). He came in soon after that. He indeed had wanted a picture with me, but wasn't allowed to ask.

We eventually did catch up with the bus. Someone else had stood in for me at the first two stops, and I was able to be on stage at the last two events.

I felt bad for the scheduler, Seth Levy, who did a great job. He already had his plate full scheduling the bus route, venues, hotels, and flights, and now he had to schedule emergency room visits on top of all of that! A total of four visits for shots are needed over a certain period of time to make sure they're effective, and they need to be on specific days, so I carried my calendar around with me just to double check I was getting to the hospitals on the days I was supposed to get the shots. The first round was the worst — I received the most shots, including a tetanus shot. In addition to shots in my arms, I got a shot into the bat scratch on my chin.

Seems like I also received at least one shot in a leg on that first visit.

My stop in Mississippi was interesting, as well. The doctor actually came in to see me, and explained that he had special training with wildlife medicine (medicine for humans, not the wildlife!), so it was great to finally get to ask my questions. He confirmed that yes, even touching a bat could spread rabies, and if a bat is ever found in a house, that it's recommended that everyone who was in the house get the vaccine, even if they don't think they were touched. A couple of times during our conversation he mentioned how busy I was. Finally I asked him — *"How do you know how busy I am?"* He replied, *"Because you're running for president!*" I hadn't told him I was, so he explained that he had read about my visit in the morning paper, and recognized me (and my name) at the hospital. So I was pleased that we were getting noticed.

This was still very early in the race.

The most maddening vaccine hospital visit was in North Carolina. We entered the clinic, and were met in the hallway by a reception desk. I walked past it to head towards the waiting room and was stopped. I explained I already had an appointment (the scheduler had made sure they had the vaccine in stock). The receptionist asked if I had been tested for COVID-19, and after I said I had, she said she wasn't sure she could allow me to go to the ER! I explained the test was negative, so wouldn't that make it better than someone who hadn't been tested at all? "No," she replied, explaining that if I had been tested, there was a reason I had been tested, so that makes me high risk. I felt like I was in a George Orwell novel! We had to wait about an hour before they finally allowed us in. I was starting to panic just a little. Since rabies is virtually 100% fatal, the only sure way to make sure I don't get it, assuming the bat was rabid, which it might have been, given how it was acting, was to get my final vaccinations on that day. What if there was not another hospital with the vaccine within driving distance? Would they keep me from getting a vaccine for a 100% fatal disease, because I just tested negative for a disease that had about a 2% fatality rate? Unbelievable. Eventually, they did allow us in.

The day I was scratched by the bat, and the following couple of days, there were big discussions in the campaign staff meetings (campaign manager, deputy campaign manager, social media, communications) about whether we should reveal it. I didn't hesitate at all — I thought we should let everyone know. First, I tend to be very open about things (perhaps that's a reason "genuine" was the word that most described me on Facebook). Second, I figured any publicity (within reason) was good. Some in the campaign were very hesitant, though, especially since it was the beginning of COVID. Some voters were terrified of this new, deadly virus, potentially related to exposure from a bat — how would they react to find out I potentially came in contact with a different fatal virus? Viruses had an especially bad name at the time.

It took a couple of days before everyone was on board to announce this, and we were shocked at how fast the news spread and how much publicity we got. A magazine in Europe even wrote about it! People were coming up with memes and t-shirts. There were jokes about my becoming a vampire, to which someone close to me said, *"Don't they know you're already a vampire?!!"* - because of my very late hours at night, and my surprisingly dark house (blackout curtains, as explained in the sleep section, which mostly remain closed during the day even in the living room). We had a lot of fun with it. I received a lot of bat jokes along the way, and even with some hand-crocheted bats.

Because I have the type of high-deductible insurance I promote on the campaign trail (I practice what I preach!), this bat episode cost me $3600 out of pocket. I jokingly said the campaign could pay for that and come out way ahead, given all the free publicity we received for this. Much more than $3600 could ever pay for!, but I paid it out of my HSA account. Anything for the cause!

Being bitten by a bat on the campaign trail and having to cancel events and coordinate injections was a bizarre experience, and it added a fair amount of stress to a time in my life that really didn't need more. But with support from friends and a healthy reframing, I was able to keep that stress in perspective. Years later, the bat incident is one that we can recall with rueful laughter. Many of your life's trials will pass in the same way. Just do the best you can, for now. And then do the same tomorrow.

Stop Stressing Out About Politics

Given my professional choices, you might expect me to tell you that following professional politics is very important, a necessary investment of time. After all, every politician and every branch of government wants to control so many aspects of our lives. They have so much power — don't we have a responsibility to be vigilant?

Yes, and no. The vast majority of the ways people consume political information do not lead them toward constructive change, nor restoring the consent of the governed. Instead, we consume media driven by the already-powerful, and advertisers. We're fed clickbait, and outrage *DuJour*. 24-hour news and up-to-the-minute social media are feeding us an endless diet of stressors, and it's really starting to take a toll. It has recently been especially hard on left-leaning voters who were fed a steady diet of "democracy is dying" and "*this time* we're going to get Trump" for years.

More than half of Americans say politics is a significant source of stress in their lives, according to repeated studies.

Half of American adults say exposure to politics causes them fatigue (can't argue there), loss of sleep, loss of temper, compulsive behaviors, or physical health symptoms. One in five Americans reports losing sleep or suffering depression, and four percent claimed they had contemplated suicide as a result of politics.

I point to the demographic data that accompanies this study not as an accusation, but as an expression of concern about our collective future. The people most likely to report negative mental health relating to politics were statistically younger, left-leaning people (during both the Trump and Biden administrations) who described themselves as "politically engaged" and "interested in politics." We're at serious risk of stress from political media burning out people who could otherwise be genuine political activists.

The same study identified people who were "politically knowledgeable" by asking five questions including, which party holds the majority in Congress? and how many votes are required to override a Presidential veto? People who were more knowledgeable reported less political stress and fewer negative health impacts, perhaps because they better understood the process.

Based on this data, taking a civics class might be a novel, but effective, approach to improving your mental health.

National politics — and mainstream coverage of it — is built to manipulate our emotions. Particularly in the era of 24-hour cable news, our discourse has become increasingly polarized, and polarizing. These long-term, tense, anxiety-inducing political climates make for riveting television and engrossing Twitter fights, but they have real physiological costs. Bigotry, crime, and violence are stressful to witness, but media reporting relies on "if it bleeds, it leads." The negative and dramatic stories, no matter how overblown or rare, are likely to get the most attention.

Because the news is framed as "true," it can be easy to forget that news companies are profit-driven. They deliver what customers want, and we've proven by our choices that we want drama, bad news, and controversy. So that's what the companies provide us, because the more people tune in, the more they can charge advertisers, and the better the media companies' bottom line.

I spoke to young people who felt genuinely endangered by trends they see reported on the news. Young people are increasingly estranged from their families based on political differences. In many cases, these strong stress responses are making politics completely unapproachable, and compromise impossible, for too many of us.

Political campaigns aren't much better. Advertising, whether for the candidate or against a rival, often relies on fear to manipulate you into either voting or staying home on election day. Our brains are hardwired to prioritize threats, which is a good tactic for staying alive in an evolutionary environment. In our mostly calm, comfortable world, though, threats are minimal unless they are fed to us by political strategists and attention-driven platforms. Campaigns' claims that a policy "will destroy the schools," or "let murderers go free" are designed to grab your attention and hold it; stress is an excellent way to do that. It's the political equivalent of the ads for home alarm systems that show a shadowy figure breaking into a house.

Stress and anxiety about the political environment isn't helpful to you, to your health, or to the people you're worried about being negatively impacted by change. "Doom scrolling" social media or listening to partisan podcasts will have your alarm system firing over a thousand things that don't actually matter. Learning the particulars, watching the footage, from the latest incident of police brutality *should* cause you outrage. But is that the best use of your emotional energy? Once your body is all fired up for the fight, do you just feel more helpless? Do you fire off a social media 'hot take' that leaves you feeling drained and under attack? Would it be more helpful to get in touch with your local DA, or volunteer with a citizen advocacy group? Research suggests you'll feel more empowered, and calmer. How would your body and brain feel different, and the issues you care about be different, if you built toward meaningful goals instead of letting the stress response paralyze and depress you?

No doubt about it, freak accidents happen, terrible injustices persist, and there's a lot to be anxious and outraged about. But your evolutionary alarm system is being manipulated by politicians and powerful media outlets with their own agendas. Your feeling overwhelmed and unable to function, but staying glued to the steady stream of doom and gloom, is politically useful to those already in power. Stress is being directed at you, pushed on you, partially to scare you into surrendering your power, and partly to make you feel too helpless and discouraged by the system to change it. Detach from the stress responses they want to force on you. Choose your health and happiness, over politics, every time.

Stress Less (Actionable Advice for Managing Your Stress)

Some stress isn't avoidable. Some may even be desirable, like the pressure of a deadline helping you to be more productive. But understanding how stress impacts you, and how to address it, can be life-changing.

<u>Watch out for these habits of stressed thinking</u>:

Dichotomizing means separating the world into just two categories, and ignoring the large middle ground where most of our experiences exist. *Overgeneralizing* is imagining that one example defines our whole selves, like failing a test makes you feel like you're also no good at athletics, music, and will never get a girlfriend or boyfriend. *Catastrophizing* is making a mountain out of a molehill, so failing a test makes you think, "Uh oh - I'm probably going to fail this course and not going to graduate which means I'll never get a job." By the way, my dissertation chair told me to stop catastrophizing several times while working on my dissertation.

See if you can recognize these patterns of stressed thinking in these situations.

You're rejected for a job interview, and you fear that you're unqualified in your field, that you'll never get a good job, that you'll be poor and sleep on someone's couch forever.

Your partner breaks up with you, you decide you are unlovable and unworthy of having a decent relationship.

You encounter turbulence on an airplane, and suddenly worry that the plane will crash horribly, killing all passengers.

You need knee surgery, but fret that it will go wrong and you'll never walk again.

You lose sight of your child in a store, and feel suddenly convinced he's been abducted by a crazed murderer.

Do any of these sound like you?

These cognitive distortions cause us much more stress than the real situation generally requires. When you're activating your stress responses over things that are very unlikely to happen, you're wasting energy that could be put to better use.

And don't think that being intelligent will protect you from these biases. Smart people just have more brain power with which to generate unlikely worst-case scenarios.

<u>Practice mindfulness</u>

One of the most-studied ways to manage stress is mindfulness. Lots of research focuses on meditation, specifically. While it may sound woo-woo-crunchy-granola, the science definitely backs up the practice as a way to take control of your thinking and regain a sense of balance and power over your environment.

Get this paragraph out again when you're ready to give it a try.

Sit comfortably. You don't have to be cross-legged in a garden, just keep your spine mostly straight so you're not hunched or closed off. Focus on your breath as it goes in and out. It may help to say to yourself, "in" and "out" as you notice the sensations. When your attention wanders — and it will — notice that. Forgive yourself, and return your thoughts to the breath. Start your practice at five minutes. You can set a timer on your phone so you won't be tempted to check how long it's been. Then just try to be still, and notice where your mind goes, and gently bring yourself back. It takes discipline, but it builds discipline, too.

<u>Confront your problems directly</u>

While it might feel tempting to "sweep it under the rug," ignoring your stressors doesn't help you in the long run. Even if you're too overwhelmed to act right away, writing out a calendar of action-oriented steps is still an action that moves you forward. It might even be a relief to see a road map of how you'll conquer (or at least cope with) your stress. On the campaign trail I was fortunate enough (or maybe unfortunate, depending on how you look at it!) that the campaign staff filled in my calendar. Even when the bigger emotional stress would start to weigh on me, all I had to do was focus on the next thing that needed to get done. One step at a time and keep moving forward.

<u>Get some social support, if you don't already have any</u>

Friends and family can greatly decrease stress. Of course, they can cause stress, as well, so don't fall into the trap of thinking that any kind of social contact will help you in stressful times. It could actually make things worse.

<u>Reframe, but at the right time</u>

If you are going for a goal, sure, telling yourself how important that goal is can be motivating. If you don't reach your goal (you're not chosen this season's American Idol), then reframe, by telling yourself that it's not the end of the world if you didn't come in first. Because it's most likely not the end of the world! Be sure to reframe at the right time, though. I point out to my students to please don't reframe two weeks before final exams that a grade in final exam isn't that important. Two weeks before finals you want to tell yourself that how well you perform is important! Telling yourself a few weeks ahead that it's not important might just result in an F on an exam. If you study and still get the F, then remind yourself that you most likely won't end up homeless because of this one grade.

You might protest a bit, asking if that isn't a bit dishonest to tell yourself two weeks ahead of time that it's important, but then afterward telling yourself it's not important. Yes, you're correct - it is a bit dishonest. But that's one way we protect ourselves to get through a harsh world. Defense mechanisms, such as rationalization and denial, work because we are deceiving ourselves. Most people tend to look at themselves in a slightly better light than they actually are, but that's a way of coping. And it's considered healthy.

<u>Exercise</u>

If you don't like exercise very much, I have two pieces of good news for you:

1. It's better to not do too much (30 minutes, 3 times a week is enough to help reduce stress)

2. While aerobic is better than anaerobic, it's best to do the kind of exercise you like, even if it's anaerobic.

The good news is that you don't have to exercise every day. In fact, research has shown that marathon runners actually tend to increase their amount of stress. Exercising every day can seem like having another job, which adds another layer of stressful cues. The happiness/stress relief gained from exercising tends to last anywhere from a few hours to a full day, so it's better to space out your exercise. (Sorry, you can't exercise Monday, Tuesday, and Wednesday to "get it over" for the upcoming week if it's stress you're trying to fix, although consecutive days might help physiologically). Much better to have at least a day in between each day of exercise. The minimum amount for psychological benefit is 20-30 minutes, three times a week.

Last, it doesn't have to be high-intensity, losing your breath exercise. Walking is fine (and the best option if you like walking much better than all other types of exercise). For myself, I've "run" for much of my adult life. "Run" is in quotes, because it's actually a very slow 1970s-style jog, if even that fast! Mothers pushing baby strollers pass me regularly, and not just those jogging kind of strollers. My mom's friend drove by me once and asked me what I was doing – "*What – is that some kind of walk-run thing you're doing?*"

I do know it helped me on the campaign trail. Yes, I "ran" at least three times each week. Not only was it exercise, it gave me a chance to be alone and gather my thoughts. Being on the campaign trail can be very noisy – around people all the time. The physiological and psychological benefits of exercise and alone time combined to really reduce that experience of stress, even at one of the busiest and highest-pressure times in my life.

Stress is a huge contributor to poor mental and physical health. Our stress isn't brief and physical, like our ancestors outrunning predators. It's physiological, based on the things that are happening in the social world. And it isn't fleeting; it's chronic. For this kind of life experience, our evolved physiology is maladaptive. It's doing us more harm than good.

When you're facing an angry mama moose, an underactive stress response can get you killed. When you're facing life in the 21st century, an overactive stress response can kill you. And likely will, one day.

Getting a handle on stress doesn't always mean reducing the stress-inducing parts of your life. If you want to achieve great things — or even small things — you're likely to encounter stressful times. But processing that stress in a healthy way can be key to living a long, happy life.

Say No

I don't mean *"just say no,"* like Nancy Reagan's anti-drug campaign (which inspired my 1992 U.S. House campaign slogan, *"Just Say Jo"*). What really frightens me about drugs is becoming dependent on something. I don't even drink coffee, because I see how it impacts people: they don't feel like themselves until they've had their morning coffee, or they have to prioritize finding coffee when they're traveling or need to do an important task. I can't stand the idea of not being in control of that, not being able to decide to say no. (I am distressingly dependent on lip balm, though.)

You've got to be able to say no. I've quit jobs. I've changed careers. I've fired people. I've ended business partnerships and relationships. I divorced my plastic-surgeon husband when our daughters were in grade school.

While persistence and determination are good to have, there's a crucial power in knowing when to close a chapter of your life. There can be a lot of pain in making the choice, but it really can be better on the other side.

When my ex-husband and I were getting divorced, we were sitting at a table with the lawyer, who was acting as mediator, as we divided our assets from 17 years. He requested some number about dividing up the assets, and my husband and I each had calculated a different number. The lawyer asked, *"So, which number should I use?"* and my husband replied, *"Use Jo's. She's always been better at math than I am."* (I must point out that he was still very good at math, and graduated with a higher GPA than I did.) The lawyer got very quiet, laid his pen on the table, and said, *"I have no idea why you're getting divorced or what problems you think you have, but I'd like to suggest you go back and make it work. You two get along better than most of the couples who come in here for just some random contract, who don't even have divorce on their minds."* We even went on a double date with some friends, well after we signed the initial paperwork.

It wasn't that the relationship had become unbearable, or that we hated each other's guts and just couldn't live together. But we got married young, my husband was 19 (still a teenager!) and I had just turned 20 two weeks earlier. We got together young and then kind of grew up together. Many psychologists believe that the consistency of personality is overrated, and it is. We were not the same people that we were when we married each other. Each of us was ready for the next chapter, but we were on totally different pages.

South Carolina doesn't make it easy to get divorced. The only way to obtain a no-fault divorce is to live separately for a full year. To get the timer started, I moved out. My friend allowed me to sleep on the couch so I would technically be living somewhere else (I also changed my drivers license and other details). I know you can just lie; probably that's what people do. But I actually played by the rules in that regard, as I often do. Many people are surprised by how much of a rule-follower I am, given my strong Libertarian streak.

After the kids went to bed, I would leave the house, go sleep somewhere else (after a month at my friend's house I found my own place), and then come back before they woke up. My ex-husband had been in practice less than three years, and was working all the time to build his new practice, not able to take them to school or their activities. We didn't have a 1950s attitude about our relationship (while he was in medical school, I was the breadwinner) and he would have liked to have been more involved. But he was always working and had been for almost a decade at that point. So for more than a year, I would wake up somewhere else, go directly to his house, make breakfast for the kids and pack their lunches, and take them to school. Then in the afternoon I'd pick them up from school, take them back to his house, and do all the normal mom things with them, while also doing laundry and getting dinner on the table. For the first several weeks, I would wait until they went to bed before leaving. I had actually moved out of the house a month before my kids even knew it.

The lawyer was right. We did get along great, which is why this arrangement worked so well, even if just for sheer convenience. He never had to worry about child-care, even when he got called into the emergency room late, which was happening a lot because his practice was new. I never called in sick. The kids got to be in their home, and I continued to raise them. I stayed as late as I was needed, often later than needed to share dinner, which was a little bit traumatic as we transitioned, but I was still spending more hours with them than lots of working moms. My business was very flexible, and my business partner was himself a father who had strong feelings about family, so he insisted I leave by 3 p.m. to pick them up. Eventually, I also had "my days," in which my daughters spent some days and weekends at my place.

This arrangement worked so well while we waited for the year to pass (which ended up being eighteen months) that I thought it would go on for years. In fact, I would never have agreed to the terms of our children staying with him if those terms didn't include my being there every day. I hated that house, though, and since I didn't request nor receive alimony, I couldn't afford anything nearly that large (I left my friend's couch for a one-room efficiency). And, again, the children had been living in this house for three years, so it was their home.

Then the divorce became final and his girlfriend felt it was safe to start making demands as her talons were firmly into him, the first one being that his ex-wife should not be coming to his house. I mean, I can see where the girlfriend was upset. How dare we be this functional? I was blindsided by how fast he acquiesced. He felt comfortable getting a former neighbor to step in as their caregiver, since he had known her for many years.

A bit of advice: get everything in writing. Since things were going well between us and the arrangement was working so well for both of us for over a year, it didn't even occur to me to get it in writing. That I would continue to raise them, but it would just be at his house because this was our daughters' home and I wouldn't have a suitable place for a while. Besides, he had been the typical 1950s dad, out of necessity for his job, so I thought I would be indispensable. Shortly after he finished his training, when he actually had time to run an errand, I asked him to pick something up for me at the store, and to take the kids with him. He looked at me in bewilderment. "*Both of them? I can take one, but I'm not sure I could handle both of them.*" (Did he not realize during all those years of training that I was taking both of them to the grocery store with me? I certainly wasn't leaving a 1-year or 2-year old or even a 6-year home alone!) Yes, he did successfully take both of them, but you can understand why I hadn't expected that he would boot me out of the picture anytime soon.

So, for a few years, I was limited in my parenting of my kids, which was beyond painful. I realize I was totally to blame, though. Of course, there's no expectation for ex-spouses to continue agreements — many spouses don't either. I had quit my career to stay home with them when they were small as soon as we could afford for me to do so. Part of that involved my "flipping" the house we lived in, and I was able to do most of the painting, tiling, and other tasks during naptime or at night. I didn't "have to" work anymore, but I got bored very quickly and in less than a year ran for U.S. Congress (as you do). Then I was back to working again. Luckily, soon after my ex-husband married his girlfriend, our daughters came to live with me. One of the happiest days of my life.

I didn't need to desperately get away from him, and he was never home anyway. My life didn't get any easier in the immediate aftermath of divorce, but I was happier. Freer. I didn't have the weight of expectations, and my own sense of failing to meet them, dragging me down anymore. I never viewed our time together as wasted, nor that I regret marrying him — certainly I have two beautiful daughters as a result, one of them the spitting image of her dad — but I recognized that it wasn't how I wanted to continue to spend my time. I'm not suggesting you leave a serious relationship for trivial reasons, especially when children are involved, but we had some deep, personal incompatibilities that we simply couldn't overcome. Back to that question of trade-offs momentarily.

Steve Clark, the lead guitarist for Def Leppard died that year. He was only around 30 years old. I was a huge fan at the time. (I even went to see Def Leppard a few days after my daughter was born — so soon that my mother had to drive me to the concert like I was some teenager, because in those days you weren't supposed to drive for a week after giving birth.) His death shocked me, somehow. So sudden, at only 30. And I had this sharp realization that you're not guaranteed time. I imagined dying that young — would I be happy with how I'd spent my time? Within a year I'd asked him for a divorce.

Trade-offs are everywhere. They can't be avoided. But weighing potential options, and understanding the costs, benefits, and trade-offs, takes real practice. We're not intuitively good at it. There are, fortunately, tools you can use to improve your understanding of your options, empowering you to make better choices and improve your life in all kinds of ways.

What the Research Tells Us about Decision Making

Behavioral economics (which combines my love of economics and psychology) tries to understand why people make the choices they do. Israeli psychologists Daniel Kahneman and Amos Tversky, through a rocky, but fruitful partnership, published extensive work on *"the framing of decisions and the psychology of choice."* Kahneman would later win the Nobel Prize in economics for the work he did with Tversky, but only after the latter's death. Some of their most interesting work surrounds how people think about sunk costs.

Sunk costs are the time, energy, or money that you've already put into something, the investment you can't get back. Even very smart business people really have trouble with this concept. We overvalue sunk costs. Business school professors say it's one of the hardest concepts to get across to students, and while in my MBA class, I remember students in our class having a very spirited debate on it.

Kahneman and Tversky gave participants in their study a hypothetical scenario. A company that had budgeted $1 million for a project, and was now facing a decision of whether to invest an additional $1 million to continue the project, or cut their losses. Participants who were told that the original $1 million had already been spent and could not be recovered were more likely to recommend continuing the project. In other words, when they believed the project was already underway, instead of merely being budgeted in advance, they were more likely to recommend doubling the spending. People were considering the sunk costs differently, and weighting them more heavily, even when that information is irrelevant to the decision of whether it was worth investing the additional million.

Rationally, in that hypothetical situation, you should cut your losses. But we're intuitively drawn to throwing good money after bad, because we're emotionally motivated to hang onto what we've chosen. We don't like loss, and somehow putting in more money, time, and effort in an attempt to stave off the inevitable feels better. At best, putting in more resources delays the loss, but more often, compounds it.

If you're still hanging onto the pair of boots that are too uncomfortable to wear, because you "paid good money for them," you've been a victim of the sunk cost fallacy. Or perhaps you've continued to sit through a whole movie you don't like, because you paid for the tickets. Would you have left sooner, if someone had given you the tickets for free?

Some people stay in relationships that they know aren't good for them, just to avoid the pain of divorce, or having to admit they've changed, or acknowledging they probably shouldn't have gotten together in the first place. Have you heard someone say — "yeah, we should probably break up, but we've been together so long!" Sunk costs! It's true you can't get that time back, but that's no reason to go on wasting it on something that isn't working.

Sometimes we overvalue sunk costs when considering career options. Over half of young women who become lawyers want to leave the profession after their first year. Yes, law school and the bar exam are huge investments of time and money, but if you discover that the work makes you miserable, or there isn't room to advance, or you'd rather be home with your kids, should you continue on for thirty years in a career you hate? Many do. A really extraordinary number of people hate what they do, and drag themselves through it, and live for the weekend. It's a terrible fate. But no one can give you that life sentence except you.

While people tend to overvalue sunk costs, we routinely underestimate, or fail to consider *opportunity costs*. Opportunity cost is what you lose when you choose. It's the other, next-best option; The potential benefits you would have gained if you'd made a different choice.

Kahneman and Tversky found that people have trouble figuring out what the opportunity cost of a decision is, especially when the decisions involve risk. People routinely make choices that leave them worse off, if they don't really understand what they're giving up. If we don't know what we're saying no to, our choices are more likely to be wrong.

One reason I was able to leave a relationship that was not working is I had other things going for me, according to the investment model theory, which explains why satisfaction isn't the only thing that keeps couples together. There are three components to this model. First, Satisfaction (how satisfied are you with your partner or how much do you like him); Second, Alternatives (do you feel you have any out there besides your current partner?); and Third, Investments (sunk costs, as described above). Satisfaction alone doesn't predict who stays married and who doesn't, but all three components combined do. Luckily, I tend to not fall prey to sunk costs (even before my MBA program explained to me what I understood intuitively), so that didn't keep me in it. Looking back, and I have to laugh at #2, because I thought that being in my mid-30s meant I was really old and would probably have a really hard time finding someone! Oh, I wish those mid-30s days were back for many areas of my life! Even if I didn't think I could ever find another partner again, I felt I had alternatives in a career, so I could at least support myself, even if it became lonely at times.

One point to make about "alternatives," listed above. Luckily, I've never experienced this, but many women have. Their current partner repeatedly drills into their heads that no one else would ever want them, and that they're lucky they even have this emotionally abusive partner at all. It's easy to be persuaded by a message that you hear on a continuous loop, without any challenges to it. An abusive partner will try to skew your calculations on whether to stay, by sowing doubt and feeding your fears.

Speaking of satisfaction, I think many women go into relationships humming the Spiral Staircase song (later recorded by Sonny & Cher) "More Today Than Yesterday," with the chorus, "*I love you more today than yesterday.*" While it's nice to go into relationships with such a positive attitude, research has shown that the trick to a long-term relationship is to keep the relationship from declining. Many in good relationships think their relationships do improve each year, but a closer look at the data shows no improvement, just a lack of decline.

We can't have everything we want in life. We have to choose. Taking into consideration sunk costs and opportunity costs helps us decide how to use scarce resources. Every time you say yes to something, you're saying no to something else.

Working long hours means we don't have those hours to spend with family, or on hobbies or leisure. Going to lunch with an old friend costs time and money we could have spent taking our grandmother to the movies. Yes, we can do both, but not infinitely. There is only so much money, and only so many afternoons.

We only have a certain number of years allowed to us. With good diet and lifestyle choices, decent healthcare, and a bit of good luck, you're likely to live around 80 years on this planet. That's around 700,000 hours, in which you must do all the things that will ever make your life *yours*.

Our time, energy, and attention are limited, often more than we consciously realize — at least until our favorite rock star dies. We have only so many hours in the day, to distribute among the things we must do and those we choose to do. That means each thing we choose to allocate time or attention or effort toward leaves little bit less for everything else. Everything has an opportunity cost. My generation was sold the lie that, "you can have it all," but really, everything is a choice, and it's up to you how to distribute your limited resources.

The opportunity cost of marrying one partner might be the potential for a primary relationship with anyone else. But only those who are actual alternatives — marrying my husband didn't have an opportunity cost of not marrying Steve Clark, because that option wasn't actually available. Actually, Steve wouldn't have been my first choice of rock stars (I'll keep that one to myself!), but it did stop me from marrying someone else I knew, or living alone, or dating. Staying married, living with my husband, had the opportunity cost of the happiness I could have living on my own, or with some other partner. Staying would have meant sacrificing all that could be, and also denying him the chance to be with someone who was really excited about being married to him, which he eventually did find.

We weren't strangers to making hard choices. Getting my MBA so I could pay the bills while my husband went to medical school meant not getting my Ph.D. in Behavioral Statistics, which was my first choice. Taking time away from computers to raise my kids meant technical knowledge raced ahead without me. I had less income and slower professional gains than I might have had if I'd stayed in that job, even though I didn't like it. Leaving my husband meant I wouldn't be around for the years when there were nice vacations, fancy restaurants, or the house with two water heaters we always said we'd buy. (Yes, he later did get the two water heaters.) But the sunk costs before, and the opportunity costs after, the marriage were both well worth paying. I would rather have lost all that, than my freedom, peace of mind, and happiness.

Two of the most important questions you can ask yourself in making a decision are:

1. What is the probability of the outcome?

2. How much do I really value it?

Probability of Outcome: One disservice my generation has done to the younger generations (although I'm not guilty of this myself), is to tell young people things like "if you can dream it, you can be it" or "if you can visualize it, you can have it." Nope, not true. I think that's one of the biggest disservices that my generation put on their kids. There can only be one American Idol per season. I have no doubt that a million people can dream of being the next American Idol, but there are only so many slots open for that title.

Likewise, you need to realistically assess the outcome for the downsides, as well. You want to open a restaurant, and you have a great theme, a few good recipes, and the perfect location. But you need to go into this with your eyes wide open, with estimates out there that over half of all restaurants fail within the first year. Does that mean yours will fail? No, but you need to do your homework. We are not very good at setting aside our emotions when looking at probabilities. One of the examples drilled into my head during my doctoral training was the example, "*You decide to buy a car. You do the correct thing of doing your research by going to Consumer Reports and other places. Based on overwhelming evidence, you decide on a car that has great reliability with loads of stats to back it up. Then you go to a party, tell your intention to someone else there, who tells you that she has a friend who used to own that car and it was nothing, but problems and got rid of it. So what do you do? Unfortunately, people will pay more attention to that one anecdotal example than the research done on thousands of that same car.*"

We are also prone to confirmation bias, discussed in the curiosity chapter, in which we look for things that support what we already believe and disregard information that doesn't. That means that even if you take the time and go through the trouble of looking up objective numbers, your brain might pay too much attention to some small bit of information while ignoring glaring evidence that should play the largest role.

What is the value to me? People suck at figuring out what they want and predicting what will make them happy. An experiment demonstrating this was also drilled into my head during my doctoral training. A booth was set up on a college campus for students and faculty members to sign up to receive free yogurt the following week. All they had to do was fill out a card predicting how much they would enjoy the yogurt. Some said they thought it would be off the charts great while others had a lukewarm "eh." When they got their yogurt the following week, they rated how happy it made them. Ratings still ranged from "eh" to off the charts, but not by the same people who made the predictions. Many of the original "eh" raters were ecstatically happy with it, while others who had been looking forward to it all week weren't nearly as happy as they thought they'd be.

I experienced something like this. I recently splurged on two items - a fancy kitchen knife (that cuts vegetables very finely) and a battery hedge trimmer (gas trimmers are messy, and my old electric one had broken, but instead of getting another electric one with the cord in the way, I got a nicer one with a battery). I had no doubt the knife would make me happier. First, I no longer had to struggle with tomatoes and bell peppers, and, second, hedge trimmers equal work. Hot, sweaty work, since I bought it when temperatures were in the 90s. I was surprised when I looked forward to the hedge trimming over the vegetable cutting. It felt so rewarding to see those hedges getting cut back along my driveway, further and further away from my car. Yes, my first few times using the knife were delightful (I think might've even giggled), but surprisingly the hedge trimmer beat out the knife.

One thing to keep in mind with the yogurt study (or my hedge trimmer) is that it was on a fairly simple item (liking yogurt), and not a major life decision, such as whom you marry and what career you're going into. Which brings up another decision trap that people fall into when making both large and small decisions — using the wrong decision-making method. We should use a different method when deciding on a career than when choosing a couch. Sometimes we rely on emotions too much in one case and not enough in another. Yes, that's right — sometimes you might not base your decision on emotion enough!

A classic happiness study was done by giving out free posters to college students. (Gee there's a lot of free stuff being given out on college campuses! Yogurt, posters…) Again, the catch was that students would have to give a rating on their choices later on. There were two basic options — a choice of an impressionist painting art (two options, both landscapes) or a humorous cartoon poster of a cat (three options). Participants were divided into two groups — "Thinkers" and "Nonthinkers." The Thinkers were asked to look at both types of posters (impressionist/cartoon) and examine why they liked it. In deciding which free poster to take, they were to ask themselves which one would fit the room they planned to hang it in (does it match the wall color, etc.). The nonthinkers were told, "Just go with your gut." Basically, they were to choose the poster they liked looking at.

A couple of weeks later, the new poster owners were contacted to find out how happy they were with their choices. The Nonthinkers were happier with their choices than the Thinkers.

Is this the way you should choose a new career, which college to attend, or which city to live in? Absolutely not. In that case, it's best to do the old-fashioned Ben Franklin T-method, of drawing a T for each option, listing the Pros on one side and the Cons on the other side.

If that way works so well for large decisions, can't it be used for smaller, more emotional decisions? Wouldn't it be better to analyze our emotions? No! Let's say you're going to buy a new couch. If you were to draw up a T for each couch and list the pluses and minuses, you are becoming aware of any downsides. Say you end up choosing the couch with the best "score" based on the T, but in the negative column is the one downside, which is legs that are too short. Now that you've analyzed all the features, including the one glaring negative, every time you walk into the room and see your new couch, your mind will be focused on that one negative thing, instead of all the positives. We are programmed to look out for bad stuff; that's how we survived as a species. Instead, it's much better to simply walk through the furniture store and be a "Nonthinker," picking out a couch that makes you feel good. Sometimes emotional decisions really do make us happy.

One way to evaluate your decisions and your values is to observe your own behavior to deduce what you're thinking, known as self-perception theory. Sometimes we change our attitudes towards things or have a stronger opinion about something without even realizing it. This happened to me a few months ago.

My kitchen faucet broke, beyond repair, so I went shopping for a new one at a local plumbing supply house. I decided to splurge a little, to get a faucet that would have an old-house feel and seamlessly fit into my 100+-year-old kitchen. I was immediately drawn to a somewhat outlandish faucet that was way over my budget. It was the coolest faucet I had ever seen (a bit steampunk-ish), but, unfortunately, out of the question. In the back of my mind I thought perhaps I could buy it when I renovated my kitchen in a year or two. I ended up picking out the faucet right next to it, which did fit into the kitchen nicely, and had a 6-8 week delivery schedule, and left.

Within a week, after thinking about the other, way cooler faucet, I decided to stop in and take a picture of it so I could show a few people. After showing the picture around to people, like showing baby pictures to others, I took a step back and observed myself. I must really love this faucet a heck of a lot more than I realized! I mean, who goes around showing a picture of a kitchen faucet like it's a baby picture? By this time I was eight weeks into the wait for my original faucet, and for once, I was thrilled with a delay. I'm not sure if they were still blaming COVID, but there was a delay in my faucet (which was a real pain, since my kitchen faucet didn't work), and I started a serious inquiry about switching my order to the baby-picture faucet. Being able to get that faucet almost immediately was the tie-breaker - I did end up getting that gorgeous faucet, and got it faster than waiting for the other one. Had there not been the delay, I wouldn't have had the time to observe myself going crazy over a kitchen faucet and make the upgrade that was, apparently, worth it.

Now, every time I go into the kitchen, I get a smile on my face when I see that faucet. I'm not sure how long that will go on — hopefully my smiles will last longer than the restaurant meals and many other discretionary things I'll be giving up to pay for it — but it makes me immensely happy. I didn't buy it because there was a designer label on it. In fact, I doubt anyone who sees it will be envious of me for my faucet, but I bought it emotionally for me, and no one else. I know what I said no to, and what I said yes to, and I couldn't be happier.

Sometimes our calculations are right, and sometimes they are wrong, and we cut corners someplace that comes back to bite us. We don't finish one relationship before starting another, perhaps having an affair that we think will increase our happiness, and end up ruining a much more meaningful relationship. Or we get caught up in daily life and forget to stop and smell the roses with our children while they're young. Or we skip an oil change to save money, and end up with costly engine damage.

Sometimes we just break even — like trading months of sleep and sanity for the chance to appear on ballots in all 50 states!

Government Distorts Our Decision Making

Government policies routinely distort our ability to understand opportunity costs. Subsidies and price controls disrupt our calculations of our best available alternatives. And when we see that a program isn't solving the problem it was supposed to solve, government always wants to throw more money at the problem, instead of acknowledging the failure.

The US Department of Agriculture routinely pays farmers to pour milk down the drain, because supply is restricted to keep prices stable. It's impossible for either individual producers, or the industry as a whole, to accurately assess the true cost of producing milk, which leads to misallocation of resources. Perhaps 10% of dairy farmers should be producing something else — the opportunity cost. Americans also, then, are routinely paying more for the milk we do drink than we need to, at the opportunity cost of whatever else was on our grocery lists.

Nowhere are the opportunity costs and sunk costs of government policy higher than in government-run education. We pay an astronomical price — not only in dollars and resources spent, but in human potential wasted — for letting government run a system while paying the costs ourselves.

Student loans, backed by the taxpayer and sometimes forgiven, make it more difficult to assess the opportunity costs of getting a college degree. This means that someone who would have thrived in technical school will struggle through a college degree instead. Someone who could have started a business, or gotten a four-year head start on a promising career, might end up racking up debt and dropping out without a degree. Thousands of high-paying, non-degree jobs go unfilled, while one-third of college graduates end up working in a job that only requires a high school diploma. Graduates loaded with student debt lose the chance to buy a house in their 20s, or travel. The opportunity cost of a college degree might rival the sky-high tuition.

But well before they get to college, students are paying the opportunity costs of decisions the government decided to make for them. The ninety percent of kids who go to government schools will never know what their next-best option was.

Government doesn't just limit your choices, sticking you with the cost. It's also bad at calculating the costs of the choices it makes. Cut an afterschool program for at-risk kids, and end up paying to incarcerate them later. Emphasize test scores above everything else, lose recess and music and art class and gym.

But even for reformers, the sunk costs of government-run schools can feel too high to turn away from. We have spent billions upon billions, built vast infrastructure and hired millions of teachers. We've been doing it this way for a century, we're committed, people believe. Psychologically, the costs of admitting government education is a mistake may seem unthinkable. We have already sacrificed generations of kids. Our own childhoods. Our own children. If we admit we're wrong now, will we have to calculate the costs?

So we struggle on, for the same reason you still own those boots you know you'll never wear again. We keep doubling down on what we know doesn't work — more standardized testing, more homework, more hours behind a desk. More years of forced attendance: There are constant movements for government to provide Pre-K programs and college as well. We keep throwing good money after bad, and ignoring all of our next-best options, or never even considering that we are free to make a different choice.

Freedom has its costs, too. When we choose for ourselves, we sometimes misvalue things. We change our minds. We feel cheated. It isn't only government that makes mistakes. We make plenty of them ourselves. But individuals can correct for these mistakes, if we are attentive to them. We can choose a different job, or get divorced, or go back to school. When we realize that a particular trajectory or outcome is no longer serving us, we can let go. We can say no. We can make a different choice.

Government doesn't want you to be able to say no. Government wants you to limit your choices, and impose its values on your life, regardless of what it costs you, or what you actually value.

It's easy to feel trapped by choices we've made, or tolerate a situation way too long when we feel we have no choice. The power to say no is the power to choose.

Whenever you're facing a choice, before you say yes, understand what you're saying no to. Learn to calculate opportunity costs, and be less sensitive to sunk costs. Consider the consequences of your choices, and do a cost-benefit analysis before you decide. Say no to the things — whether old or new — that will stand in the way of what you aspire to become.

Wherever possible, say yes to individual liberty, and no to government promises of handouts or short-term security. Say yes to the things that make you happy, not what advertisers and influencers say you should want. Say yes to authenticity and no to living by someone else's values. Say yes to individuality and no to conformity. Say yes to yourself — by learning how to say no.

Do What You Love

I love to drive. Fast. Faster than I should. Faster than I should admit to in this book, because I'm not sure what the statute of limitations is. When I asked those who know me best, "*What's the one thing I should include in my book so that readers really get to know me,*" the reply I got more often than anything else was, "*Your driving!*"

I've always had stick-shift cars, since I was a teenager, because back in those days you could drive faster, and accelerate faster, with a stick shift. You had more control back then. Automatics have since caught up, but nothing beats a manual transmission. (Now in the electric cars it doesn't matter — they've taken all the fun out of the game).

I've been called AJ, after AJ Foyt the legendary race car driver. I've been called Mario (after Mario Andretti). I once skidded into a parking space after giving a coworker a ride who said, slightly wide eyed and slack-jawed, "*I should give you a quarter for that.*" My mom's best friend, after riding in the car with me, said, "*Jo really doesn't like it when there are cars in front of her on the road.*" Yes, I pass lots of cars.

The distance doesn't matter. I'll try to beat my time on routine errands (which I loathe). On the very rare occasions on my roundtrips to campus that I grab fast food (about twice a year, max) — which doesn't really conform to my food preferences at all — and eat it, I don't even realize I'm driving a stick shift. Five lanes of traffic, people stopping, and turning, for four or six miles, shifting with the bottom three fingers that aren't holding my sandwich. This causes some degree of alarm to my passengers — which is something of a theme when you're riding with me.

I offered to drive a friend home from a colonoscopy, because he needed someone to pick him up, and he said, *"Okay, but you have to promise you're not going to drive like you normally drive."* What did he mean — less...fun?

My driving habits seem to be something people learn about me early on. When I was all of 24, I got a new manager at IBM. I didn't know him very well. But we gave a presentation to a prospect who said, as we were walking to the elevator, *"well I'd better be off, because I'm going to be late for my next appointment."* Without missing a beat, my new manager said, *"You should have Jo drive you. She'll get there on time."* Somehow my reputation as a driver had preceded me up to the fifth floor. Once, a fellow IBMer from a different division would later seek me out on my floor only minutes after I arrived to work to tell me, *"Don't ever do that again. You're going to get killed."* I have certainly done it again, and so far, have survived. (It had to do with changing lanes right before a lane ended near our office.)

Years later, I was driving my daughter and one of her friends, trying to be on my best behavior, as I always do with other people's children. Habits are hard to break, though, and turned a corner at my usual speed. Her friend said, *"that corner was fun!"* to which my daughter replied, *"aaaaalll the corners are fun in my Mommy's car!"* I don't care about going 90 on a long stretch of highway. That's boring. What's fun is taking tight corners at 45 miles per hour, grand-prix style.

I'm not a jerk driver. I'm a very respectful driver. I've never purposely cut someone off and certainly never caused anyone an injury on the road. But I'm impatient in most things in my life. When I get into the elevator I hit the door closed button before I hit the floor that I'm on because I figure I've just saved a split second. Get the doors closing and then we'll worry about what floor. (Yes, I know about the ADA requirements that make some of those buttons moot, but I swear I've found a few elevators that do make a difference. I have to hit both buttons anyway, so I'm certainly not losing anything.) Going faster makes me happy. I find it satisfying and exciting. Even when other people don't really seem to understand what motivates me (and even if they're white-knuckled in the passenger seat), I want to pursue what makes me happy.

Both of my daughters were born at a birthing center. I did not want them to be born in the hospital. And keep in mind, I was married to a medical doctor. He was okay with the birthing center since it was owned by two doctors from my OB-GYN group. It was right across the street from the hospital. If you ran into any problems, the ambulance would ferry you right over.

Basically, this was a three-bedroom house that they converted. There was no food; you had to bring your own. It had three bedrooms total, a shared living room and kitchen, and here, have a baby.

A couple weeks before my second child was born, I told my doctor, *"Okay, just to warn you, I'm going to have her on Sunday, January 10th, so it might be a good idea to not make any plans."* He quickly looked through the notes and said, *"No, you're due on the 6th."* I replied, *"I know my due date is the 6th, but I'm not going to have her till the 10th, because I want to have her during the Bears playoff game."* Maybe this will only make sense to Chicago sports fans, but I intended to be watching the football game, to hopefully distract myself from the pain.

Long story short, I had her on the 10th. My first daughter had been late by a few days and I thought, well, maybe this will be me again. And it was!

So, I brought my little black-and-white, 11-inch TV with the rabbit ears (this was long pre-internet, there was no way to stream games) because the birthing center didn't even have a TV.

I have a political story I can tie to this to. I remember telling my friends at the time how great it was to use the birthing center and I even said, *"And it's really cheap!"* A birth there was about $900 at the time, where it cost over $3,000 at the hospital. And I remember somebody telling me, *"I don't care about saving a couple of thousand dollars because insurance pays for it anyway. And didn't you hear? They redid the rooms."* And yes, I had seen them talking about each room receiving a $600 comforter on the local news. (Keep in mind – these comforters were $600 each in 1980s dollars!) And, I remember thinking, like, how sad. Our healthcare system is really messed up. It would be nice if there were an incentive to save money in the healthcare system, and spend that extra $2,500 on what you wanted. Go on a vacation with your new baby when your baby is 6 months old…wouldn't it be great to have that choice?, but insurance, along with state mandates on what insurance policies must cover, takes those choices away from us.

I rather enjoyed having a baby at the birthing center. I realize why some people wouldn't, but for me, it was more intimate. There weren't nurses I didn't know, around the clock, whisking my baby off to the nursery. Now people are having more home births, but at the time, as a professional in suburbia, it wasn't done very often at all. The doctor was present, but from the reactions of a few of my friends, you'd have thought I was giving birth out in the street, for heaven's sake.

There was another woman giving birth at about the same time and it just so happened that her husband was a Redskins' fan (the team the Bears were playing). And he was thrilled that this other pregnant woman in the center had brought her own TV, because he didn't think to bring a TV and again, no streaming. Perhaps he thought he'd have been told off for bringing a TV, that the story his wife told forever would be that she had their beautiful child and he'd brought a TV.

But my husband was still in his residency, and was being quizzed on rounds. He had so much to study. He was reading textbooks and journal articles, to get prepared.

So my husband studied at the kitchen table in the birthing center, and another pregnant woman was in a bedroom laboring, and that woman's husband and I were in the living room watching a football game with rabbit ears. I was cheering for the Bears and he was cheering for the Washington Redskins — I'm sorry, I know it's crazy, but that's what they were called back then.

It might have backfired, though, because I was so stressed out by the way the Bears lost, and that was Walter Payton's last game. I was actually in much more pain for the second child than my first child, and I think it was the stress of the football game and that they were losing.

After the game, I finally got up and walked the halls, which is supposed to assist in labor, and I found that the other woman was walking with a nurse, because her husband was still celebrating the win. My daughter was finally born, hours after Walter Payton's last game.

Just four days after that is when I went to the Def Leppard concert, with my poor mom having to drive me about two hours round trip (and waiting in the car for me during the concert) because it was still too soon for me to operate machinery. And within six weeks after both births, I was back in my skinny jeans. (I sure wish I still had that metabolism! Chasing after small kids helped. And it was much easier to be skinny in the 1980s.)

My first daughter, a few years earlier, happened to be the first girl born in that same birthing center, after three boys had been born during the week. (Yes, she was born the very week it opened, thank goodness, because I don't know how my medical doctor resident and I would've compromised on that birth! I guess on some street halfway between our house and the hospital.) The nurses were so excited to finally get to use one of the pink caps on a newborn, but as they came running towards me, pink cap in hand, I stopped them, saying, "*No — you're not going to stereotype my daughter!*" They disappointedly went back and got a blue cap for her.

Life, however, had a cruel irony about my keeping that pink cap off my first daughter. Pink has always been her favorite color, very much a girly-girl. If any newborn should've had a pink cap, it was her. And thinking back to the disappointed nurses, I really should've just allowed them to give her the pink cap. I still feel bad about the nurses when I think about my small protest - this wasn't really the place to take a stand. And the irony played out to the end – I learned my lesson and allowed the nurses to put a pink cap on my second daughter, and she has always hated pink. Pink is still her least favorite color, while my older daughter is still covered in pink.

There's so much prescriptivism and pressure about how certain things "need to," or "must be," or "should be" done. Don't believe a word of it. Even the advice in this book. Consider it, see whether it fits with what you, personally, want. Maybe you'll find you want something completely different, like fast corners and football-playoff birth-plans, and Def Leppard concerts in your postpartum days.

Whatever it is, whatever lights you up and makes you come alive, do more of that, and less of everything else.

What Research Tells Us About Making Yourself Happy

It may seem circular, but being happy with who you are contributes significantly to your reported happiness. One of the most influential studies about happiness was done on 180 Catholic nuns. I know what you're thinking — nuns? The women who are sheltered away in a strictly controlled environment, with very little control over their food and schedules, who don't own personal goods, smoke, drink, or have sex? How happy could they possibly be?

But researchers saw those participants — tightly controlled conditions, people of similar values, and the consistency of environment, diet, and inputs across a large number of people — and thought it would make a perfect long-term "experiment" (it's still a correlation, but about as close as we'll get with humans for a longer period of time). The nuns were required to write an autobiography when they were preparing to enter the convent, at an average age of 22 years old. Researchers investigated those autobiographies much later, when the nuns who had written them were between 75 and 94 years old (and just over 40% had already died). The autobiographies were indexed by the kind of language each nun used, which researchers coded as positive, negative, or neutral. While we know you can learn to be more optimistic, more grateful, more positive, over time, the researchers treated the nuns' emotional outlooks as largely static across their lives. Those whose early-20s autobiographies included high numbers of positive words and perceptions were thought to have a more positive outlook, which improved their resilience and ability to cope with stress well into the future.

The results? Nuns who wrote more optimistic and cheerful accounts of their own experiences lived, on average, 10 years longer than those who had the most negative outlooks. The happier a nun was, the longer she lived. Among the very happiest nuns, 50% lived to 94, while 85% of "negative nuns" had passed away by that time.

Many of these studied nuns allowed researchers to dissect their brains after death, leading to even more interesting observations. The nuns with more positive thinking had fewer diseases, and, potentially, some natural protection against the ravages of Alzheimer's disease. Among the most positive-minded, even when there were significant clinical signs of dementia during autopsy, the nuns had shown no symptoms while alive. They weren't immune from dementia in the same way that happier people suffer fewer colds, but a positive outlook seemed to provide at least some protection against the actual effects of the disease.

What can we learn from the nuns' study? Positive emotional affect, as reflected in writings done when they were young, was strongly associated with longevity 60 years later. In a population where things like gender, socioeconomic status, social support, medical care, diet, and daily environment were held remarkably constant (by convent life), individual happiness correlated with longer, healthier lives.

So, happiness seems to be worth pursuing, not just for its own sake (and shouldn't be – more on that later), but for its tangible effects on the rest of our lives. But what actually makes individuals happy, or at least more likely to be?

As with many issues of psychological research, studies of happiness have tended to find that happiness is about half genetic, and half environmental. Often, when people hear that it's 50% environment, they think, "Too bad I didn't have a mansion and a Maserati," but wealth is a very poor predictor of long-term happiness. Even more, of that 50% environmental effect on happiness, only about 10% are circumstances (such as the mansion and Maserati), with the remaining 40% being intentional activities. Those activities are behaviors and reactions to circumstances that are completely under our control, like spending time with a supportive social network, using our talents in meaningful ways, helping others, eating well, and exercising.

So, happiness is just as much, if not more, about how we frame what happens to us, as is it about what happens to us. We aren't robots. We're meaning-making machines.

Imagine three Olympic athletes on the dais receiving their medals: gold, silver, and bronze. Who is happiest? A strictly rational view of the world might tell us that the gold medal winner is happiest, followed by the silver medalist, followed by the bronze. But empirical research shows that's not the case (and why psychology is so much fun – we're not robots!). Yes, gold medalists are happiest, having just fulfilled what was presumably a life-consuming goal. Silver medalists, however, are the least happy, because they are comparing themselves to the gold medalist, or imagining what small thing they could have done better ("geez, just a quarter second faster!" or "if only I hadn't wobbled on that final triple axel!"). The bronze medalists, by contrast, are nearly as happy as the gold winners, because they are comparing themselves to everyone who didn't get a medal, perhaps with some relief, and are thrilled to have made the cut to get a medal at all.

I find this research particularly compelling, because it shows us how much a psychological framing can impact how we experience what happens to us. Just because bystanders would expect the second-place winner to also be the second-most happy, doesn't mean we experience it that way. It also dispels the myth that psychology is nothing more than "common sense."

Several life circumstances that you might think play a role in happiness don't. Have you ever thought, "If only I were beautiful or model thin, my problems would be gone and I would be happy?" Here's the good news — attractiveness plays almost no role in happiness. There are a few exceptions (women in large cities, and taller people in some circumstances, although taller people tend to have more stress), but overall, it doesn't matter.

Other categories that don't play a large role in happiness include age, gender, and IQ.

Humans are remarkably bad at predicting what will actually make us happy (as discussed earlier in the frozen yogurt experiment). Very often, particularly in Western, consumption-oriented cultures, we assume that the things that will bring us happiness are material goods, or at least, can be bought with wealth. But research doesn't seem to bear that out.

You've probably heard, "Money doesn't buy happiness." There is some support for this. Since the 1950s, per-capita income has at least tripled, but our average rates of happiness have remained about the same. Researchers ask, "If we are so rich, why aren't we happy?"

Many people are happier with more money, but additional money makes the biggest effect at the lower end of the income scale. There does seem to be a minimum threshold of wealth below which it's a bit difficult to be truly happy. It's difficult — and expensive! — to be poor, and the headaches of choosing which bills can be paid this month, or having a car repair you can't afford and being unable to get to work, can significantly depress your ability to be happy. Having money just makes life easier, up to a point, and the reduction in stress is correlated with happiness.

Yes, money can still buy happiness even at higher levels. For years, very influential research showed that once our income reached about $75,000 in household income (2010 dollars, which is about $104,000 now), additional money didn't buy happiness. After that point, the increase in happiness associated with more income flattens out as we reach a point of diminishing returns. Once you have "enough" (the bare minimum so that lack of money isn't a constant source of stress), getting more doesn't seem to make people significantly happier.

Updated research, however, shows that for most people, more money does make them happier. Why the different results? The short answer is that's the nature of science. Researchers come up with better ways to conduct experiments, and new technology helps make that possible. An interesting finding, though, is that money still doesn't buy happiness for people who are at the bottom of the happiness scale. In fact, it stops right at about that $104,000 mark, showing the original research was correct for some people. Those who are already happier, and higher on the scale, do become happier with additional money.

So why doesn't money make people wildly happier, like they expect it to? Imagine you jump into a chilly pool or lake, where others are happily splashing about. When you first get in, you wonder how everyone else is so at ease in the cold water, because you want to climb right out again. But as you stay in the water a little bit, you adapt to it. The water isn't getting any warmer, but you no longer think it's cold the way you did when you got in.

Contrast that with the day you got an acceptance letter to college (or achieved some other goal you'd pursued for a long time). Maybe you jumped up and down and waved your acceptance letter around. You laughed, shouted, or even cried a little. It felt like the most meaningful accomplishment ever, and you were sure that it would make you happy forever. Then you arrived at college, where everyone around you had also gotten that letter. After a while, you've literally got the T-shirt, along with the sweatshirt with your school logo. Two semesters in, you probably don't feel that same overwhelming excitement whenever you pull on your college sweatshirt. You instead think of all the work that has to be done, the test on Friday, the banality of dining hall food. Getting into your first-choice college didn't magically make you happy forever, after all.

The same is true for getting into medical school. You think that will make you happy the rest of your life, but when you find yourself on call all weekend, or running double shifts in your residency, you may start thinking about how life sucks at the moment. It's no longer a big deal to be a medical student or, even, a doctor. You drift back toward the baseline rate of happiness.

Money works in a very similar way. You might think that if you had the mansion, the Maserati, the Jacuzzi tub, the annual Caribbean vacation, you'd be truly happy. But research, and actual human experience, suggest that you'll adapt to the new circumstances, just like you did to the joy of getting into college. The water no longer feels chilly.

Psychologists call this process *hedonic adaptation*. The general concept is that each of us has a general baseline of happiness, and regardless of what happens to us, we gravitate back toward that same general level. The most famous study on this was done with two groups of huge (presumably) outliers of happy and unhappy events: recent lottery winners (whose prizes ranged from $50,000 to $1 million) and victims of very recent, very serious accidents, who had been paralyzed in either two or four of their limbs. The results, generally reported with a kind of, "who'd have thunk it?" vibe, were that lottery winners were, on average, slightly *less* happy than those who had recently been paralyzed in a terrible accident. Lottery winners quickly got used to the pleasures their new wealth afforded them, and no longer took significant joy in experiencing them. The recently paralyzed, however, continued to take joy in the little things in their lives. Maybe they even appreciated a conversation with a friend, or a sunny afternoon, or a hot breakfast a little more, because they were recovering from something that had seemed disastrous.

Most of us won't experience either the (ostensibly) highest-high of the lottery win, or the lowest-low of a life-altering injury. But we will have many good and bad things happen that feel as if they will adjust the tone of our lives, but relatively quickly fade beyond our notice.

Related to hedonic adaptation is *hedonic treadmill,* in which the "neutral point" of feeling like things are basically okay and you have "enough," is constantly moving up. I tell my students, "*After living with roommates in college, you're going to be thrilled living in an apartment by yourself. You know when you wake up in the morning, there'll be milk for your cereal because there aren't three other people eating out of the same fridge. Then, after a while, you get used to it, and you think, 'If I only had a house, I'd be happy,' so you get a three-bedroom, one-bath house. Then you see your friends with a five-bedroom, three-bath house, and think 'If I only had a house like that I'd be happy.' The problem is, it never stops. You can have three homes, including a mansion, a beach house, and a house in the mountains, and say, 'If I only had a 50 ft. yacht instead of my 25 ft yacht, I'd be happy!' It never ends!*"

Speaking of nice houses, there is some interesting research showing that yes, when people live in a nicer house, their "housing happiness" does go up. Surprisingly, though, their overall happiness doesn't go up. Yes, I know the math doesn't work out with that, and the math part of me doesn't like that, but humans aren't rational. Besides, some research shows that people who rent tend to be happier than people who own homes, but there are a lot of variables going on there.

I'm not sure why, but it seems to take me longer to adapt than most people, which has made me happier. I was thrilled with the "Dr." in front of my name for several years. It took quite a while for that neutral point to move up. Perhaps it was because I got my Ph.D. at a later age and had gone through 45 years without it, but I still don't take it for granted. A fellow faculty member, acting as an outside observer (just as a lawyer who represents himself has a fool for a client, same with psychology), believes it's because in addition to getting it at a later age, earlier in life I had a job that I wasn't suited for, at all. I know what the alternative can be because I've been there. This is something I had wanted for quite a while.

My house also makes me absurdly happy, even though I've lived here for almost 30 years, and it was already an old house when I bought it. Actually, that's why I bought it. I love old houses. The only must-have I told my realtor was to have a house that was old enough for push-button light switches, and still had them in working order. I am the proud owner of a now 112-year-old house with very old light switches.

Part of my continued happiness with the house was not doing the HGTV-style makeover, in which they remodel the entire house into a dream home. Yes, the initial excitement of something like that must be overwhelming, to have it all transformed at the same moment. Literally like a dream, walking from the dream kitchen to the dream living room to the dream master suite. But, I've always wondered, what about a year from then. Or the following year? Hedonic adaptation has to set in sooner or later.

Being a do-it-yourselfer (since the early 1980s, long before HGTV and YouTube videos, which really impresses my daughter), I've been completing projects for the almost 30 years I've been here. For example, I sanded, stained, and polyurethaned the front hall about 10 years after I moved in. A few years later, I finished the upstairs hall floor, and later on, the living room floor. I'm still not halfway done with the floors. Each time, I glide along the newly polished floors like I'm in some kind of floor polish commercial, and after I get used to that floor, then I do another one.

If you're thinking, "Finishing three floors in 30 years? That doesn't sound like much!" Well, I've made plenty of other changes, too. The first major change I made was installing kitchen cabinets and countertops. A few years after that, a few more kitchen cabinets. Several years after that, a kitchen island, adding lots of food-prep counter space, along with a vegetable sink that solved a lot of cooking headaches (after all, with happiness, it's getting rid of the headaches that makes a difference). The first five years that I lived here was without a dishwasher (macro living doesn't include dishwashers anyway). I went six years without a washer and dryer, too, hauling my stuff to either my ex-husband's or the laundromat, like a college student.

Other changes that came after that: installing a spray hose shower head to the old-timey claw-style bathtub (the bathtub faucets are towards the bottom of the tubs, to the dismay of my houseguests who complained they couldn't rinse their hair since the faucet is underwater), turning a bedroom into a closet since you need a microscope to see the closets in old houses, changing light fixtures (this may sound like a small victory, but I found a goth-style "chandelier" for the front hall that was a bit small, but bought it anyway because I loved it so much, and years later found a larger version, so I moved the smaller one upstairs and have matching chandeliers).

I tiled a bathroom floor, tiled the kitchen countertops and backsplashes, but left the plumbing and electrical to others (I've got a renovation fixation, not a death wish). I've painted every room at least once, some of them twice, and sewed new curtains for each room.

And that island I installed almost 20 years ago? About 10 years later, I added a new shelf in the cabinet underneath, doubling that shelf space. Then, of course, that new kitchen faucet, followed by a really cool stove that meant taking a cabinet out. And this might sound strange to anyone who's only lived in modern houses, but over the years I've taken down three doors. They loved installing doors in old houses, even in places they weren't needed.

I haven't put in central air conditioning yet, and probably never will. I'm not a huge fan of air conditioning (no pun intended!). It took me three years just to install the first A/C window unit, and that was only at the urging of a houseguest who begged me, *"Make it cool in here, Jo!"* (After first moving into the house, I confided in a friend that I thought the old place, with all its flickering lights and noises, might be haunted. He replied, *"I can understand the place being haunted — what I can't understand is living in a house in South Carolina without air conditioning!"*)

So while I've lived in the same house for almost 30 years, I have yet to fully adapt to it, because it keeps changing. As the neutral point keeps moving up, I'm traveling up right along with it! Who knows when I'll have all the floors sanded — it may be a decade or two. Running for vice-president and president, while running a company and working a full-time job with side jobs doesn't leave much time for sanding floors.

Starting out by having less gave me the opportunity to make big, appreciable jumps along with many small ones in my "hedonic neutral" which I continue to be grateful for.

And those were just the internal features. I did a little landscaping and, for a big jump in happiness, added a pretty advanced raised bed garden of seven different beds, most being four by four feet. And the changes continue. I just planted a pomegranate tree a little over a year ago (turns out South Carolina has ideal conditions for growing them), am now planting pawpaw trees this year (it's the largest native fruit in North America, but most people haven't heard of it because it's too fragile to ship and sell at grocery stores). Over the next several years, I will gradually change my typical front lawn (grass) into something more native that I won't have to mow, so that'll be a nice change. And supposedly it's better for the environment.

Last, without my participation or effort, the neighborhood where my house is — where no one would dare deliver a pizza when I first moved in, and my friends hesitated to visit — has become a trendy area. My down-on-its-luck neighborhood, like my neglected house, has given me scope to grow into happiness here. There are more restaurants within walking distance, and they keep getting better. Our small town is starting to be ranked by some travel organizations. And, best of all, it's now safe to run down Main Street after midnight, and plenty of people for me to dodge on the sidewalks.

How to Be Happier at Work

In high school, I took one of those tests that claims to tell you what field you'll be happiest working in, what career you're suited to. Some outside folks were invited in to give all the students the career test. Now I realize I'm aging myself here, but it had a paper overlay, and you'd poke the pin into the paper to make a hole for each response. They repeatedly emphasized, "It's impossible to cheat on this test. Be as honest as you can. Don't worry, there are no wrong answers, will be no grades, and you can't cheat, okay? It is as simple as choosing what interests you."

The questionnaire asked things like, "which would you rather do: bake a cake or make a butterfly collection?" and you'd stick the pin in your choice, making a hole, which records your answer (how did we get along before computers?).

I thought, *"Well, that's really interesting, why are we poking holes? What are they going to do with this?"* So I picked up the little booklet, and turned it over to the other side, and discovered different shaded areas. Turning the paper over back and forth, I realized there was a pattern — whichever shaded area you had the most pin pricks in was what you were supposed to do for a career.

Being the competitive and determined teenager I was, I turned it back over, and I made sure that no matter what the question asked, the holes that I poked lined up with whatever the box was that said I'd make a good medical doctor. I knew what I wanted to be!

Afterwards I told Bambi what I'd done. She said, "*I don't believe it; the test where they tell you it's impossible to cheat, you figure out a way to cheat on it!*", but I was worried that if I answered all the questions honestly, it would come up with the result that I should be a chemist or a teacher (heaven forbid!), and they would somehow keep me from doing what I wanted to do.

I didn't end up becoming a medical doctor. Perhaps if I hadn't gamed the test, it would have told me something different? What's really interesting is that I ended up getting a Ph.D. in Industrial/Organizational psychology, which, among other things, involves testing people in the workplace. I've actually designed and administered a testing system to help management determine which employees would be better suited for certain jobs. Perhaps I was actually just showing my aptitude for my Ph.D. very early in life.

In retrospect, yes, you could cheat on that test: I cheated myself out of that insight. It just makes me so mad that I cheated, because now I really want to know what my results would have been.

Perhaps it would have shown me teaching, which I didn't come to until over 30 years after taking that questionnaire, but is clearly part of my life's calling. In retrospect I'm dying to know what career my little teenage brain was showing an interest in. It's likely to be different than what it is now, because people change. But it seems I was very much also, already me — after all, I showed an interest in how a test works. It probably wouldn't have shown me, "Candidate for President of the United States." I did, however, take a career test about 10 years ago that showed, as my top career match out of 200+ careers, a government job. CEO was second on the list, which I've been. Psychologist was #7, so that was a pretty good match given there were over 200 careers, but the most interesting thing is that "lawyer" came in ahead, at #4. Friends and family have told me I missed my calling in being a lawyer, because I like to argue. I'm sure lawyers would contest that definition of their profession, but after feeling my eyes glaze over in a business law class in my MBA program, I know that I would've never made it in law school.

The job I love, and it's clear to me I have always been meant for, came to me rather by accident. It started with an email out of the blue from my dissertation chair, a few years after I had graduated. At the time, he was serving as interim Department Chair for a year and found himself suddenly short of an instructor. The subject line of the email read, *"Think about this before you say no"* (how intriguing!), with the email asking me if I'd step in and teach a semester. The offer was to teach one, or several, sections of an undergrad Intro to Psychology course.

Teaching was the last profession I would have ever considered! I received my Ph.D. in Industrial/Organizational Psychology in order to be a management consultant — go around the country and help companies, just as my statistics professor had done. At the time I was still earning a living duplicating computer software (although it was winding down) and had a few consulting clients. In fact, I had gotten an MBA almost 40 years earlier and had worked in the corporate world. Academia was the last place I would fit in, especially after receiving complaints from my dissertation chair while I was a student that I spoke too much like a layman, and not enough like an academician. I didn't use long, fancy words used in a profession. I still spoke like myself.

I didn't hesitate at all before agreeing to do it. After all, he did get me through my dissertation despite my lack of focus — I definitely owed him one. I ended up teaching three sections to help out as best I could. If I didn't teach these sections, being a state university, they would've had to go through a long, arduous process to hire a permanent employee — making sure the job listing is posted in all the correct spots and that they demonstrate they aren't discriminating. Having me fill in as a temporary adjunct would save all the bureaucratic headaches, and I was certain that it would definitely be temporary.

Now, I'm about the least academic Ph.D. out there, and I never had any interest at all in going into academia. In other words, the main reason I said yes was as a favor for him (and for a little extra cash as I built my consulting practice). By three weeks into the semester, though, I discovered that this was the best job ever. Now I've been doing it for almost 20 years, including while I was running for president, and I still think to myself, at least once a week, how much I love my job and how lucky I am to have it. When I'm writing an exam at 1 a.m., thinking about how flexible my job is; when I'm explaining something really fun in class and I see the 'ah-ha!' faces (or feel the 'ah-ha' on my own face because

I just made a connection with material from a different class and just learned something new myself!); or when I'm building out lessons for a new class and I think how great it is that I'm being paid to learn new stuff… and especially when I set my alarm for 10:43 a.m. on a weekday! A weekday that I work, no less.

I'm a few years past the normal retirement age and have no plans to retire, at least, anytime soon. I've already told my Department Chair that I plan to work until I'm 85, so he may end up sending me out the door on a stretcher. I probably won't be working full-time by that age, but I hope to be teaching something somewhere. Yes, research shows that retirees tend to be happier than those who continue to work, especially if they can put their skills to use, but not for those with interesting and well-paid jobs. I wouldn't classify my job as "well-paid," but there are many weeks of vacation throughout the year that normal jobs don't have, so taking actual hours into account, I feel I'm well-paid. Also, the flexibility more than makes up for that — I love getting to travel on non-peak travel days for holidays, or going to the store while everyone else is at work. Best of all, my job is definitely interesting; I'm always learning more about how people think and act.

Also, my dissertation chair and I created a new work personality test (along the lines of the MBTI, but much better) and have just joined forces with someone else who's been successful in the testing world. By the time this book is published, it should have hit the market. So I've got other endeavors to keep myself busy, as well.

There are a few things to look for in work that tends to make people happier. A job, in which you work only to get a paycheck, is self-focused. One step up is a career, which while also being self-focused does offer rewards outside of pay, including prestige and increased power. The ideal, however, is a calling, which is other-focused and gives a sense of purpose or contributing to make the world better. The good news is you don't have to be a doctor or philanthropist to have a calling (in fact, many doctors find their profession to be a job, because pay is the motivating factor). You can turn just about any profession into a calling by focusing on the endpoint. In our society, janitors are often used as the bottom-rung of jobs, but my junior high school janitor treated it as a calling. He looked at it as helping to keep us kids safe. Other-focused.

My career is definitely a calling and sometimes, as in my case, there's an element of chance or serendipity or whatever. A lot of people go through life never knowing what their passion is. And, I wouldn't have known mine if I hadn't received an email that said, "Think about this before you say no."

Probably one of the biggest predictors of happiness at work is autonomy. Do you get to decide what you want to do and when you want to do it, or is someone above you micromanaging you? This is one of the best parts about my job. I get to decide when to check and reply to email, when to write exams, and when to prepare lectures, as long as it's done in a timely manner. There are plenty of times that I'm perfectly happy writing a test on a Saturday night, because I want to do something else during a weekday. In fact, my sister, who is a flight attendant, and I often remark when we're on the phone in the middle of a workday how nice it is that we don't work 9-to-5.

A few other things that are shown to influence how happy we are at work are having a good supervisor (you probably didn't need to have me tell you that, but it's in the research), being a part of a cohesive work group or team, being given clear expectations with proper training, working in a fair environment (pay, work distribution), and having good friends at work.

There's also something in it for your employer, if you're in a higher-level job. Early research showed that being happy on the job had no influence on performance, but updated research has shown that it depends on the job. If you are working on an assembly line, unfortunately your happiness probably won't make you a better worker (although you'll be happier!). For jobs requiring creativity, such as engineers and accountants, it does help. Workers tend to be more creative on their happier days. In fact, doctors given candy (making them happier) did a better job at diagnosing, were quicker to diagnose, and had an increase in flexible thinking. (Yes, the researchers knew what they were doing and set it up so the doctors ate the candy after the appointments – it wasn't the sugar in the candy doing it!)

More Government Means Less of What Makes You Happy

When you earn money, you decide what to spend it on. Gas for your road trip, flying lessons, dinner out with friends, concert tickets, a collectible you can't live without, materials for your next creative project.

But when more and more of your money has to go toward taxes — around 20% of what all Americans earn — you no longer get a say over what it is spent on. Politicians decide where to spend it. And they often spend it on priorities that aren't what people really want or need, but instead what politicians think will help get them re-elected or gain more power. Worse yet, what they spend money on often ends up hurting people. When government spends money to generate short-term political gains, rather than long-term economic growth and stability, "malinvestment" of resources occurs. Over time, malinvestment means less-happy lives for most people, most of the time.

Sometimes politicians promise what we think we want, like investing in healthcare for low-income seniors, or equal educational opportunity for every kid, but spend money in a way that actually results in less of those things than if we'd kept the money in our communities and allocated it ourselves. The states send billions of your dollars to Washington every year to fund the federal Department of Education, which establishes a bunch of hoops that schools have to jump through in order to get even a portion of that money back. At the state and local levels, taxes intended to educate kids are often directed toward programs and initiatives that aren't evidence-based, or don't align with the priorities of local communities. Funds are increasingly being spent on administrators instead of teachers. This means taxpayer dollars are ultimately wasted, because the things that would make us happy — better outcomes for more students — aren't where the money ends up being spent.

The same is true of Social Security, where the promise of "saving for retirement" was outsourced from individuals to government, with disastrous results. Seniors are living on a fraction of what they could have had if they'd been allowed to privately invest the 6.2% seized from their paychecks, instead of paying FICA taxes and leaving it to the whims of Washington.

Social Security yields a 1% to 1.5% return at best, vs. 4% for a conservative investment portfolio. Retirees were robbed of their future happiness by people who promised they knew better how to invest that money. They didn't.

It might stroke a politician's ego to fund a new airport with his name on it, or push for a new highway interchange that makes a splash in local news, but it's likely that boring, unglamorous maintenance, like caring for existing infrastructure, would actually benefit more people.

Economic development projects very often become exercises in vanity, with millions in local taxes being diverted from whatever individuals would have spent their own money on, toward stadiums, inefficient public transportation projects (like the Big Dig in Boston or the Gravina Island "bridge to nowhere" in Alaska) and other skewed priorities. Lobbying might keep prisons or military bases open long past their usefulness, because protecting those few jobs looks good politically, even if the money would be better spent in helping the people employed there to find other work.

If you buy something from a company, like designer sunglasses or a top-of-the-line kitchen faucet, you decide individually that you value that product more than you value keeping your money for some other purpose. No doubt, sometimes we make bad choices — perhaps I'd be better off putting a little bit more away for retirement than treating myself to red wine and decent bourbon on a regular basis. But when I give my money to a company voluntarily, that company can produce more of what I've told them I want. When politicians control how my money is spent, they are more likely to offer tax breaks or big-budget contracts to their cronies and supporters, who may or may not be producing anything useful. There's less left over for me, and millions more like me, to spend on what we value.

When you spend your own money, you have a strong incentive to spend it wisely, and to care about the quality of goods you get in return. When politicians have a constant stream of other people's money to spend, they care much less about whether the projects they spend on will actually serve constituents in the long run, and more about whether that spending can be used to generate media coverage, political support, and votes. Government collects too much in taxes, and tries to do too many things; We end up getting a lot more of what makes politicians happy (including power and social control) and less of what would actually benefit us.

When you're the one spending the money, instead of the government, you have more power, and more choices. Education, especially during the pandemic, is a great illustration of that. We saw images of a California politician taking his own child to private school while insisting that public schools stay closed, a picture of a Chicago teacher on the beach somewhere warm, talking about how great her Zoom classes were because she could teach from anywhere, and the teachers union fighting to keep schools closed. Twice as many private schools stayed open during the pandemic as public schools, because that's what parents wanted. They didn't want their children to fall behind in academics, and they were comfortable with the tiny risk of illness in small children. Government didn't have to listen to parents. Private schools did.

Another huge problem with government spending is that politicians routinely want to spend on whatever they value, far more than they can actually collect in taxes. The ratio of tax revenue the government can collect in the United States seems to be mostly consistent: around 20-25% of GDP, regardless of how tax brackets and policy change.

When Congress (or, increasingly, a Presidential administration) floats a budget, they generally want to spend more than they can actually cover with taxes. Tax increases make us unhappy, and if we were actually on the hook for every pork barrel project that politicians want to prioritize, we might get angry at the amount we have to pay out, and vote someone out of office. Instead of raising taxes or cutting spending, then, politicians increasingly borrow money to cover what they want. If you and I did that, we'd quickly be miserable: financing a lifestyle you can't afford with credit cards carries high penalties — figuratively and literally. But government carries more and more debt over time, and charges us the fees to finance that debt (the federal debt is projected to hit 110% of total GDP in the years immediately following this writing).

Borrowing money requires spending tax revenue on loan interest, indefinitely into the future: probably not a spending choice that's likely to make you or I very happy in the long run. Failing to pay the interest on that debt will cause even worse pain. The net effect of borrowing like this, and carrying high debt, is to charge current spending to the account of future generations of taxpayers. If you took out a credit card in your infant child's name and ran up a big bill spending on things that made you happy, we'd see that as morally wrong. It's a way of getting your happiness at the expense of someone else's future happiness. But a child born in 2023 will have a $78,089 share of publicly held federal debt, dollars long since spent on some politician's pet project. That's how government operates, and will keep operating, for as long as we let them.

How to Do More of What Makes You Happy

It may sound like well-meaning, but impossible-to-follow advice: *just do what makes you happy. But* it's certainly not that simple, especially when we factor in delay of gratification, and the investment of real, hard work it can take to create things that bring you true joy. While the recipe for happiness will be highly individual (chances are you don't get as much happiness out of grand-prix-style turns and kitchen fixtures as I do), there are some good general principles that can help set you up to enjoy your time on this planet more — both now and in the future.

<u>Make friends and see them</u>

Since social relationships are the top cause of happiness, be sure to include friends in your life. Quality matters more than quantity, but the ideal number of close friends has been estimated at between four and six.

And don't just rely on social media to interact with them! Early studies of those on Facebook were correlational, showing that people on Facebook were less happy than those who weren't. But perhaps those who chose to be on Facebook were already less happy, because they got on there to compare how their lives were to others (a situation you'll never win). Later research, though, determined it was Facebook causing the unhappiness, and not the other way around. They took people who had never been on Facebook (I think this research was done in Denmark — perhaps they couldn't find enough Americans who weren't on it yet?) and randomly assigned them to either join and participatc in Facebook or just not get on it. Those randomly assigned to Facebook became less happy.

Yes, it is possible to use Facebook to become happier, but most people don't use social media in that manner. My sister is a great example of how to be on Facebook. Her Facebook friends are only people she knows, and knows fairly well. She gets to see pictures of her great nephews' birthday parties, see pictures of close family members or friends' vacations (those she wouldn't compare her vacations to), and only post pictures for joy, and not downward comparison. For instance, when she would visit our mom out of state, she would jokingly send me a photo of the Swedish pancakes our mom had just made for her breakfast (a real treat for both of us), and teasingly say, "Hey — look what I got for breakfast!" Never meals from fancy restaurants. Connection, not comparison.

<u>Get a job you love</u>

Work is a close second to social relationships for happiness. The old adage, "if you love your job, you never work a day in your life" is true. The good news about being happy at work is those who are happier at work tend to have a higher income, get more pay raises (even at lower levels of pay), get more promotions, and get better ratings from supervisors, giving you a better chance of keeping the job you love.

Hate your job? If you're 36 years old, there's good news. That tends to be the age that people have the lowest job satisfaction, with satisfaction heading up after that. It's a U-shaped curve, with younger people and older people tending to have higher job satisfaction.

Work takes up a big chunk of our week, and of our lives. If you work a "full time job" in America, you're likely to work 40 hours a week, 50 weeks a year, for 45 years. That's 90,000 hours of your limited time on earth, and lots of people spend it doing something they hate, or with people they'd rather avoid.

You may not be able to "do what you love" for work, or "pursue your passion" in the shallow, smooth-road ways the motivational posters would tell you. But you can definitely find work that is meaningful and fulfilling, and that gives you the kind of motivation and feedback you need to be doing your best and contributing your full value. That's where you can earn a decent living, too: because you're doing something challenging that others value.

<u>Plan ahead</u>

Roman philosopher Seneca reminds us that *"Luck is what happens when preparation meets opportunity."* That means even if you have the opportunity to do something that makes you really happy, you won't be able to jump on it if you haven't prepared yourself ahead of time. If your career doesn't provide you a lot of happiness, there are steps you can take to shift your routines, change fields, or go back to school. Perhaps you're "happy enough" with your job (because it gives you the support and flexibility to spend the rest of the time doing something you really enjoy), but don't forget to keep preparing for what's next: the "think about it before you say no" email introducing you to your dream career could be right around the corner. And be open to it.

<u>Try to find happiness in either relationships or work</u>

Typically, you'll hear vague advice about "work/life balance" or balance in other areas of your life. The key here isn't so much balance between the two (that would help, but it's hard to give a prescription to generalize all the varied lives out there), but to make sure that you have at least one of the two in a good place. This is specific advice you can start to act on today.

There is a huge interaction between social relationships and work with happiness. Ideally both are going great in your life, but if you have just one that's going great, then you'll be okay. If neither is going well, then it can be difficult to get through the day.

In general, since social relationships tend to provide a little more happiness than work, you may want to address that one first. If you can easily or more quickly fix your work side, or if you have financial problems that changing your work life would help, then that might be the better place to start.

<u>Smile more</u>

When I was grumpy as a kid, my mom used to tell me to force a smile on my face. Moms today don't do this as much, but it turns out she was right. People who hold their mouths in a smiling shape, regardless of the reason, tend to show improved mood over those who didn't. Muscles in the face send messages to the brain, and the brain listens. Yes, you smile when you're happy, but it seems you're happier when you smile, too. In fact, those with Botox injections in their faces (something I haven't done) tend to be happier afterward because their "frowny" muscles are paralyzed, no longer able to send frowny messages to the brain.

Focus on the good things

In a study of people struggling with mild depression, writing down three good things that happened to them each day for ten days generated the same improvements as a mild-antidepressant. Especially if your brain is prone to dwell on the negative, making a conscious effort to record the things that make you happy can increase their potency. And the good things don't have to be great — just good. Going to the store and not having to wait in line, getting to visit with your niece, watching your favorite reality star come out ahead over that other no-good one on last night's show will do just fine. Just be sure to do this for only about 10 days. Doing it for a month or longer becomes a chore, and can decrease happiness.

Dream big, but think small

Many of us have big life goals that we want to achieve. Maybe you want to retire young, or buy a big house, or raise llamas, or start your own company producing some novel new product. Those goals take planning. If you're spending just $28 per day on little things that make you happy (dinner out, craft beer, a dozen streaming subscriptions), that's $10,000 a year you could be putting away toward that larger goal. Don't let your simple pleasures get in the way of your big dreams. And spend less than you earn — it's the only ticket to real freedom.

Eat your vegetables

Yes, it's in the chapter on food, but I'll repeat it, just like your mom did. Eating fruits and vegetables measurably improves your mood, as well as your health.

Work on your optimism

The nun study showed that optimistic people tend to live longer. Other studies have shown that not only do people tend to live longer when they're optimistic, they tend to be happier, as well.

<u>Give thanks</u>

We take so many things for granted, because of our natural tendency to adapt to our circumstances. Things that you probably haven't thought about lately, like having a refrigerator.

My house was built around the time refrigerators were first being installed in homes, but they were expensive. Barely half of American households had refrigerators by the time my house was 30 years old, and I sometimes think how people who used to live in my house might not have had a refrigerator for quite a while. I can't imagine living like that, and I sometimes stop and think about how fortunate I am to be living in my house with so many modern conveniences.

Giving thanks doesn't have to be so existential. "Counting your blessings" for both big and small things will help prevent hedonic adaptation from setting in. Giving thanks and showing appreciation to others is associated with being less depressed and lonely and with being happier and more energetic.

<u>Focus on others</u>

We live in a very self-centered society, especially with the addition of social media. When I was growing up, we only compared ourselves to others in our small town or our small school. With such a variation in characteristics and talents (some might be better at running, others in baseball or football, while others don't compare themselves in the athletic arena at all because they excel in academics, or singing or butterfly collecting) and such a small pool to compare ourselves to, it wasn't as brutal then as it is now. Now we're being bombarded with visuals of others' vacations and "after" designer kitchens (each very well could have been put on credit cards leading to later misery, which won't be publicized).

People who focus on themselves tend to be less happy than those who focus on others. Ask others how their day is going – how it's *really* going, not just a mindless greeting. Have they read anything interesting lately or is something exciting happening in their lives? Go ahead and listen to *them* tell *you* about their vacation or new kitchen, but do it with the curiosity of a scientist. Ask some questions, and resist any urge to compare your vacation and kitchen to theirs.

Help others

Another way to take the focus off yourself in our society is to help others. Yes, it's true that it's "better to give than receive." By focusing on others, you're focusing on their problems and how to fix them and not your own problems, whether it's helping in a soup kitchen or simply volunteering at your child's school for an event. In fact, some psychologists argue that there's no such thing as "altruism," because when we're altruistic to others, we feel better. And you'll likely be around others in the process, which also gives you a boost.

Exercise

The same rules that apply for stress also apply for happiness. 20-30 minutes per day, three times per week, and focus on a kind of exercise you enjoy. If you like a wide variety of exercises, then go for the aerobic ones, but if weightlifting is your thing, then by all means, do that!

Get/stay healthy

Health isn't a large predictor of happiness, but it does make a difference. Typically, we become less happy when we become less healthy, instead of deliriously happy when we become very healthy. Stop and think of all the things you get to do because you're healthy (if you are). What would you be missing out on if you lost your good health?

If it's in your nature, practice religion

Religiosity rates are declining in our country, along with our happiness, and some of that may be due to religion not being in our lives. For years researchers weren't sure if the actual religion was making people happy, or if it was the social functions. Since social relationships are the top cause of happiness, perhaps it's the potluck lunch after the religious service rather than the religious service itself.

Later research showed that no, religion is a strong cause of happiness outside of social relationships. Some religions (those that are more positive and those that don't have or emphasize a hell) increase happiness more than other religions. Religion also has a greater effect on certain groups of people than others, and is shown to increase happiness most among Black men (sorry ladies!).

<u>Don't just go after physical "things"</u>

At least, not if you have a comfortable living. Yes, those in the lower class who are struggling will be happier spending their money on "things," such as a new dishwasher or better car. If you are struggling to pay your bills, then a newer car would improve happiness, because now you have reliable transportation and don't have to worry about calling in sick and losing your job.

Your repair bills are lower, so you don't have to worry about buying food that month or paying for children's activities.

Those in the higher classes will be much happier with experiences, such as vacations or scuba diving lessons. Why? Because experiences are more likely to be more social in nature and memories of experiences tend to improve with time. Some experiences (like flying lessons) challenge us and feel like an accomplishment after we are proficient. It can also be in line with our self-concept (after running in a marathon in another state, despite the big spend, you get to think of yourself as a marathon runner).

When you buy something, such as a new car, you become used to it (hedonic adaptation), you can more easily compare it to others' (perhaps your neighbor has an even better car), and things get old and depreciate in value (like cars!). Better to invest in things, like memories and friends, that keep getting better over time.

Doing what makes you happy, and planning for the things that will make you even happier, later, is the fastest route to a well-lived life. Yes, there will be struggle, and sacrifice, and those can be meaningful, too. But we aren't guaranteed another decade, or another year, or another day on this planet; it's never too soon to start prioritizing what you actually enjoy, instead of what others tell you is worth pursuing. Whatever it is — as long as you're not putting others in danger — give yourself permission to enjoy it.

A Final Note

I observed something interesting on the campaign trail that confirmed what I discovered early in my career - sometimes the nicest people are at the top.

When I was working at IBM, I was really nervous, even a bit afraid, to go talk to the CEO and the top-level executives of prospective companies, but I found to my surprise that they were often the nicest ones in the company. People tend to think of the leaders as being inaccessible or arrogant and egotistical. I discovered that the rude ones tended to be the lower-level managers. My guess is that the ones at the top weren't trying to guard their turf, or be more than they are, or convince me of anything. They had made it, and had nothing left to prove. Their leadership wasn't distant, it was demystifying.

Similarly, while doing media interviews for my campaigns, I've found kinder, more generous people at the top of their fields. The people who were most generous with their time weren't the mid-level network interviewers, or even the eager podcasters. It was John Stossel, Glenn Beck, and Neil Cavuto. Cavuto interviewed me live, and stayed on with me afterwards, during the commercial break. We had a little chit-chat, and he was so gracious. Granted, I had a deer-in-the-headlights moment of finding out that his son was in my class. People with that kind of clout have the opportunity to be jerks, without that costing them too much personally or professionally, and yet, they were very kind, and generous with their personal resources. They didn't have to convince me they were competent, so the conversation felt like we could all be sitting out in the backyard at a barbecue. Some of the interviewers on the next rung down (names you are probably familiar with), especially women, didn't give me the time of day. One in particular, who I knew was a Libertarian because she mentions it often in the media, didn't even bother to say hello to me either before or after the interview.

Perhaps it's harder to get to the top by being nice. Maybe you have to have a certain amount of ruthlessness. I got to the top in our little realm of Libertarian politics, and I teach at a major university, so I guess it's possible. But not easy. There's the potential to get stepped on by someone who is willing to be more ruthless; narcissists and sociopaths can do very well in business and in politics because they have few hangups about how they treat people.

My other observation about interviews is that conservative interviewers treated me much more nicely than liberal interviewers. I was appalled to find out a few days after interviewing that NPR had edited my time down by more than half. (I only found out after the campaign Communications Director asked me, after the interview was broadcast, if I had made certain points about COVID-19. I asked her if she had listened to it, because obviously I had thoroughly made all those points, and that's when she let me know that it was significantly edited.) Conservatives would let me know they disagreed with me, but they would at least allow me to thoroughly explain my thoughts. I should give extra kudos to Ben Domenech, who went out of his way to make me feel comfortable before our interview (which was fairly early on). He was the only interviewer to ask me before we started if I was nervous about this. (I wasn't!, but I don't remember how I answered his question.) He couldn't have been nicer.

So keep this in mind as you travel through life, and perhaps end up at the top. Don't fall prey to the myth that being at the top means you're kind of a jerk and don't have time for people. That wasn't my experience, at least with men. Here's one area that women may want to take a page out of the good ol' boys network - help each other out.